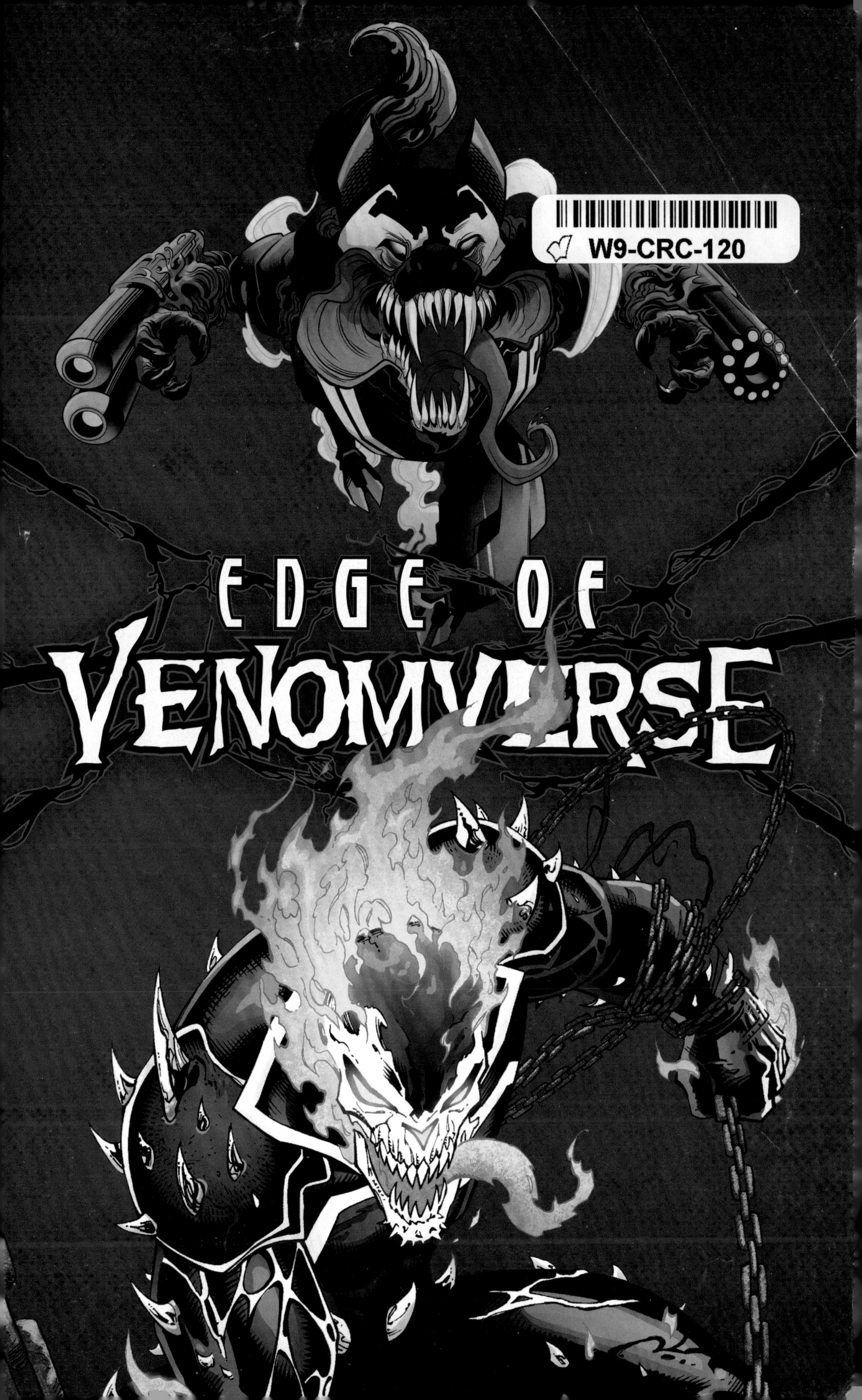
EDGE OF
VENOMVERSE

collection editor **Mark D. Beazley**
assistant editor **Caitlin O'Connell**
associate managing editor **Kateri Woody**
senior editor, special projects **Jennifer Grünwald**

vp production & special projects **Jeff Youngquist**
svp print, sales & marketing **David Gabriel**
book designer **Adam Del Re**

editor in chief **Axel Alonso**
chief creative officer **Joe Quesada**
president **Dan Buckley**
executive producer **Alan Fine**

EDGE OF VENOMVERSE. Contains material originally published in magazine form as EDGE OF VENOMVERSE #1-5 and VENOMVERSE: WAR STORIES #1. First printing 2017. ISBN# 978-1-302-90856-0. Published by MARVEL WORLDWIDE, INC., a subsidiary of MARVEL ENTERTAINMENT, LLC. OFFICE OF PUBLICATION: 135 West 50th Street, New York, NY 10020. Copyright © 2017 MARVEL No similarity between any of the names, characters, persons, and/or institutions in this magazine with those of any living or dead person or institution is intended, and any such similarity which may exist is purely coincidental. **Printed in Canada.** DAN BUCKLEY, President, Marvel Entertainment; JOE QUESADA, Chief Creative Officer; TOM BREVOORT, SVP of Publishing; DAVID BOGART, SVP of Business Affairs & Operations, Publishing & Partnership; C.B. CEBULSKI, VP of Brand Management & Development, Asia; DAVID GABRIEL, SVP of Sales & Marketing, Publishing; JEFF YOUNGQUIST, VP of Production & Special Projects; DAN CARR, Executive Director of Publishing Technology; ALEX MORALES, Director of Publishing Operations; SUSAN CRESPI, Production Manager; STAN LEE, Chairman Emeritus. For information regarding advertising in Marvel Comics or on Marvel.com, please contact Vit DeBellis, Integrated Sales Manager, at vdebellis@marvel.com. For Marvel subscription inquiries, please call 888-511-5480. **Manufactured between 9/15/2017 and 10/17/2017 by SOLISCO PRINTERS, SCOTT, QC, CANADA.**

10 9 8 7 6 5 4 3 2 1

EDGE OF VENOMVERSE

EDGE OF VENOMVERSE #1

Matthew Rosenberg
writer

Roland Boschi
pencils

Roland Boschi with **Adam Gorham**
inkers

Daniel Brown
color artist

EDGE OF VENOMVERSE #2

Christopher Hastings
writer

Irene Strychalski
artist

Java Tartaglia
color artist

EDGE OF VENOMVERSE #3

Simon Spurrier
writer

Tigh Walker
artist

Felipe Sobreiro
color artist

EDGE OF VENOMVERSE #4

Ryan Key
writer

André Lima Araújo
artist

Rachelle Rosenberg
color artist

EDGE OF VENOMVERSE #5

Clay Chapman
writer

James Stokoe
artist

Dee Cunniffe
special thanks

VENOMVERSE: WAR STORIES #1

"TALES FROM THE FRONT LINE"

Cullen Bunn
writer

Annapaola Martello
artist

Java Tartaglia
color artist

"BLESSING IN DISGUISE"

Nnedi Okorafor
writer

Tana Ford
artist

Ian Herring
color artist

"DEAL WITH THE DEVIL"

Declan Shalvey
writer & artist

Chris O'Halloran
color artist

"3, 2, 1."

Magdalene Visaggio
writer

Alex Arizmendi
artist

Lee Loughridge
color artist

"FORCE MAJEURE"

Aaron Covington
writer

Khary Randolph
artist

Emilio Lopez
color artist

VC's Clayton Cowles and **Joe Sabino** (*Venomverse: War Stories #1*)
letterers

Francesco Mattina
cover art

Allison Stock
assistant editor

Devin Lewis & **Charles Beacham**
editors

Nick Lowe
executive editor

1

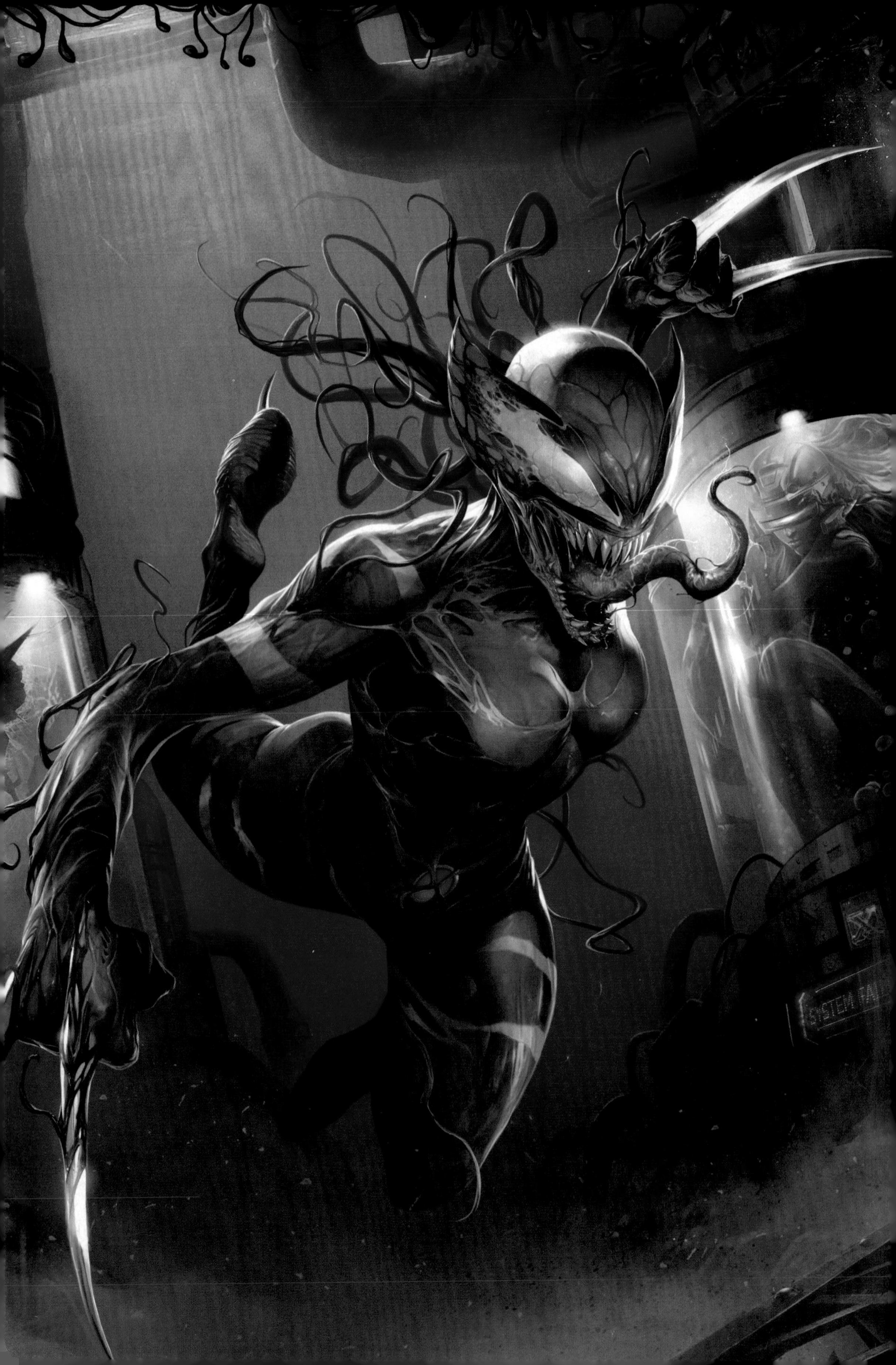

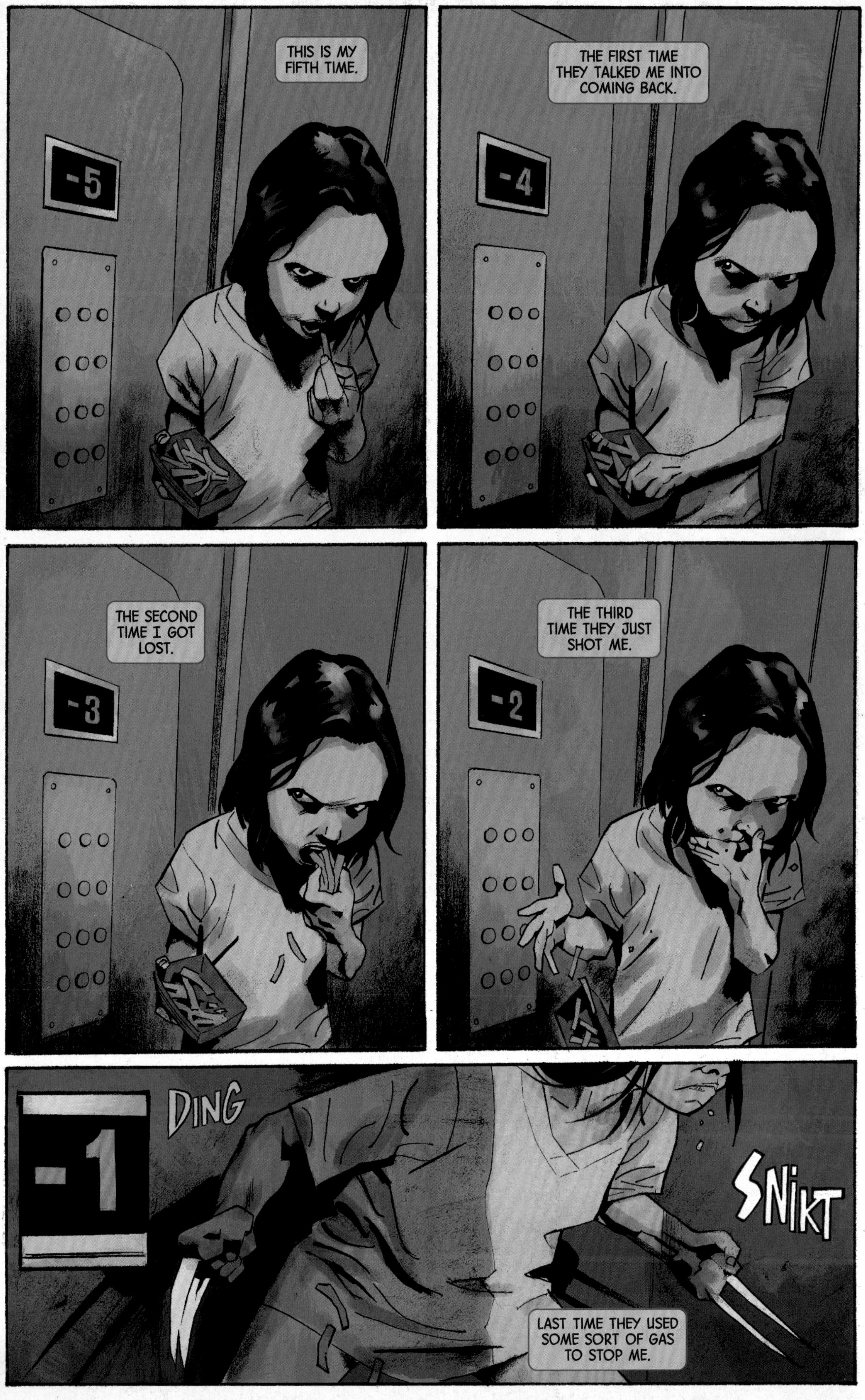
THIS IS MY FIFTH TIME.
THE FIRST TIME THEY TALKED ME INTO COMING BACK.
THE SECOND TIME I GOT LOST.
THE THIRD TIME THEY JUST SHOT ME.
DING
SNIKT
LAST TIME THEY USED SOME SORT OF GAS TO STOP ME.

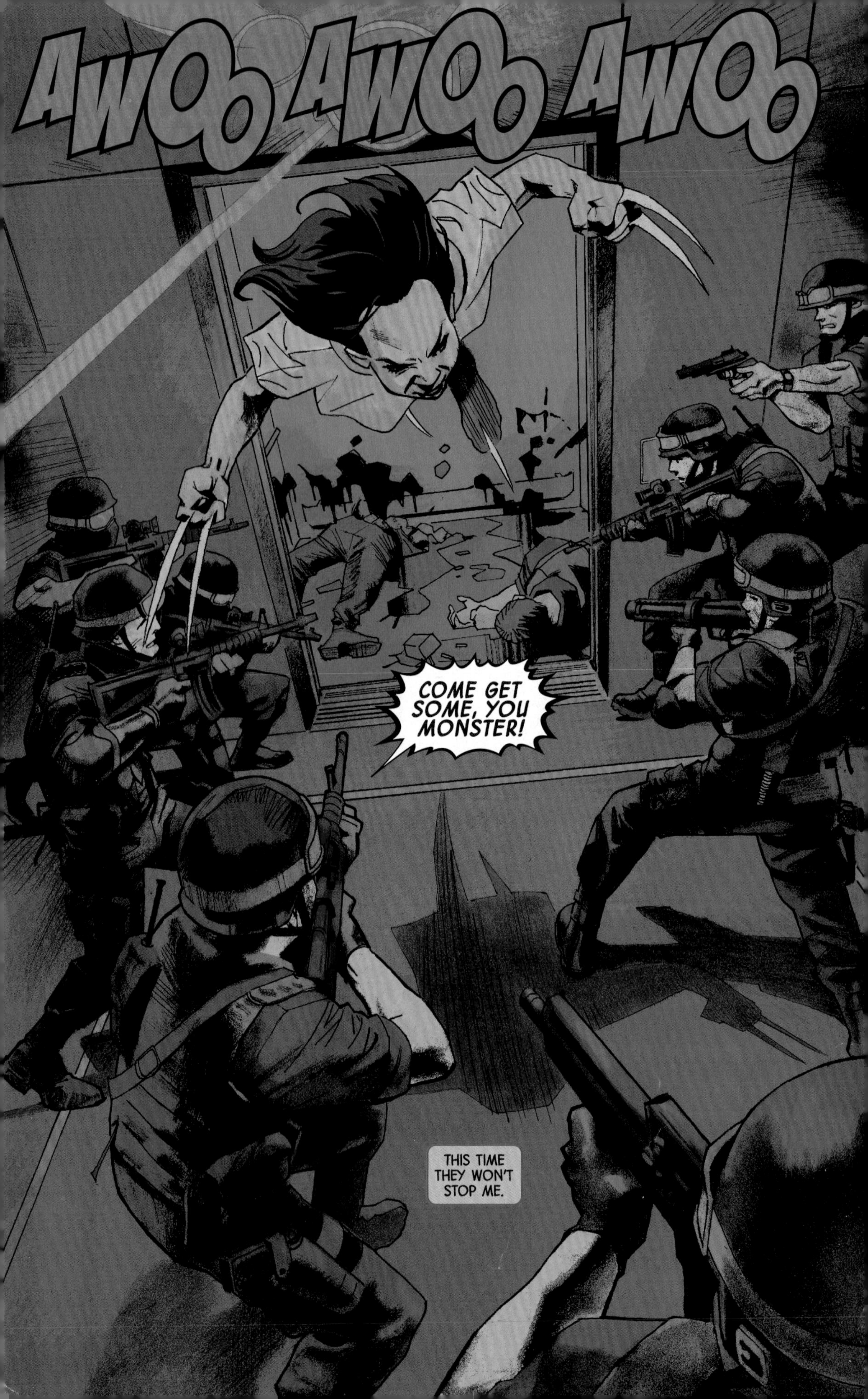
AWOO AWOO AWOO
COME GET SOME, YOU MONSTER!
THIS TIME THEY WON'T STOP ME.

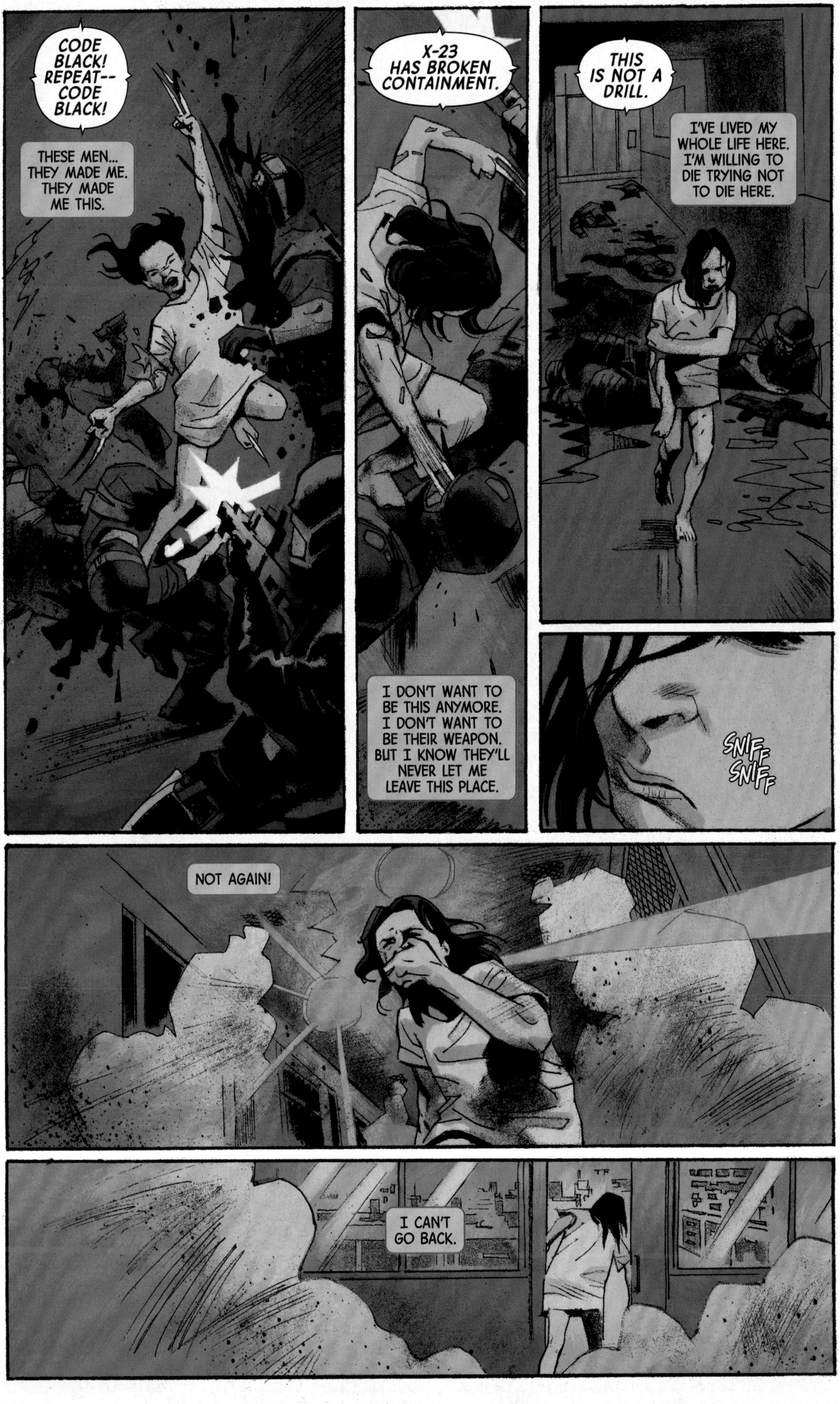
CODE BLACK! REPEAT-- CODE BLACK!
THESE MEN... THEY MADE ME. THEY MADE ME THIS.
X-23 HAS BROKEN CONTAINMENT.
I DON'T WANT TO BE THIS ANYMORE. I DON'T WANT TO BE THEIR WEAPON. BUT I KNOW THEY'LL NEVER LET ME LEAVE THIS PLACE.
THIS IS NOT A DRILL.
I'VE LIVED MY WHOLE LIFE HERE. I'M WILLING TO DIE TRYING NOT TO DIE HERE.
SNIFF SNIFF
NOT AGAIN!
I CAN'T GO BACK.

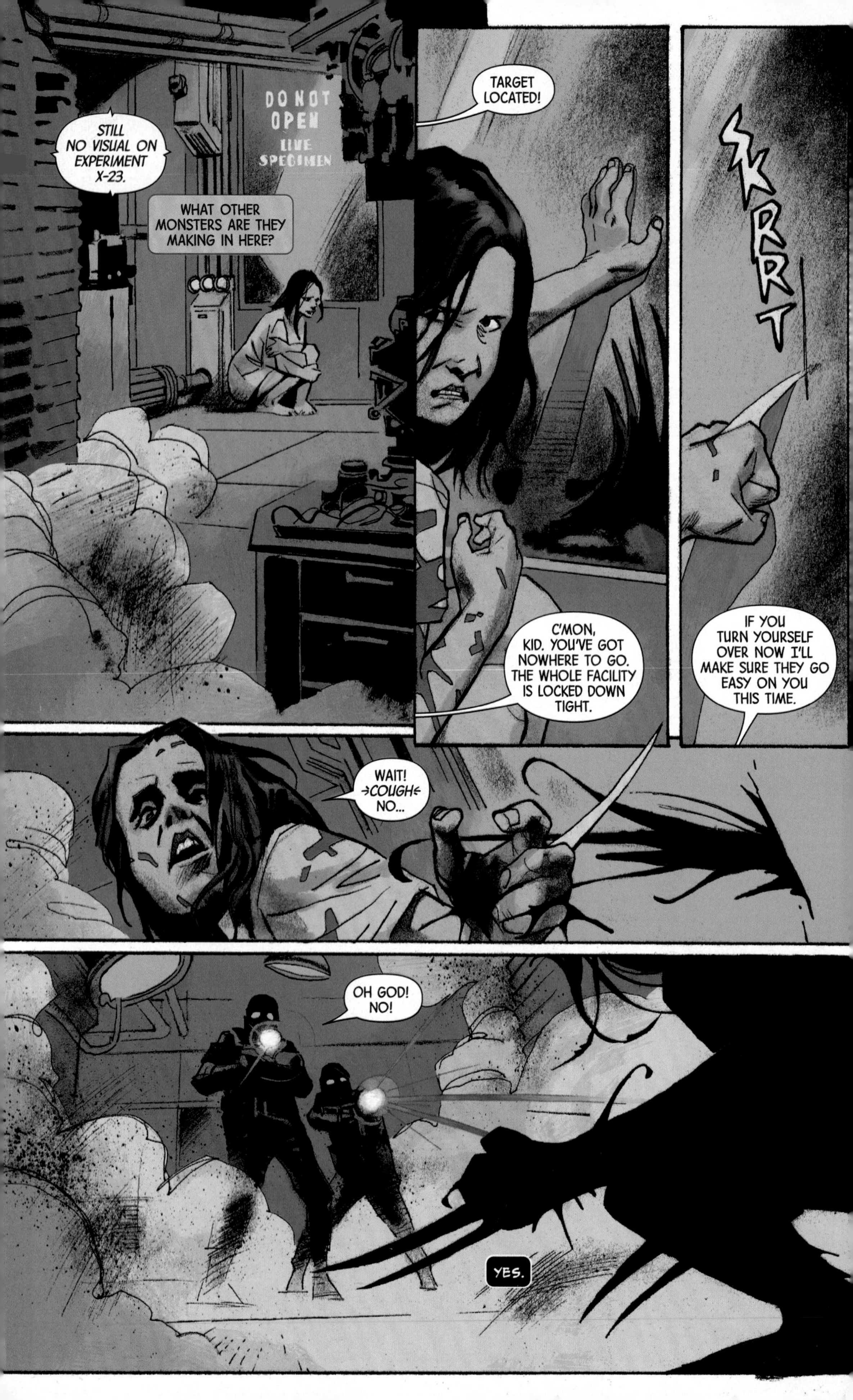
DO NOT OPEN
LIVE SPECIMEN
STILL NO VISUAL ON EXPERIMENT X-23.
WHAT OTHER MONSTERS ARE THEY MAKING IN HERE?
TARGET LOCATED!
SKRRT
C'MON, KID. YOU'VE GOT NOWHERE TO GO. THE WHOLE FACILITY IS LOCKED DOWN TIGHT.
IF YOU TURN YOURSELF OVER NOW I'LL MAKE SURE THEY GO EASY ON YOU THIS TIME.
WAIT! *COUGH* NO...
OH GOD! NO!
YES.

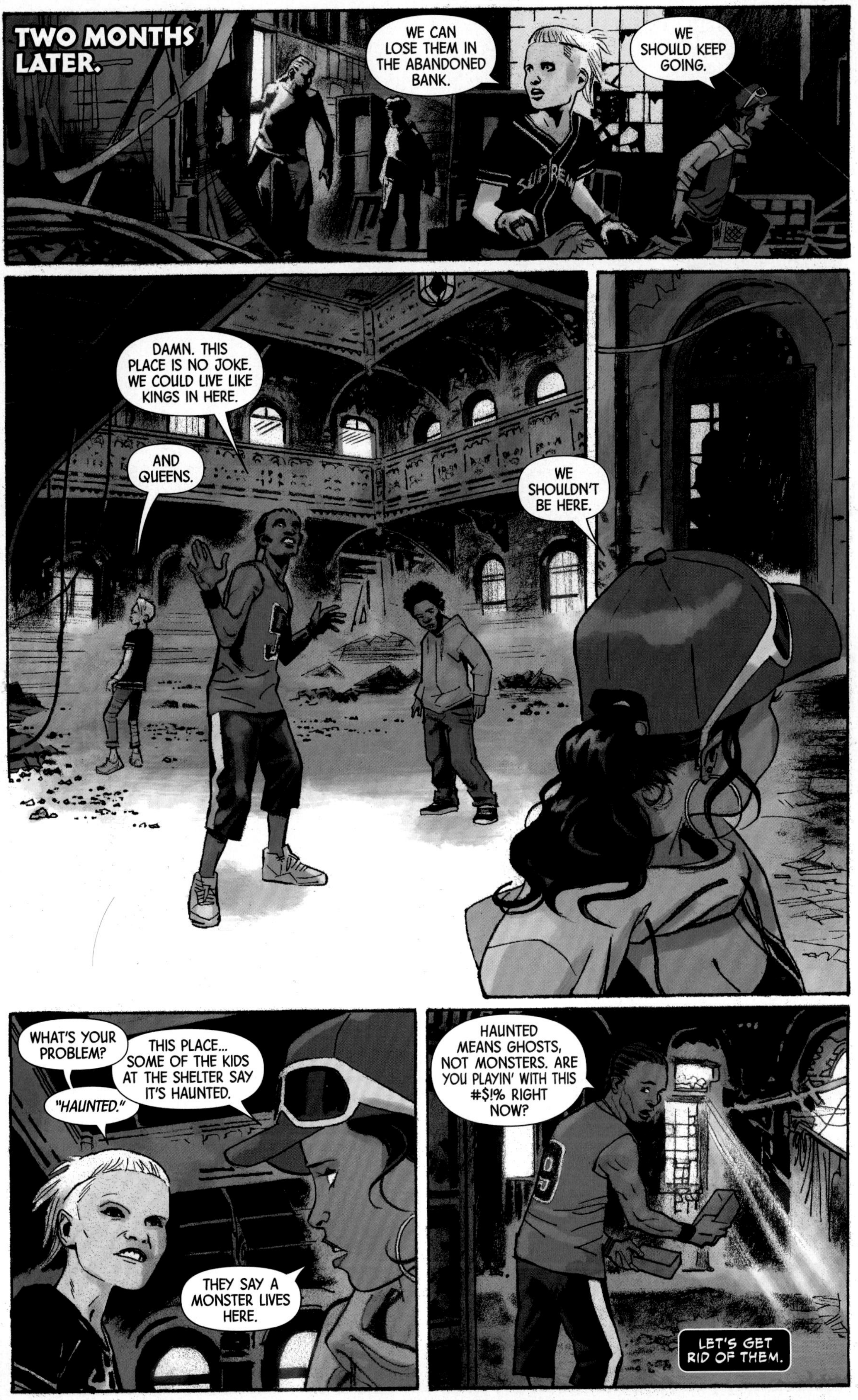

TWO MONTHS LATER.
WE CAN LOSE THEM IN THE ABANDONED BANK.
WE SHOULD KEEP GOING.
DAMN. THIS PLACE IS NO JOKE. WE COULD LIVE LIKE KINGS IN HERE.
AND QUEENS.
WE SHOULDN'T BE HERE.
WHAT'S YOUR PROBLEM?
THIS PLACE... SOME OF THE KIDS AT THE SHELTER SAY IT'S HAUNTED.
"HAUNTED."
THEY SAY A MONSTER LIVES HERE.
HAUNTED MEANS GHOSTS, NOT MONSTERS. ARE YOU PLAYIN' WITH THIS #$!% RIGHT NOW?
LET'S GET RID OF THEM.

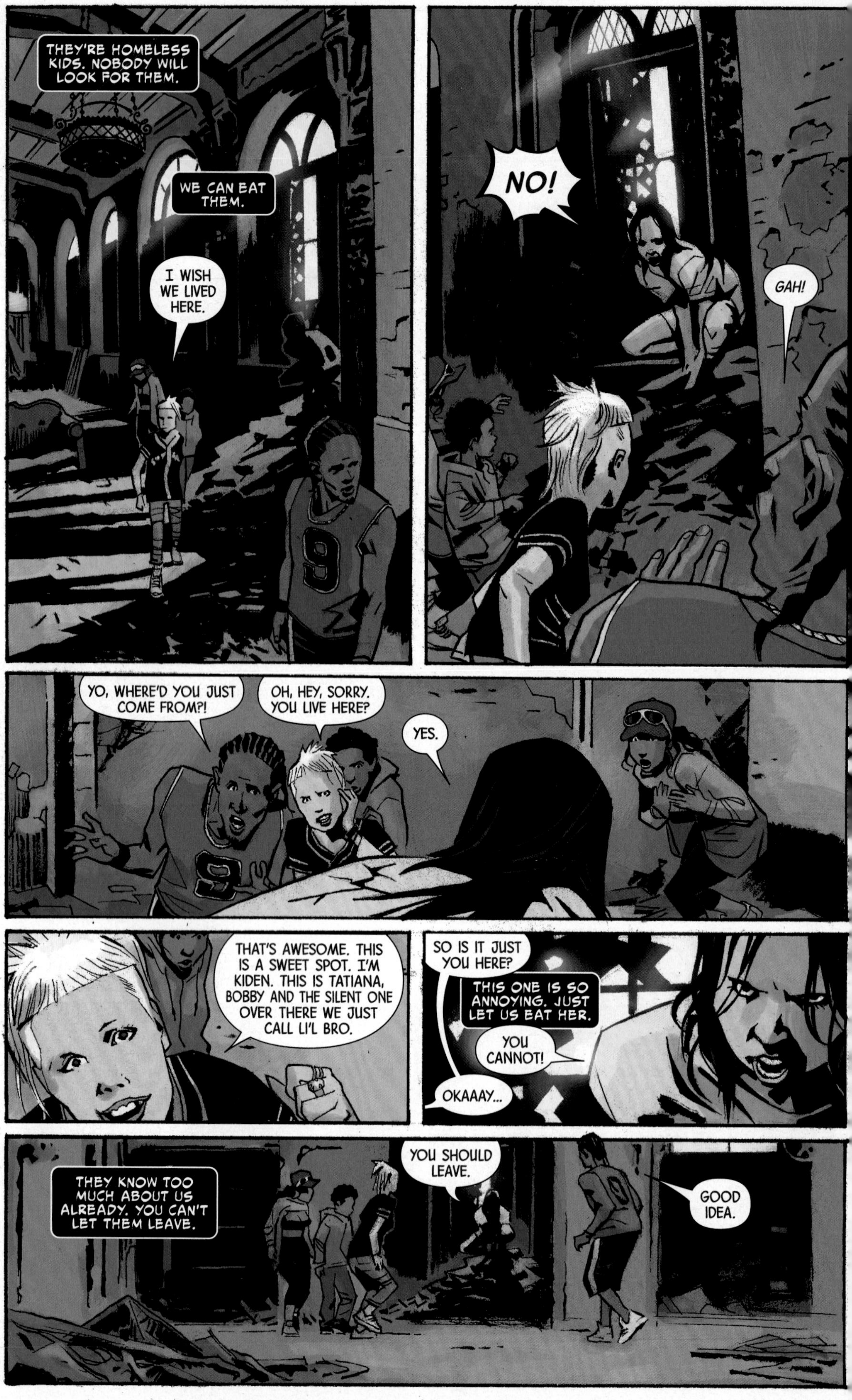
THEY'RE HOMELESS KIDS. NOBODY WILL LOOK FOR THEM.
WE CAN EAT THEM.
I WISH WE LIVED HERE.
NO!
GAH!
YO, WHERE'D YOU JUST COME FROM?!
OH, HEY, SORRY. YOU LIVE HERE?
YES.
THAT'S AWESOME. THIS IS A SWEET SPOT. I'M KIDEN. THIS IS TATIANA, BOBBY AND THE SILENT ONE OVER THERE WE JUST CALL LI'L BRO.
SO IS IT JUST YOU HERE?
THIS ONE IS SO ANNOYING. JUST LET US EAT HER.
YOU CANNOT!
OKAAAY...
THEY KNOW TOO MUCH ABOUT US ALREADY. YOU CAN'T LET THEM LEAVE.
YOU SHOULD LEAVE.
GOOD IDEA.

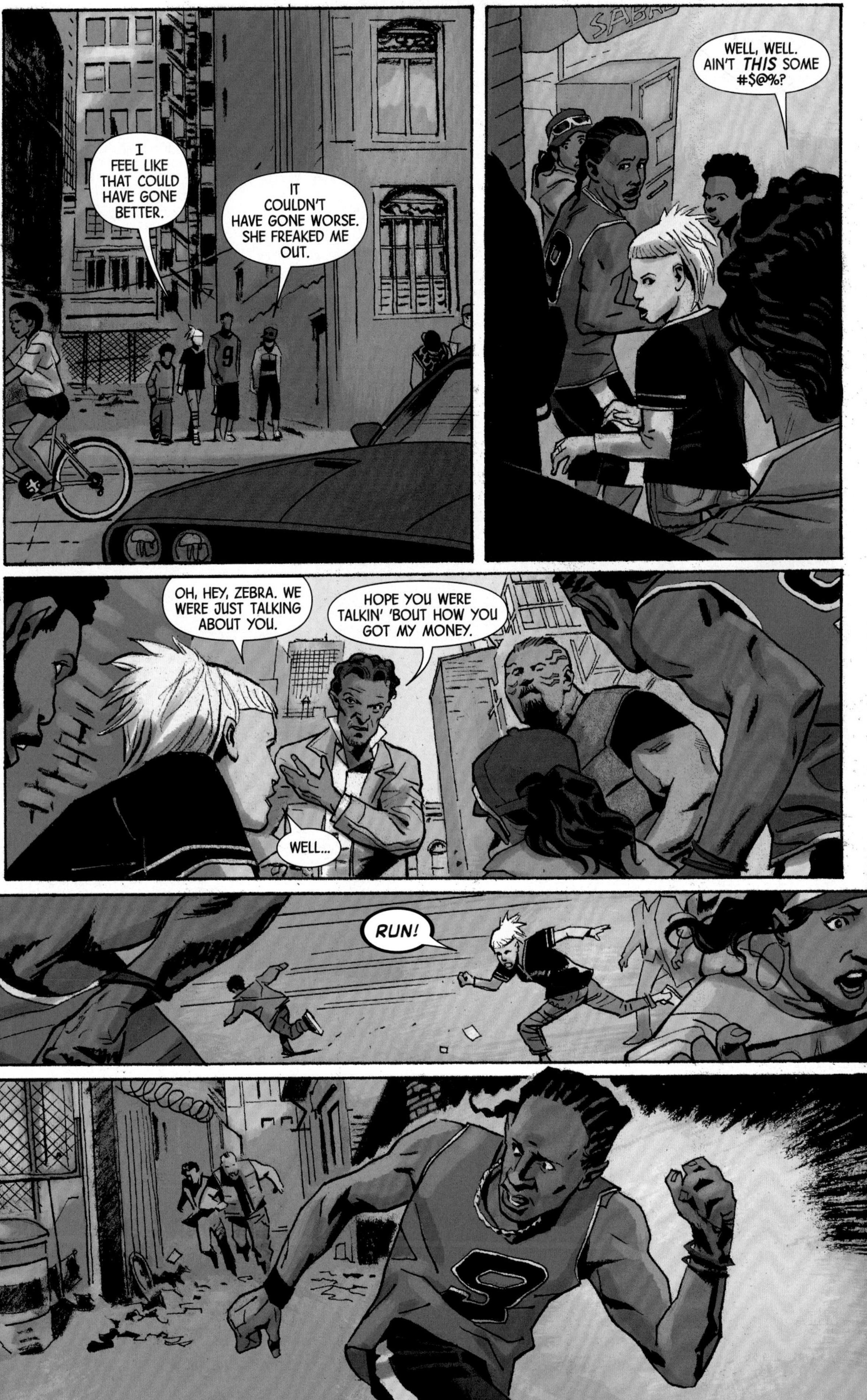

I FEEL LIKE THAT COULD HAVE GONE BETTER.
IT COULDN'T HAVE GONE WORSE. SHE FREAKED ME OUT.
WELL, WELL. AIN'T *THIS* SOME #$@%?
OH, HEY, ZEBRA. WE WERE JUST TALKING ABOUT YOU.
HOPE YOU WERE TALKIN' 'BOUT HOW YOU GOT MY MONEY.
WELL...
RUN!

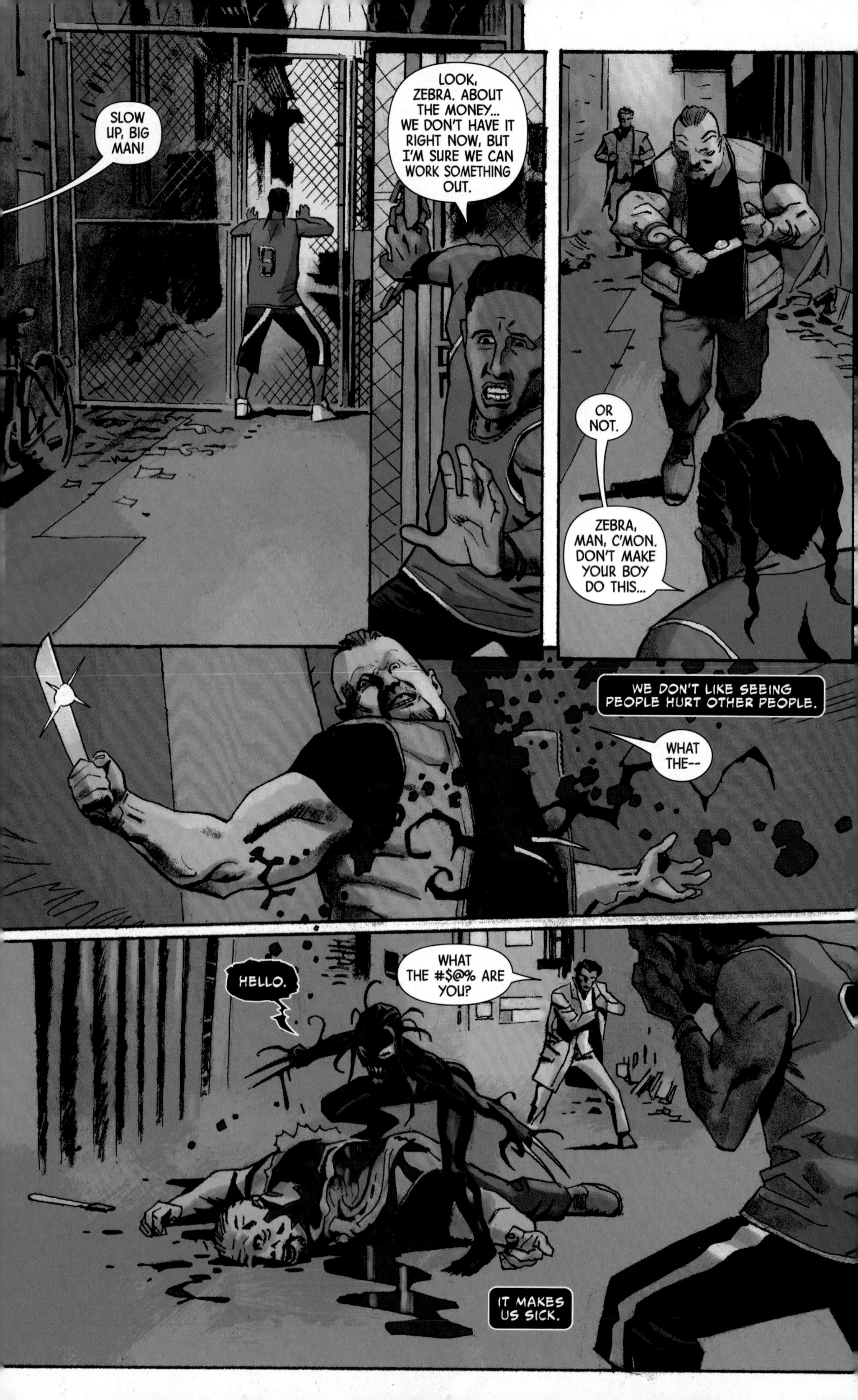
SLOW UP, BIG MAN!
LOOK, ZEBRA. ABOUT THE MONEY... WE DON'T HAVE IT RIGHT NOW, BUT I'M SURE WE CAN WORK SOMETHING OUT.
OR NOT.
ZEBRA, MAN, C'MON. DON'T MAKE YOUR BOY DO THIS...
WE DON'T LIKE SEEING PEOPLE HURT OTHER PEOPLE.
WHAT THE--
HELLO.
WHAT THE #$@% ARE YOU?
IT MAKES US SICK.

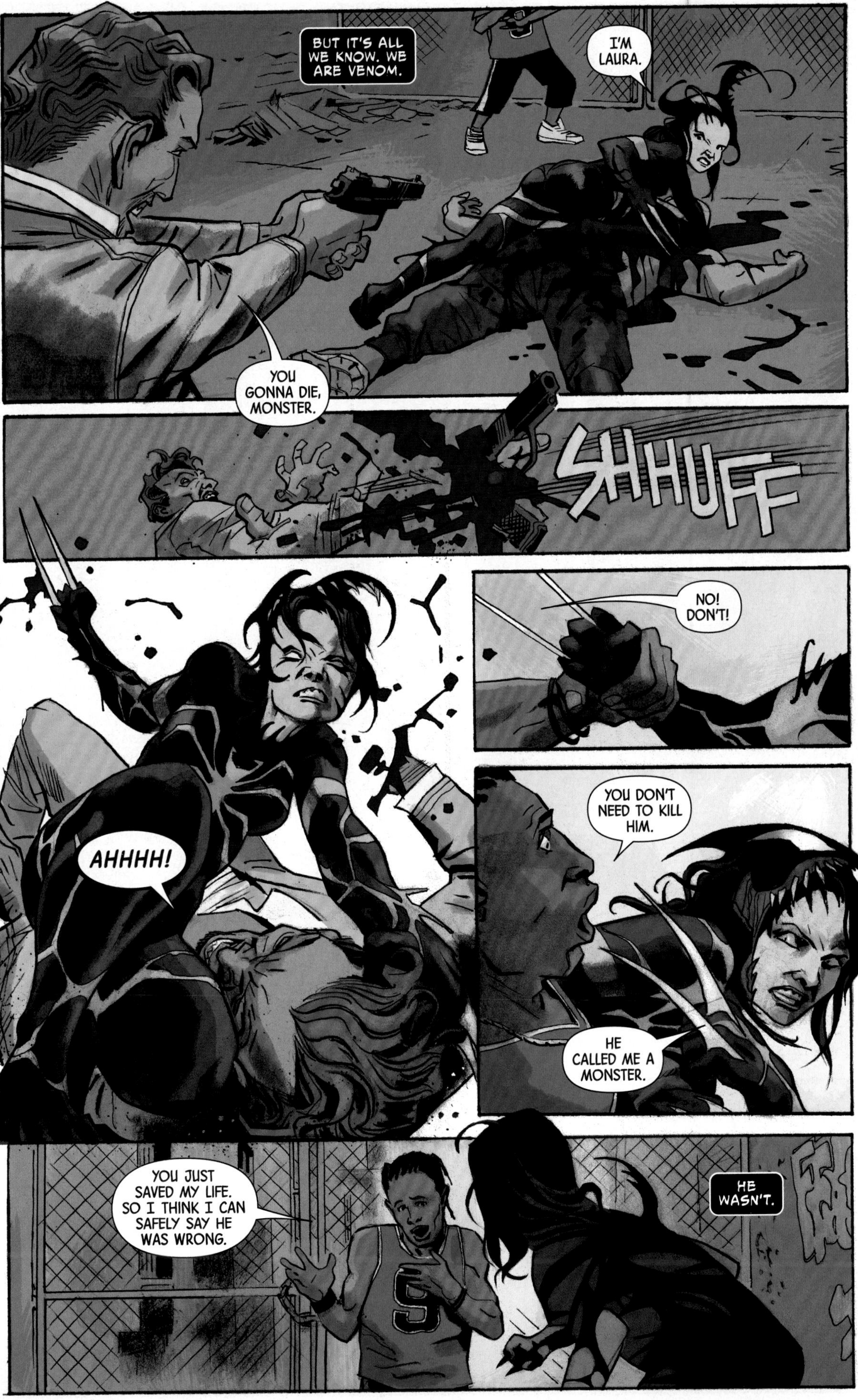
BUT IT'S ALL WE KNOW. WE ARE VENOM.
I'M LAURA.
YOU GONNA DIE, MONSTER.
SHHUFF
AHHHH!
NO! DON'T!
YOU DON'T NEED TO KILL HIM.
HE CALLED ME A MONSTER.
YOU JUST SAVED MY LIFE. SO I THINK I CAN SAFELY SAY HE WAS WRONG.
HE WASN'T.

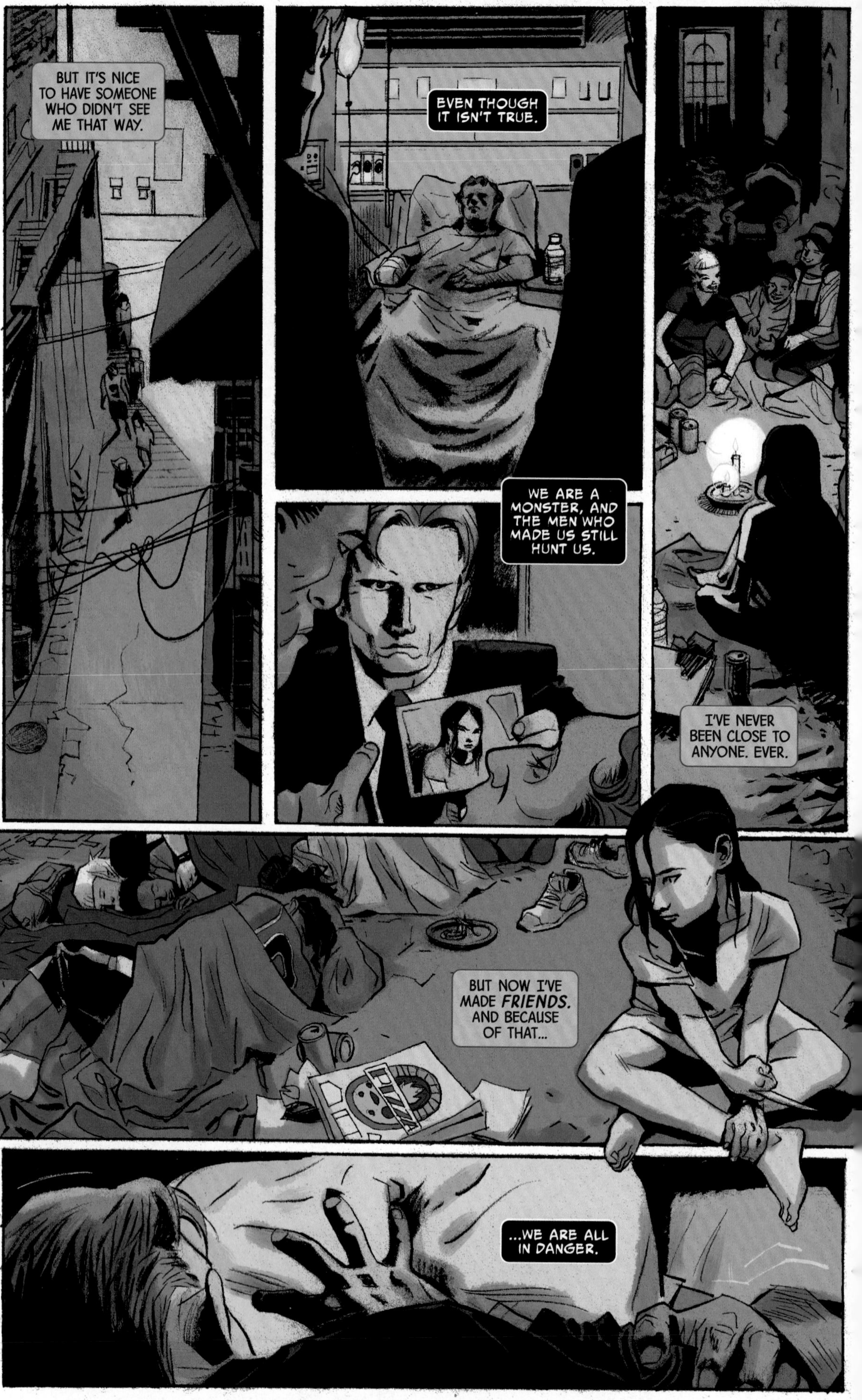
BUT IT'S NICE TO HAVE SOMEONE WHO DIDN'T SEE ME THAT WAY.
EVEN THOUGH IT ISN'T TRUE.
WE ARE A MONSTER, AND THE MEN WHO MADE US STILL HUNT US.
I'VE NEVER BEEN CLOSE TO ANYONE. EVER.
BUT NOW I'VE MADE *FRIENDS.* AND BECAUSE OF THAT...
...WE ARE ALL IN DANGER.

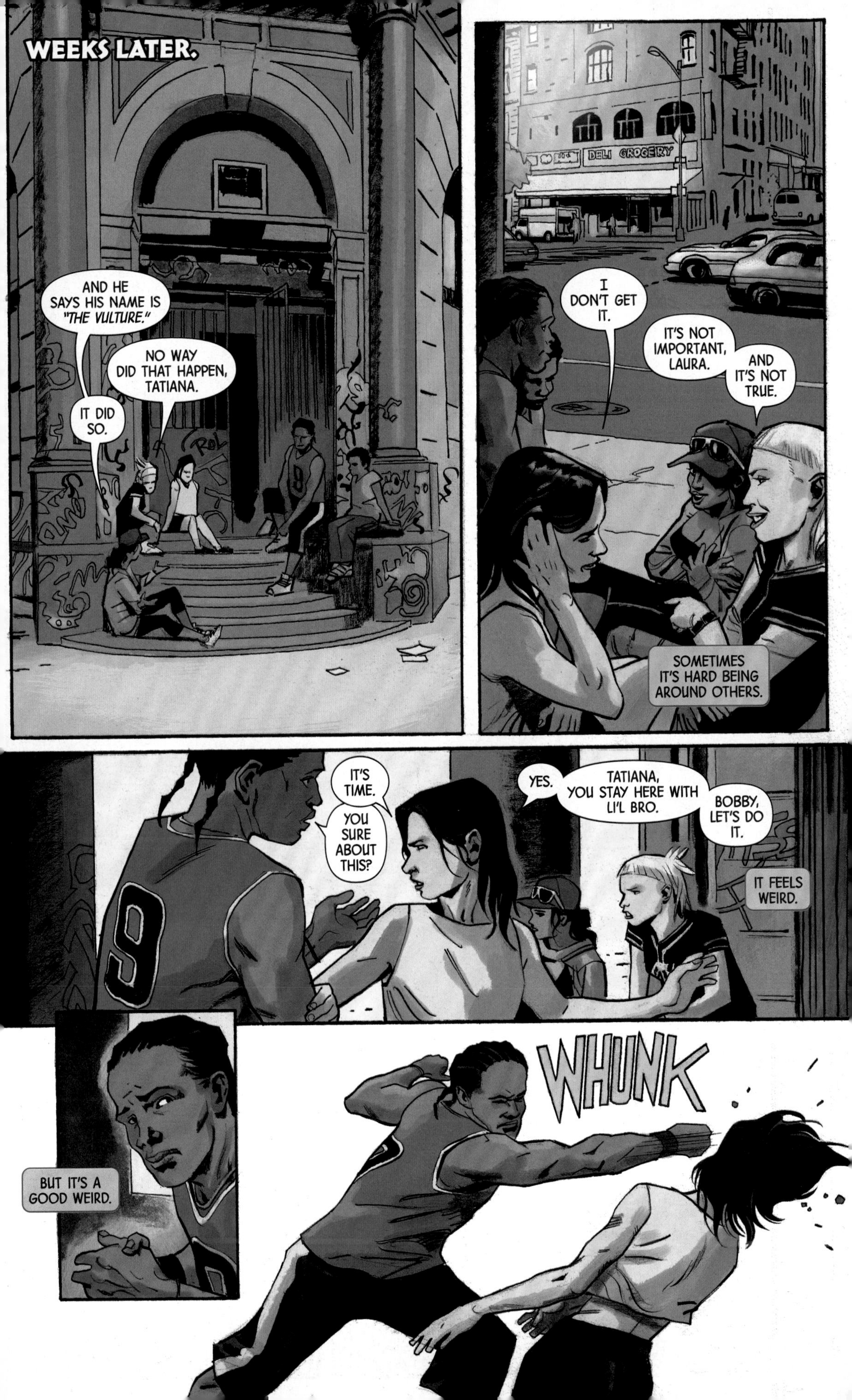
WEEKS LATER.
AND HE SAYS HIS NAME IS "THE VULTURE."
NO WAY DID THAT HAPPEN, TATIANA.
IT DID SO.
DELI GROCERY
I DON'T GET IT.
IT'S NOT IMPORTANT, LAURA.
AND IT'S NOT TRUE.
SOMETIMES IT'S HARD BEING AROUND OTHERS.
IT'S TIME.
YOU SURE ABOUT THIS?
YES.
TATIANA, YOU STAY HERE WITH LI'L BRO.
BOBBY, LET'S DO IT.
IT FEELS WEIRD.
BUT IT'S A GOOD WEIRD.
WHUNK

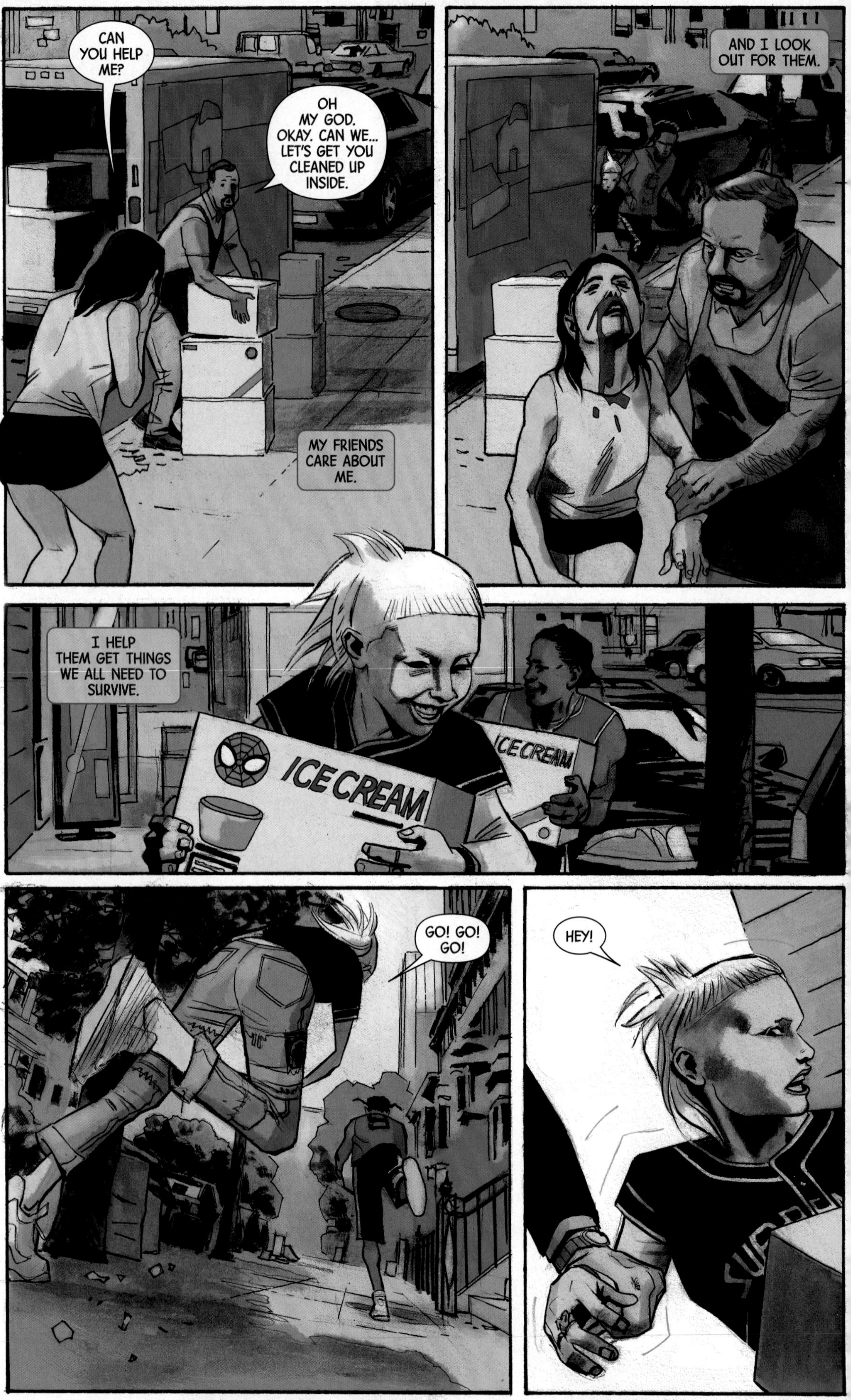

CAN YOU HELP ME?
OH MY GOD. OKAY. CAN WE... LET'S GET YOU CLEANED UP INSIDE.
MY FRIENDS CARE ABOUT ME.
AND I LOOK OUT FOR THEM.
I HELP THEM GET THINGS WE ALL NEED TO SURVIVE.
ICE CREAM
ICE CREAM
GO! GO! GO!
HEY!

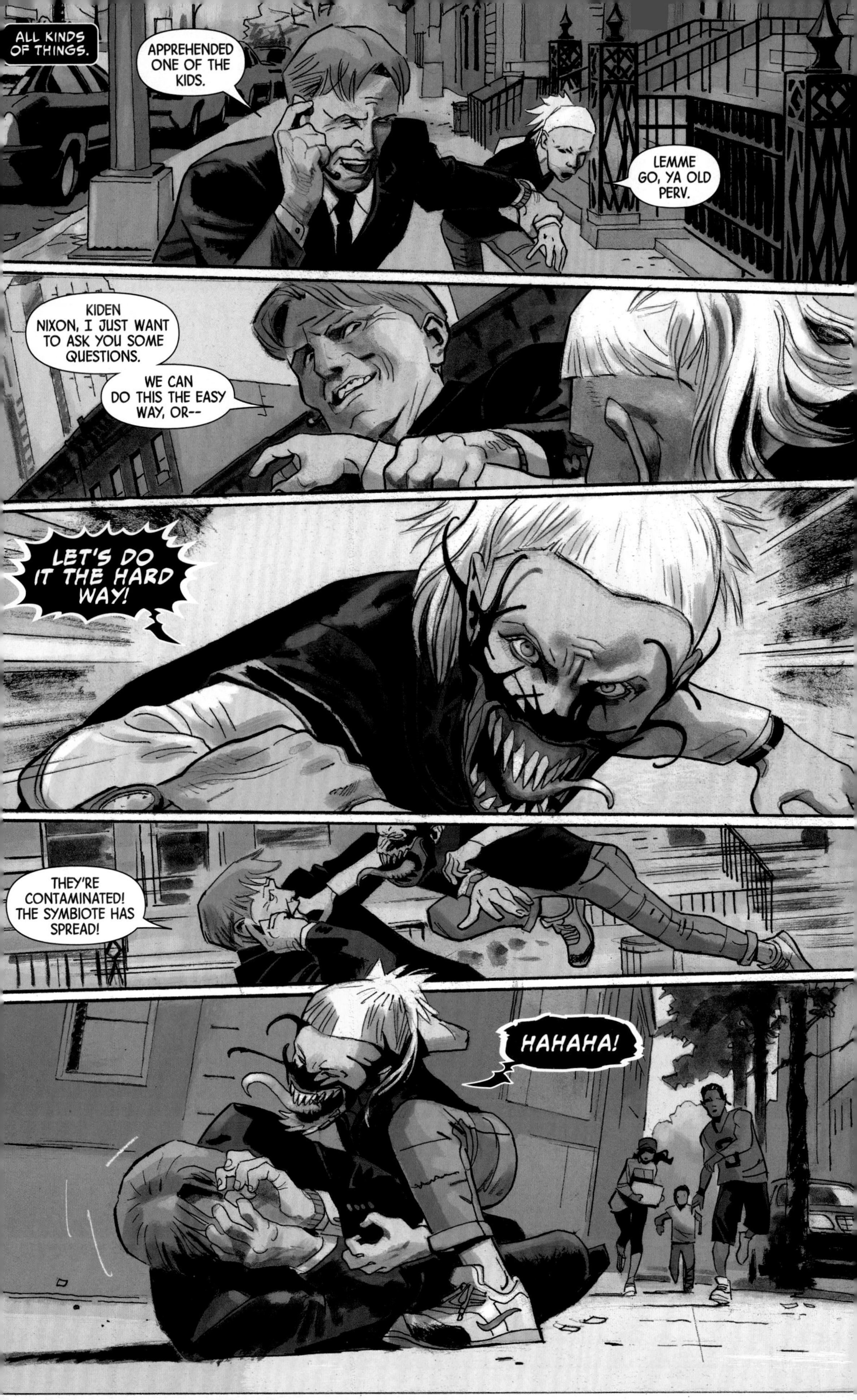
ALL KINDS OF THINGS.
APPREHENDED ONE OF THE KIDS.
LEMME GO, YA OLD PERV.
KIDEN NIXON, I JUST WANT TO ASK YOU SOME QUESTIONS.
WE CAN DO THIS THE EASY WAY, OR--
LET'S DO IT THE HARD WAY!
THEY'RE CONTAMINATED! THE SYMBIOTE HAS SPREAD!
HAHAHA!

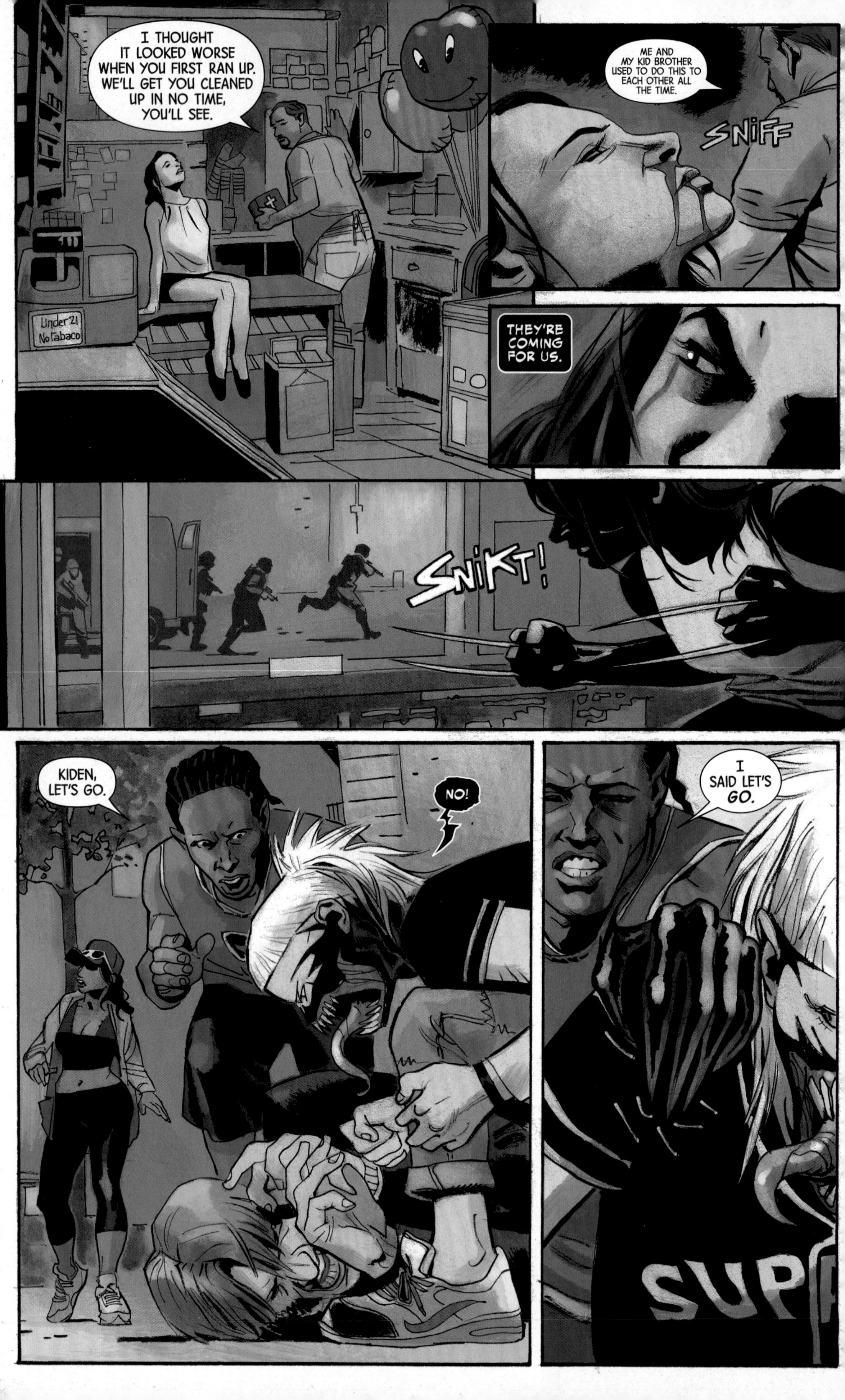
I THOUGHT IT LOOKED WORSE WHEN YOU FIRST RAN UP. WE'LL GET YOU CLEANED UP IN NO TIME, YOU'LL SEE.
Under 21 No Tabaco
ME AND MY KID BROTHER USED TO DO THIS TO EACH OTHER ALL THE TIME.
SNIFF
THEY'RE COMING FOR US.
SNIKT!
KIDEN, LET'S GO.
NO!
I SAID LET'S GO.
SUP

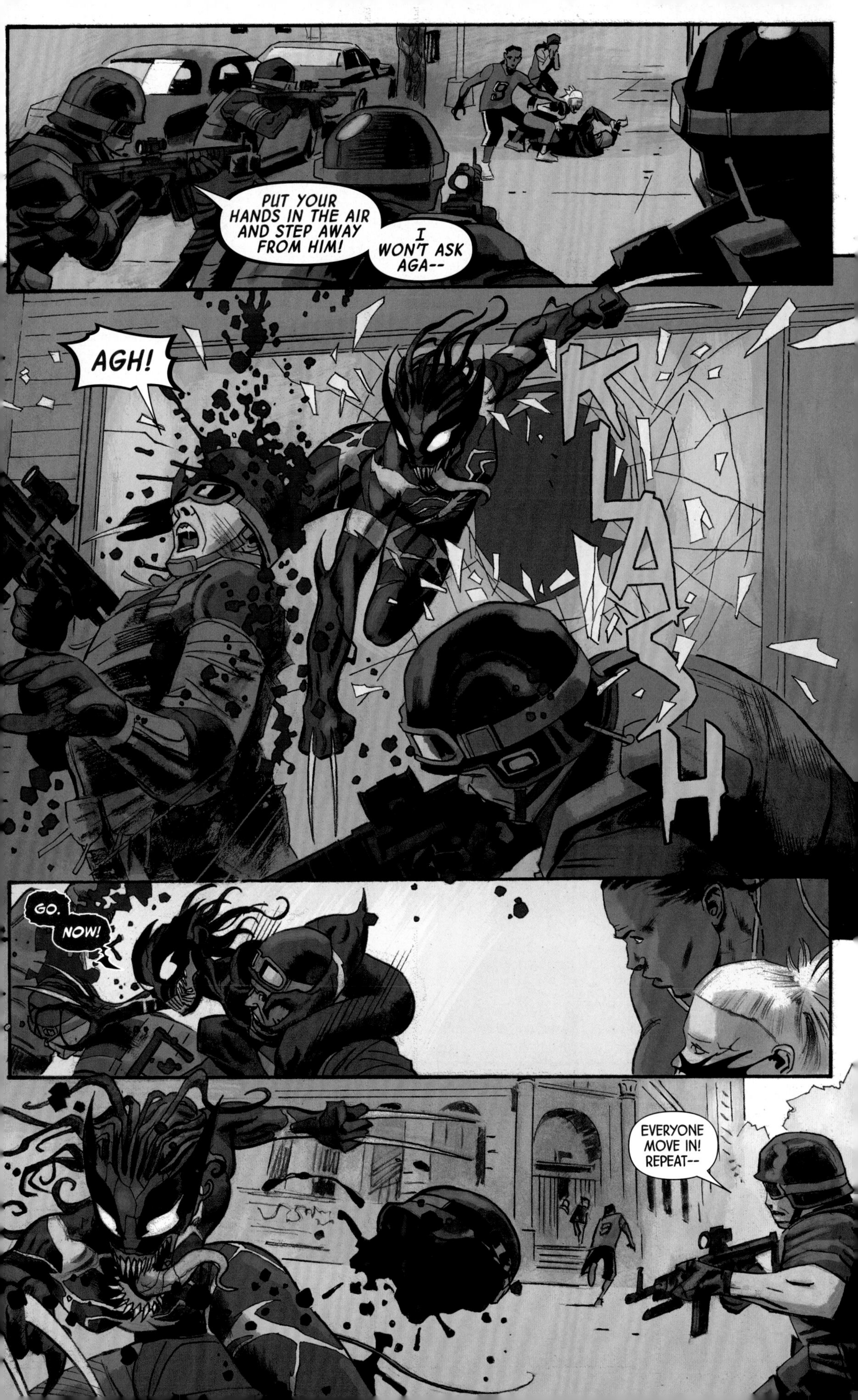
PUT YOUR HANDS IN THE AIR AND STEP AWAY FROM HIM!
I WON'T ASK AGA--
AGH!
KLASH
GO.
NOW!
EVERYONE MOVE IN! REPEAT--

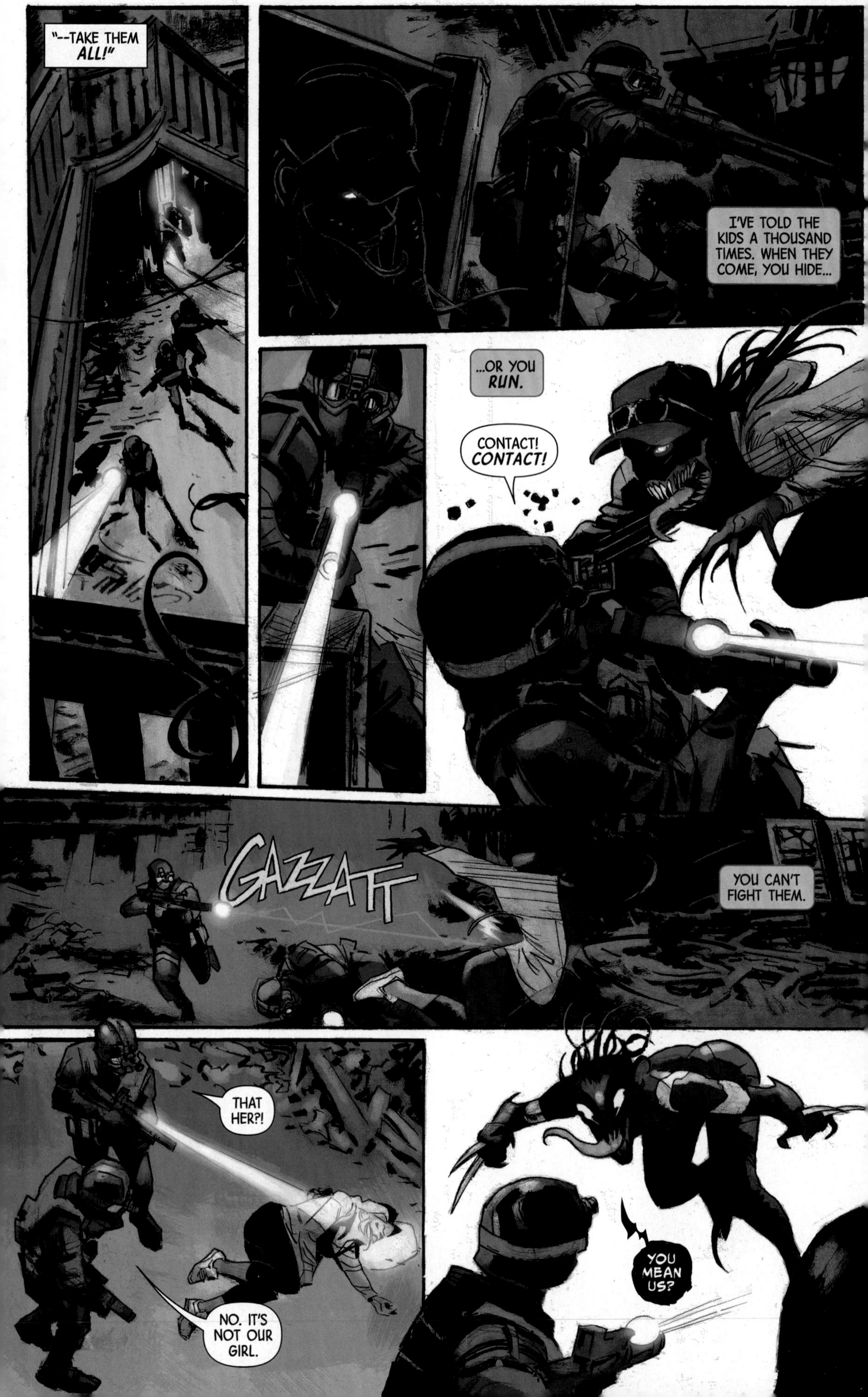
"--TAKE THEM ALL!"
I'VE TOLD THE KIDS A THOUSAND TIMES. WHEN THEY COME, YOU HIDE...
...OR YOU RUN.
CONTACT! CONTACT!
GAZZATT
YOU CAN'T FIGHT THEM.
THAT HER?!
NO. IT'S NOT OUR GIRL.
YOU MEAN US?

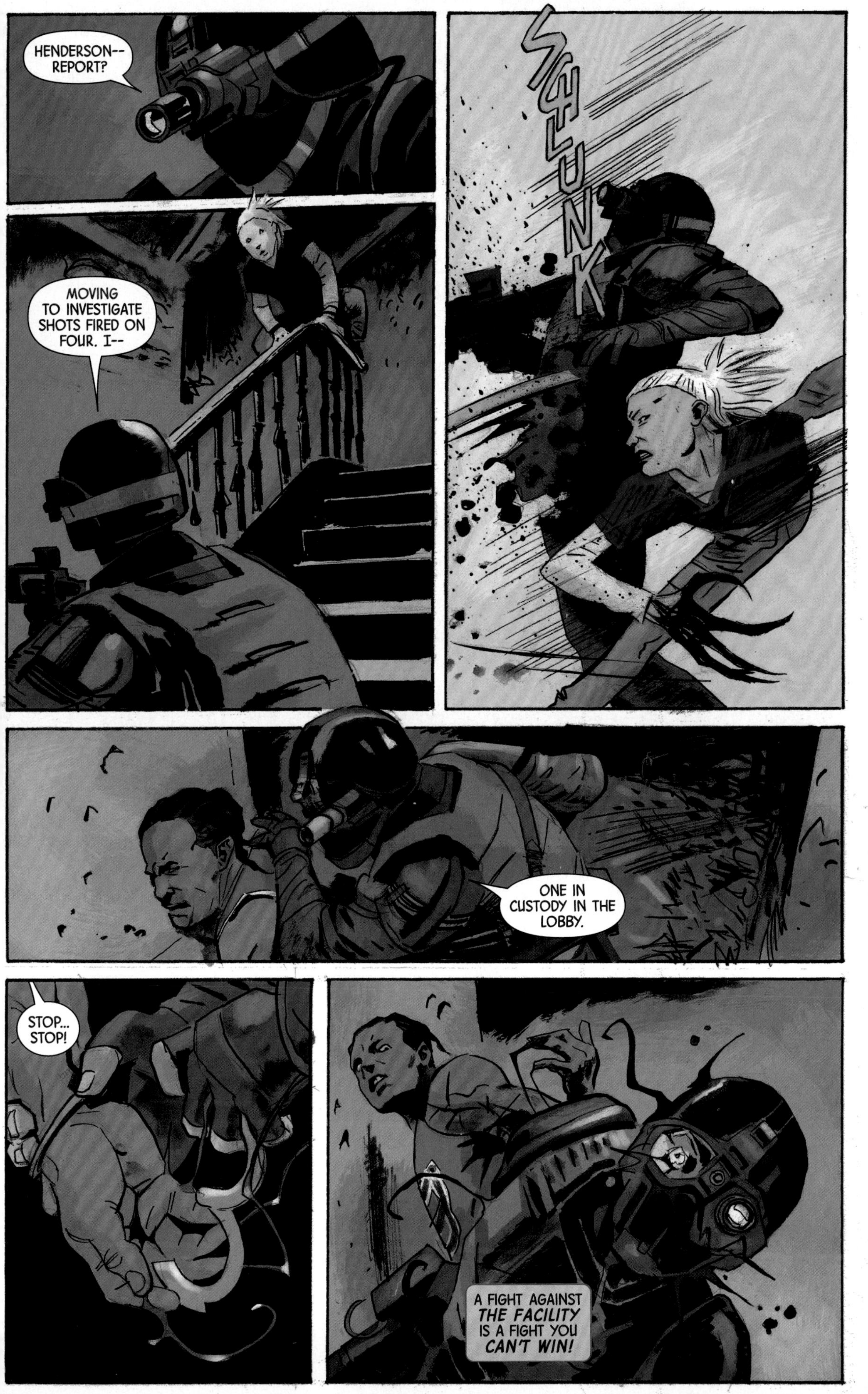
HENDERSON--
REPORT?
MOVING TO INVESTIGATE SHOTS FIRED ON FOUR. I--
SHLUNK
ONE IN CUSTODY IN THE LOBBY.
STOP... STOP!
A FIGHT AGAINST *THE FACILITY* IS A FIGHT YOU *CAN'T WIN!*

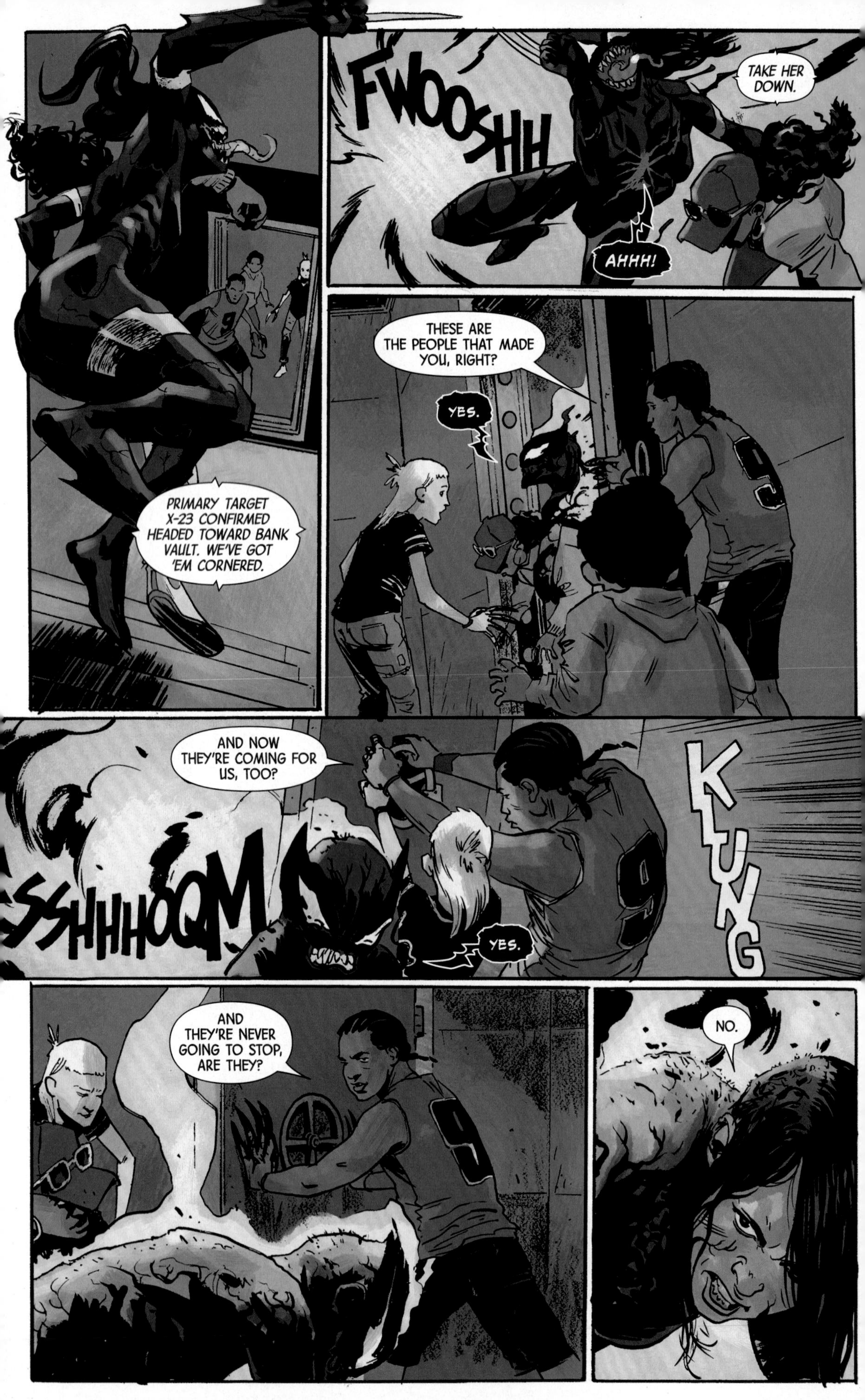
PRIMARY TARGET X-23 CONFIRMED HEADED TOWARD BANK VAULT. WE'VE GOT 'EM CORNERED.
FWOOSHH
TAKE HER DOWN.
AHHH!
THESE ARE THE PEOPLE THAT MADE YOU, RIGHT?
YES.
AND NOW THEY'RE COMING FOR US, TOO?
SSHHHOOM
YES.
KLUNG
AND THEY'RE NEVER GOING TO STOP, ARE THEY?
NO.

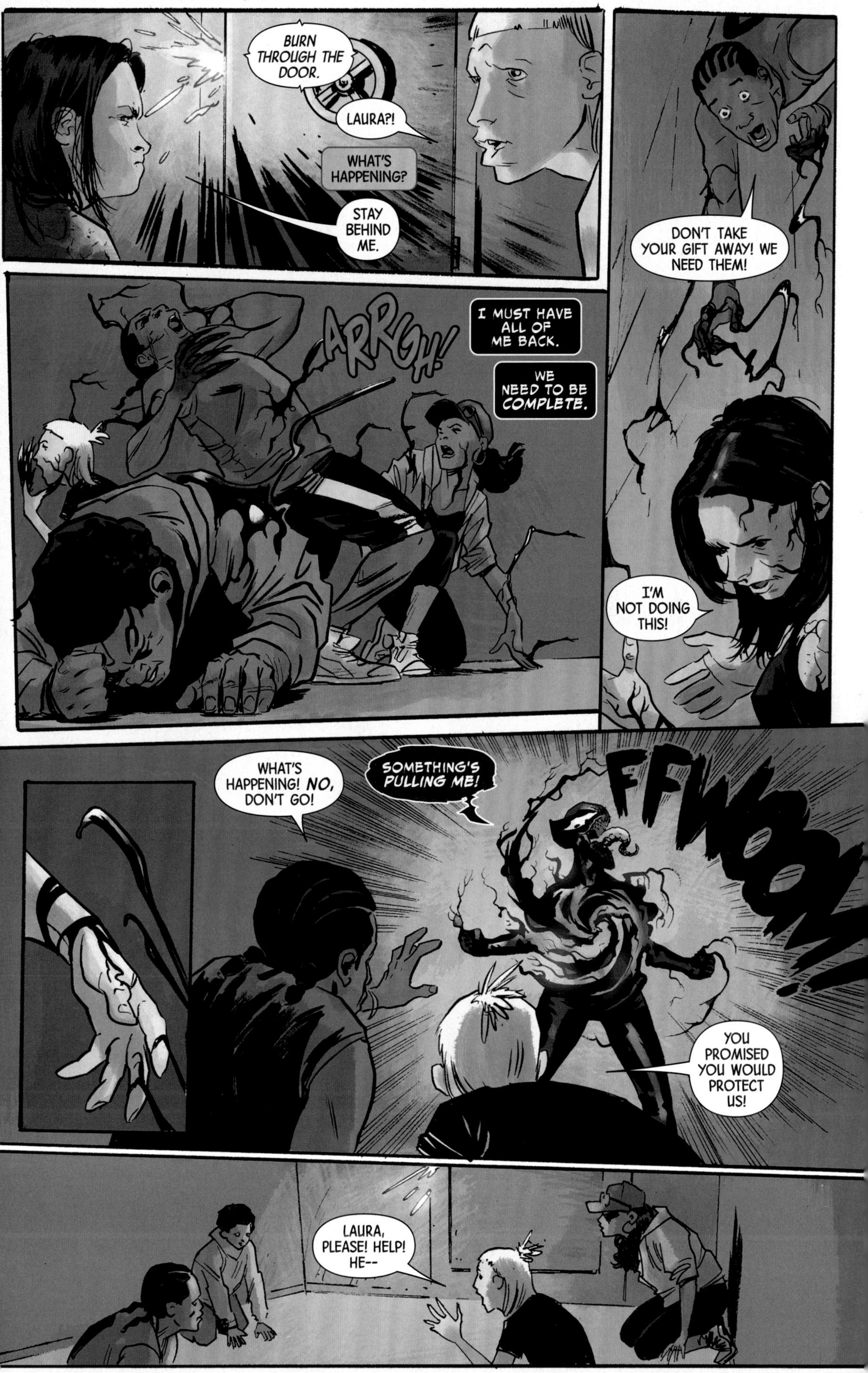
BURN THROUGH THE DOOR.
LAURA?!
WHAT'S HAPPENING?
STAY BEHIND ME.
DON'T TAKE YOUR GIFT AWAY! WE NEED THEM!
ARRGH!
I MUST HAVE ALL OF ME BACK.
WE NEED TO BE COMPLETE.
I'M NOT DOING THIS!
WHAT'S HAPPENING! NO, DON'T GO!
SOMETHING'S PULLING ME!
FFWOOM!
YOU PROMISED YOU WOULD PROTECT US!
LAURA, PLEASE! HELP! HE--

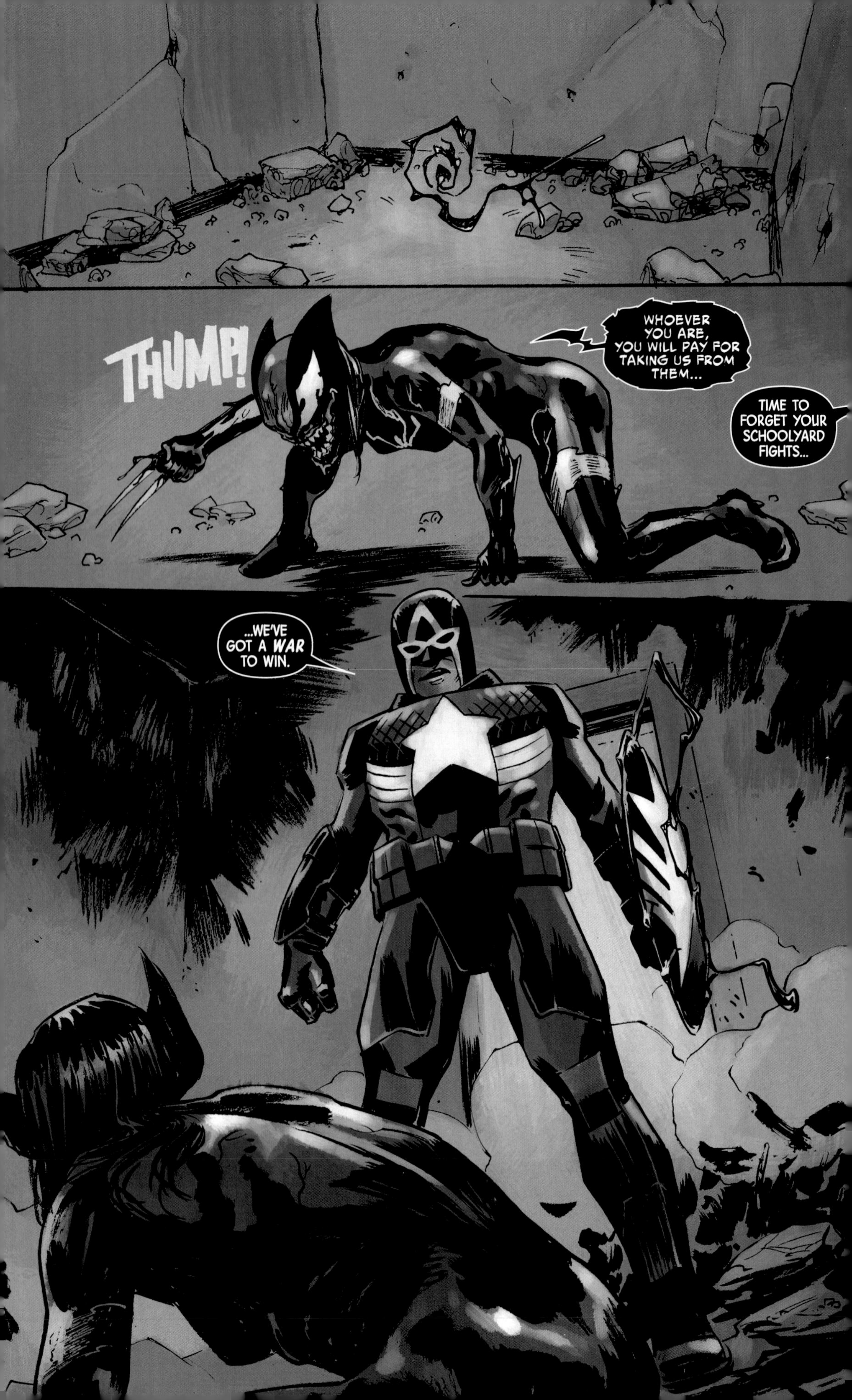
THUMP!
WHOEVER YOU ARE, YOU WILL PAY FOR TAKING US FROM THEM...
TIME TO FORGET YOUR SCHOOLYARD FIGHTS...
...WE'VE GOT A WAR TO WIN.

2

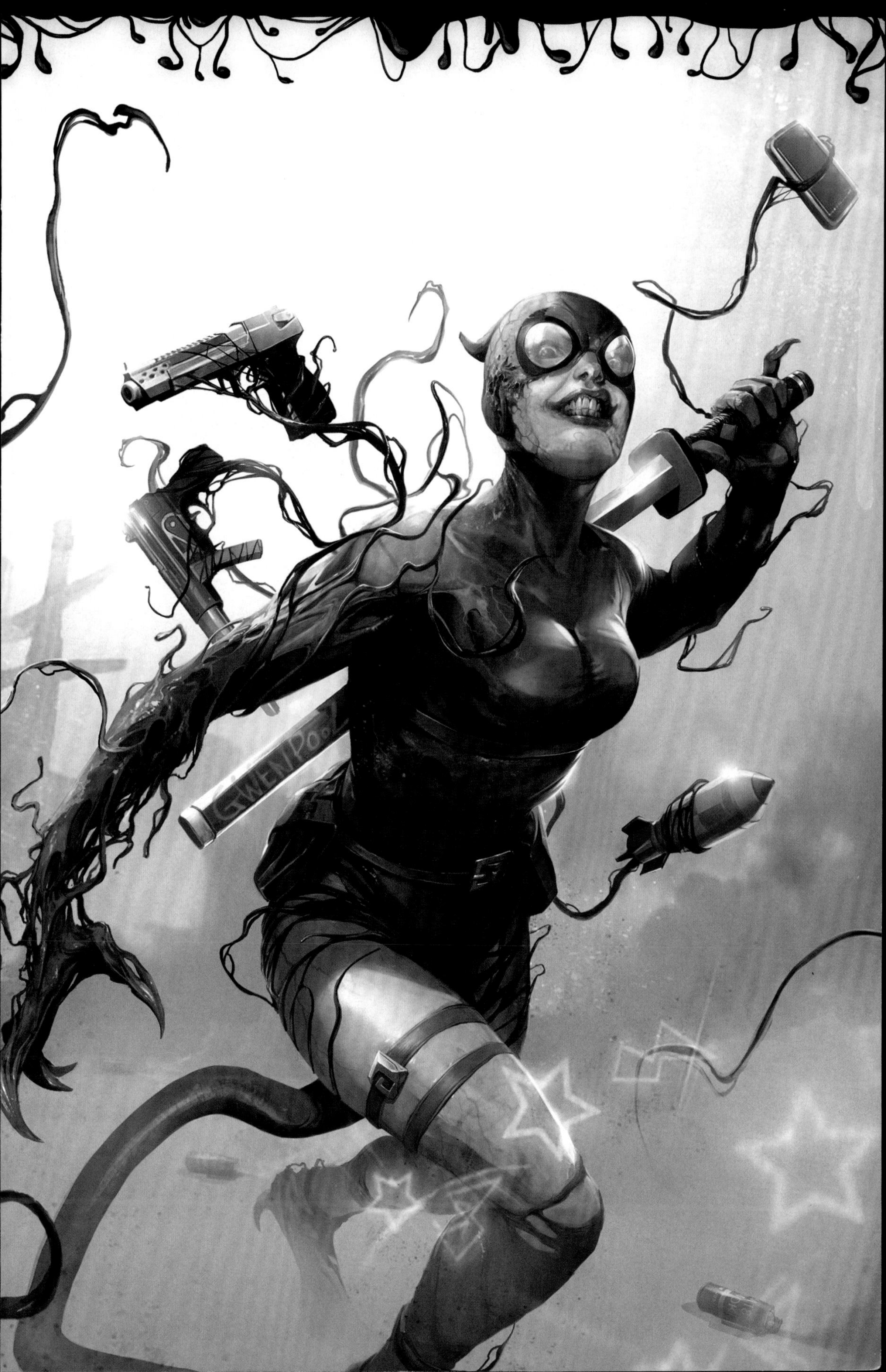

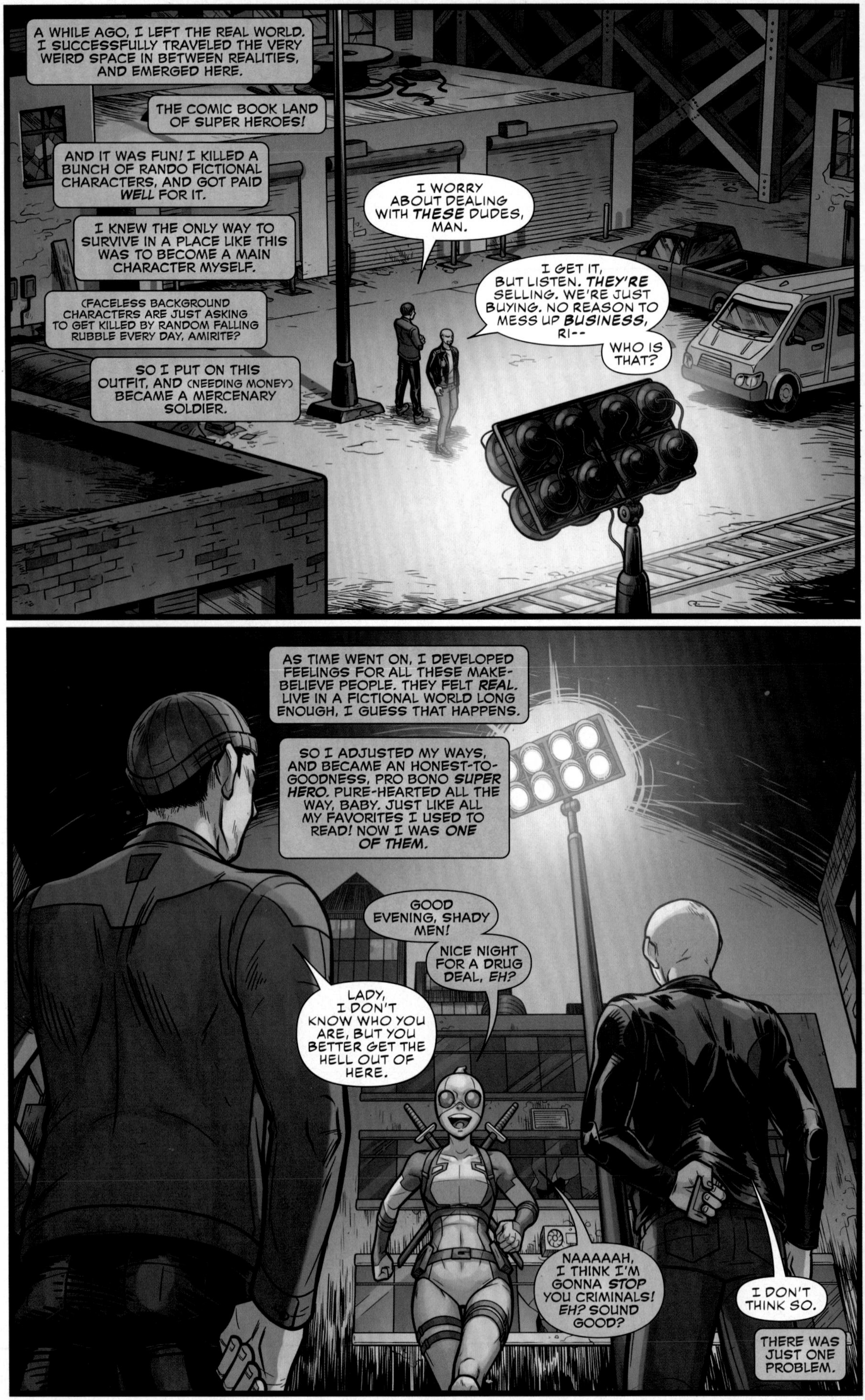
A WHILE AGO, I LEFT THE REAL WORLD. I SUCCESSFULLY TRAVELED THE VERY WEIRD SPACE IN BETWEEN REALITIES, AND EMERGED HERE.
THE COMIC BOOK LAND OF SUPER HEROES!
AND IT WAS FUN! I KILLED A BUNCH OF RANDO FICTIONAL CHARACTERS, AND GOT PAID *WELL* FOR IT.
I KNEW THE ONLY WAY TO SURVIVE IN A PLACE LIKE THIS WAS TO BECOME A MAIN CHARACTER MYSELF.
(FACELESS BACKGROUND CHARACTERS ARE JUST ASKING TO GET KILLED BY RANDOM FALLING RUBBLE EVERY DAY, AMIRITE?
SO I PUT ON THIS OUTFIT, AND (NEEDING MONEY) BECAME A MERCENARY SOLDIER.
I WORRY ABOUT DEALING WITH *THESE* DUDES, MAN.
I GET IT, BUT LISTEN. *THEY'RE* SELLING. WE'RE JUST BUYING. NO REASON TO MESS UP *BUSINESS*, RI--
WHO IS THAT?
AS TIME WENT ON, I DEVELOPED FEELINGS FOR ALL THESE MAKE-BELIEVE PEOPLE. THEY FELT *REAL*. LIVE IN A FICTIONAL WORLD LONG ENOUGH, I GUESS THAT HAPPENS.
SO I ADJUSTED MY WAYS, AND BECAME AN HONEST-TO-GOODNESS, PRO BONO *SUPER HERO*. PURE-HEARTED ALL THE WAY, BABY. JUST LIKE ALL MY FAVORITES I USED TO READ! NOW I WAS *ONE OF THEM*.
GOOD EVENING, SHADY MEN!
NICE NIGHT FOR A DRUG DEAL, EH?
LADY, I DON'T KNOW WHO YOU ARE, BUT YOU BETTER GET THE HELL OUT OF HERE.
NAAAAAH, I THINK I'M GONNA *STOP* YOU CRIMINALS! *EH?* SOUND GOOD?
I DON'T THINK SO.
THERE WAS JUST ONE PROBLEM.

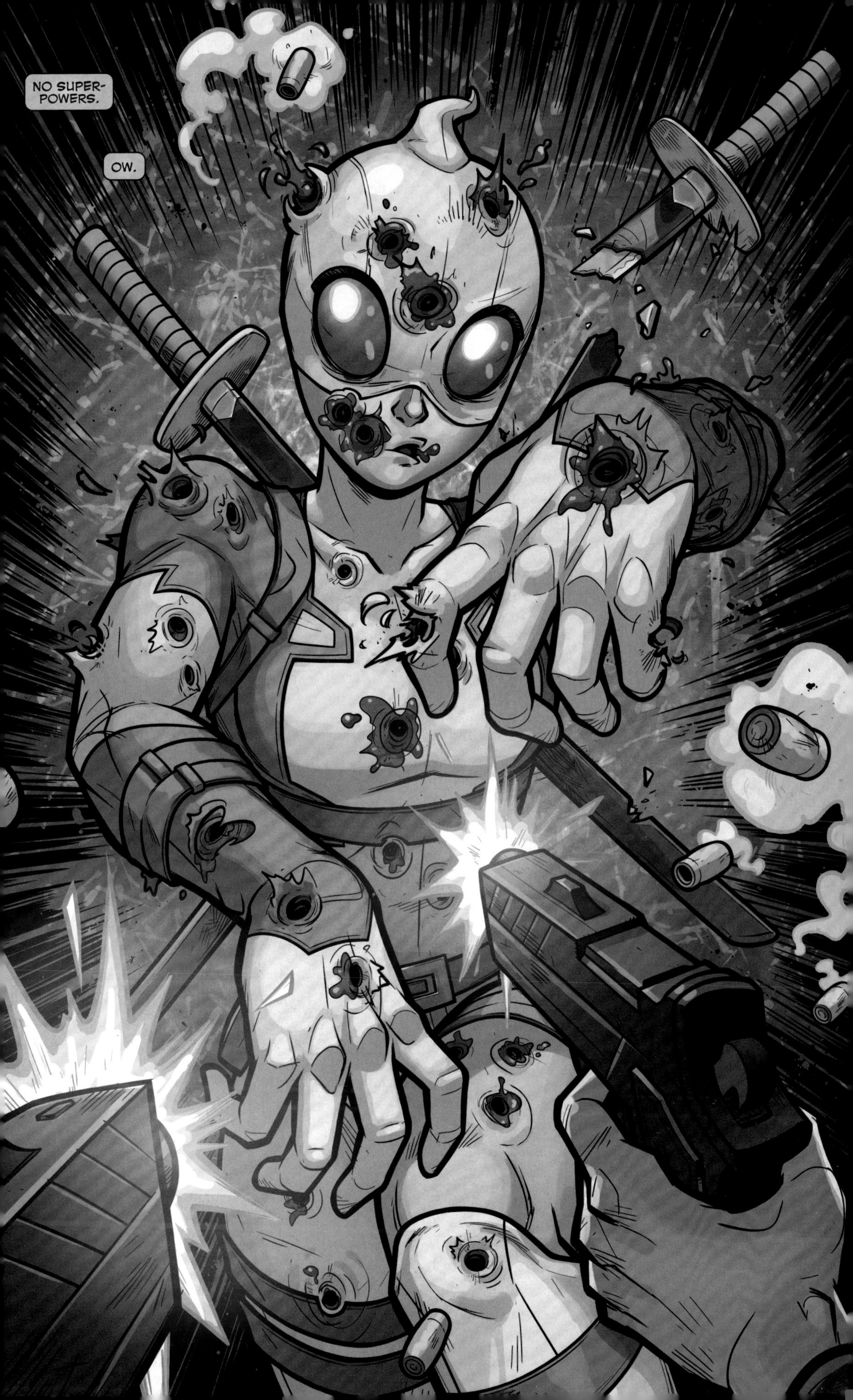
NO SUPER-POWERS.
OW.

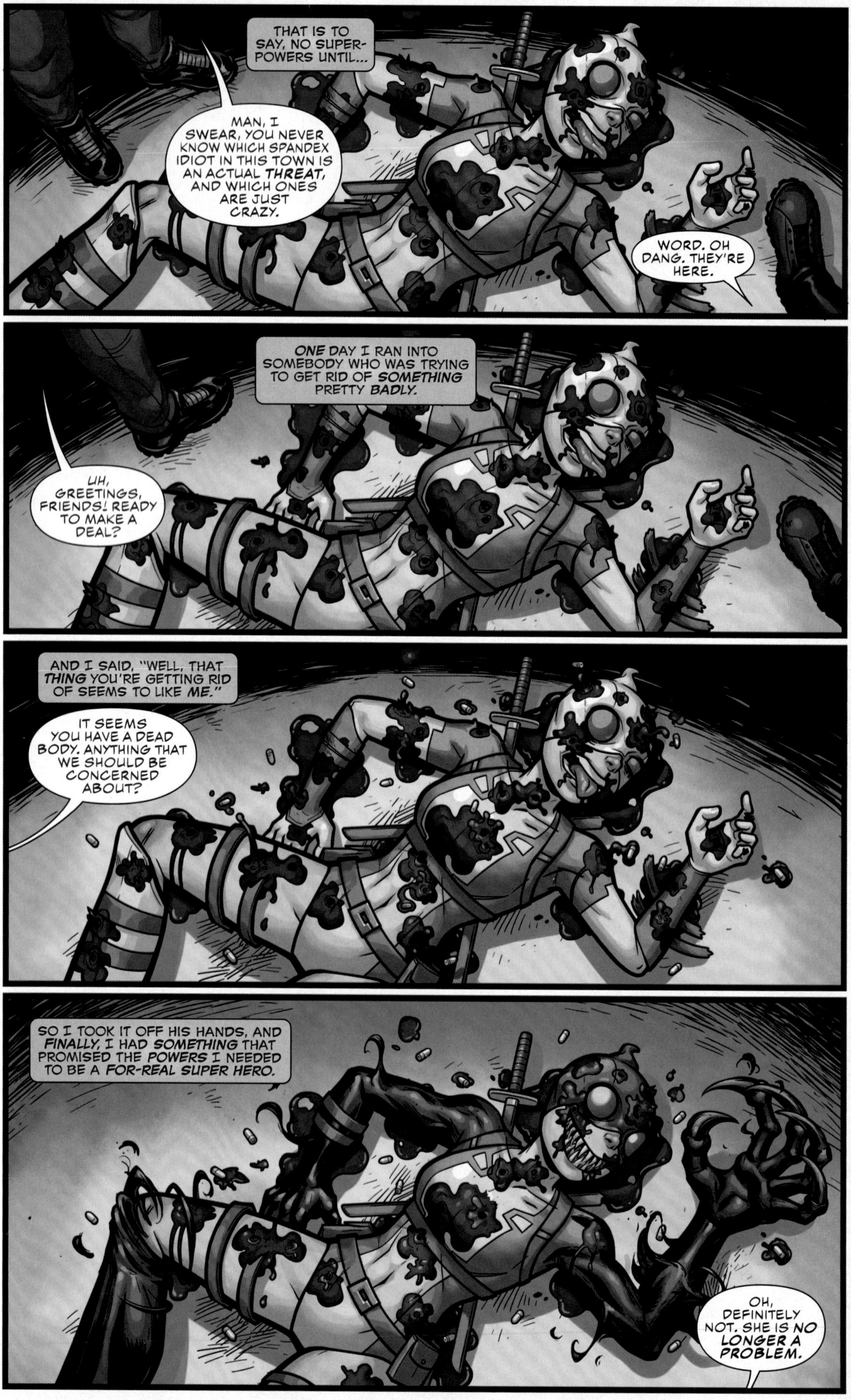

THAT IS TO SAY, NO SUPER-POWERS UNTIL...
MAN, I SWEAR, YOU NEVER KNOW WHICH SPANDEX IDIOT IN THIS TOWN IS AN ACTUAL THREAT, AND WHICH ONES ARE JUST CRAZY.
WORD. OH DANG. THEY'RE HERE.
ONE DAY I RAN INTO SOMEBODY WHO WAS TRYING TO GET RID OF SOMETHING PRETTY BADLY.
UH, GREETINGS, FRIENDS! READY TO MAKE A DEAL?
AND I SAID, "WELL, THAT THING YOU'RE GETTING RID OF SEEMS TO LIKE ME."
IT SEEMS YOU HAVE A DEAD BODY. ANYTHING THAT WE SHOULD BE CONCERNED ABOUT?
SO I TOOK IT OFF HIS HANDS, AND FINALLY, I HAD SOMETHING THAT PROMISED THE POWERS I NEEDED TO BE A FOR-REAL SUPER HERO.
OH, DEFINITELY NOT. SHE IS NO LONGER A PROBLEM.

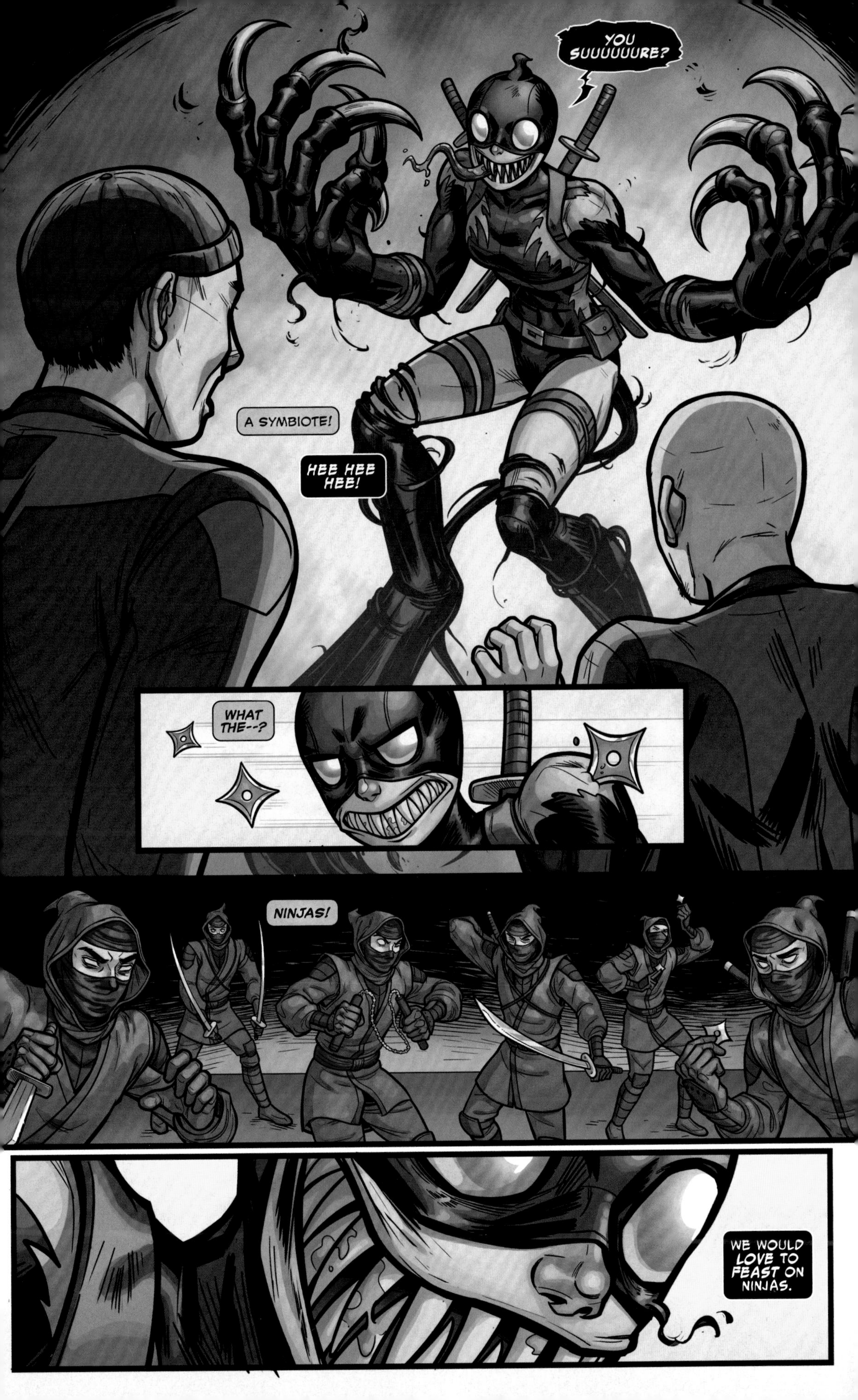
YOU SUUUUUURE?
A SYMBIOTE!
HEE HEE HEE!
WHAT THE--?
NINJAS!
WE WOULD LOVE TO FEAST ON NINJAS.

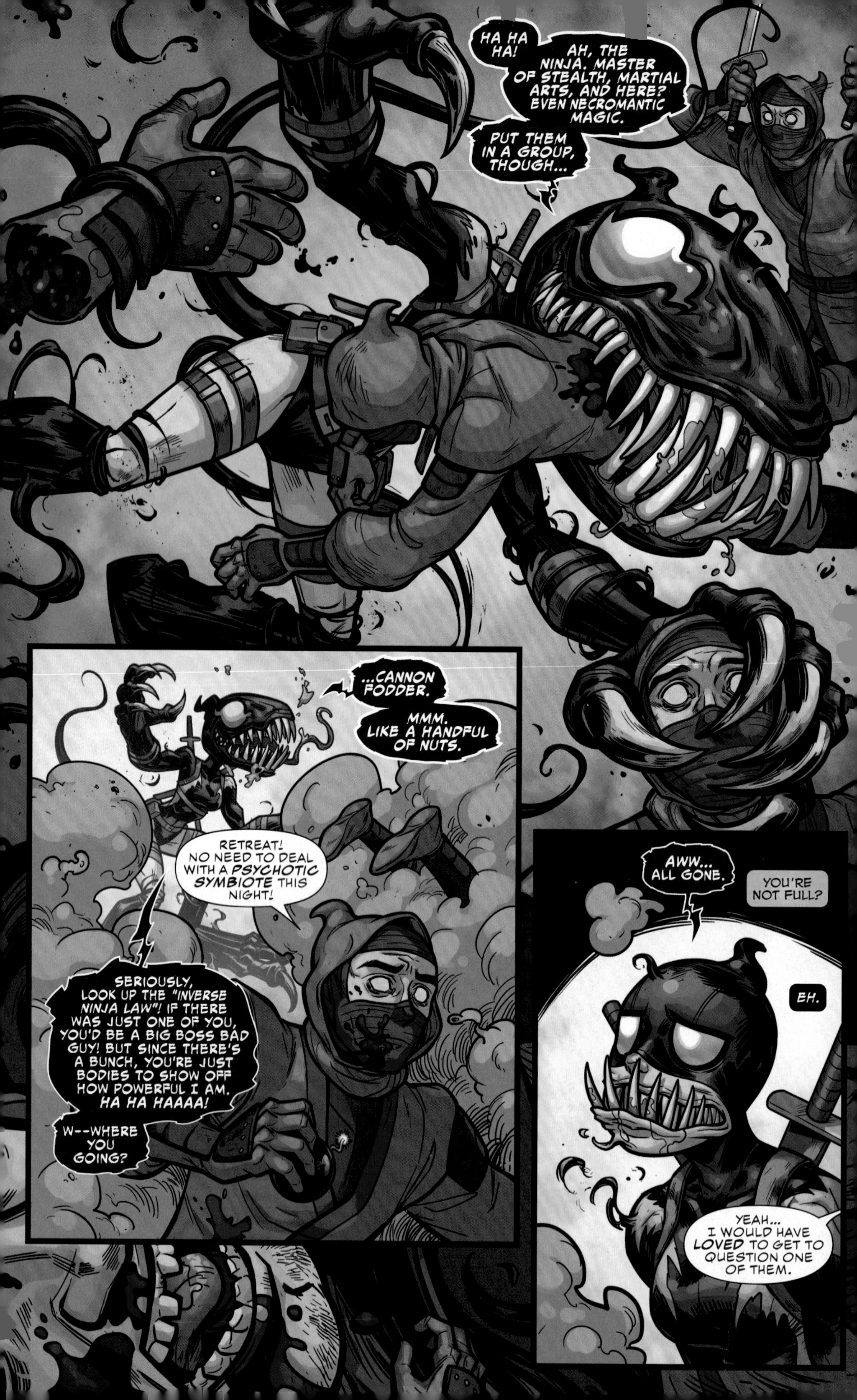

HA HA HA!
AH, THE NINJA. MASTER OF STEALTH, MARTIAL ARTS, AND HERE? EVEN NECROMANTIC MAGIC.
PUT THEM IN A GROUP, THOUGH...
...CANNON FODDER.
MMM. LIKE A HANDFUL OF NUTS.
RETREAT! NO NEED TO DEAL WITH A PSYCHOTIC SYMBIOTE THIS NIGHT!
SERIOUSLY, LOOK UP THE "INVERSE NINJA LAW"! IF THERE WAS JUST ONE OF YOU, YOU'D BE A BIG BOSS BAD GUY! BUT SINCE THERE'S A BUNCH, YOU'RE JUST BODIES TO SHOW OFF HOW POWERFUL I AM. HA HA HAAAA!
W--WHERE YOU GOING?
AWW... ALL GONE.
YOU'RE NOT FULL?
EH.
YEAH... I WOULD HAVE LOVED TO GET TO QUESTION ONE OF THEM.

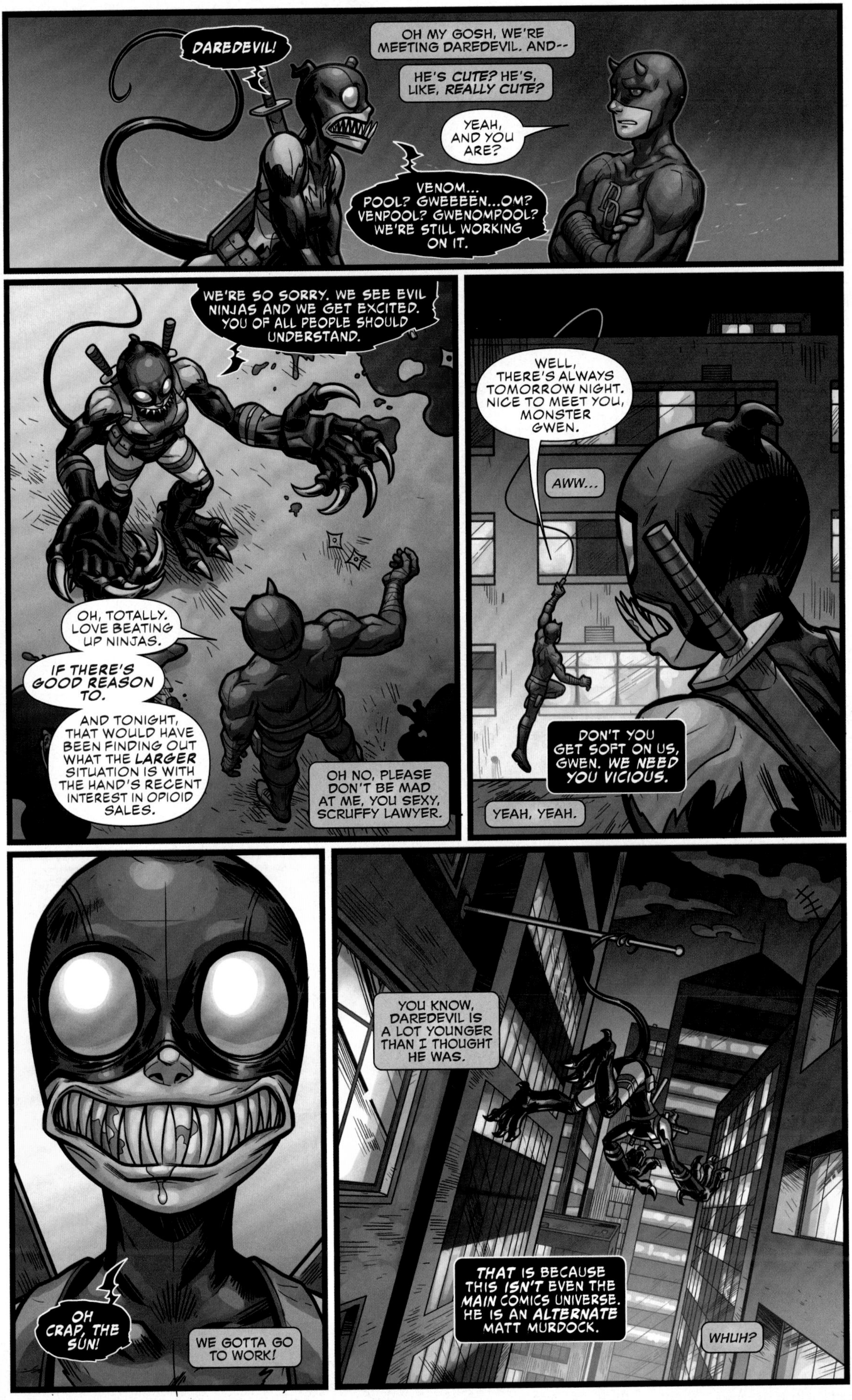
DAREDEVIL!
OH MY GOSH, WE'RE MEETING DAREDEVIL. AND--
HE'S CUTE? HE'S, LIKE, REALLY CUTE?
YEAH, AND YOU ARE?
VENOM... POOL? GWEBEEN...OM? VENPOOL? GWENOMPOOL? WE'RE STILL WORKING ON IT.
WE'RE SO SORRY. WE SEE EVIL NINJAS AND WE GET EXCITED. YOU OF ALL PEOPLE SHOULD UNDERSTAND.
OH, TOTALLY. LOVE BEATING UP NINJAS.
IF THERE'S GOOD REASON TO.
AND TONIGHT, THAT WOULD HAVE BEEN FINDING OUT WHAT THE LARGER SITUATION IS WITH THE HAND'S RECENT INTEREST IN OPIOID SALES.
OH NO, PLEASE DON'T BE MAD AT ME, YOU SEXY, SCRUFFY LAWYER.
WELL, THERE'S ALWAYS TOMORROW NIGHT. NICE TO MEET YOU, MONSTER GWEN.
AWW...
DON'T YOU GET SOFT ON US, GWEN. WE NEED YOU VICIOUS.
YEAH, YEAH.
OH CRAP, THE SUN!
WE GOTTA GO TO WORK!
YOU KNOW, DAREDEVIL IS A LOT YOUNGER THAN I THOUGHT HE WAS.
THAT IS BECAUSE THIS ISN'T EVEN THE MAIN COMICS UNIVERSE. HE IS AN ALTERNATE MATT MURDOCK.
WHUH?

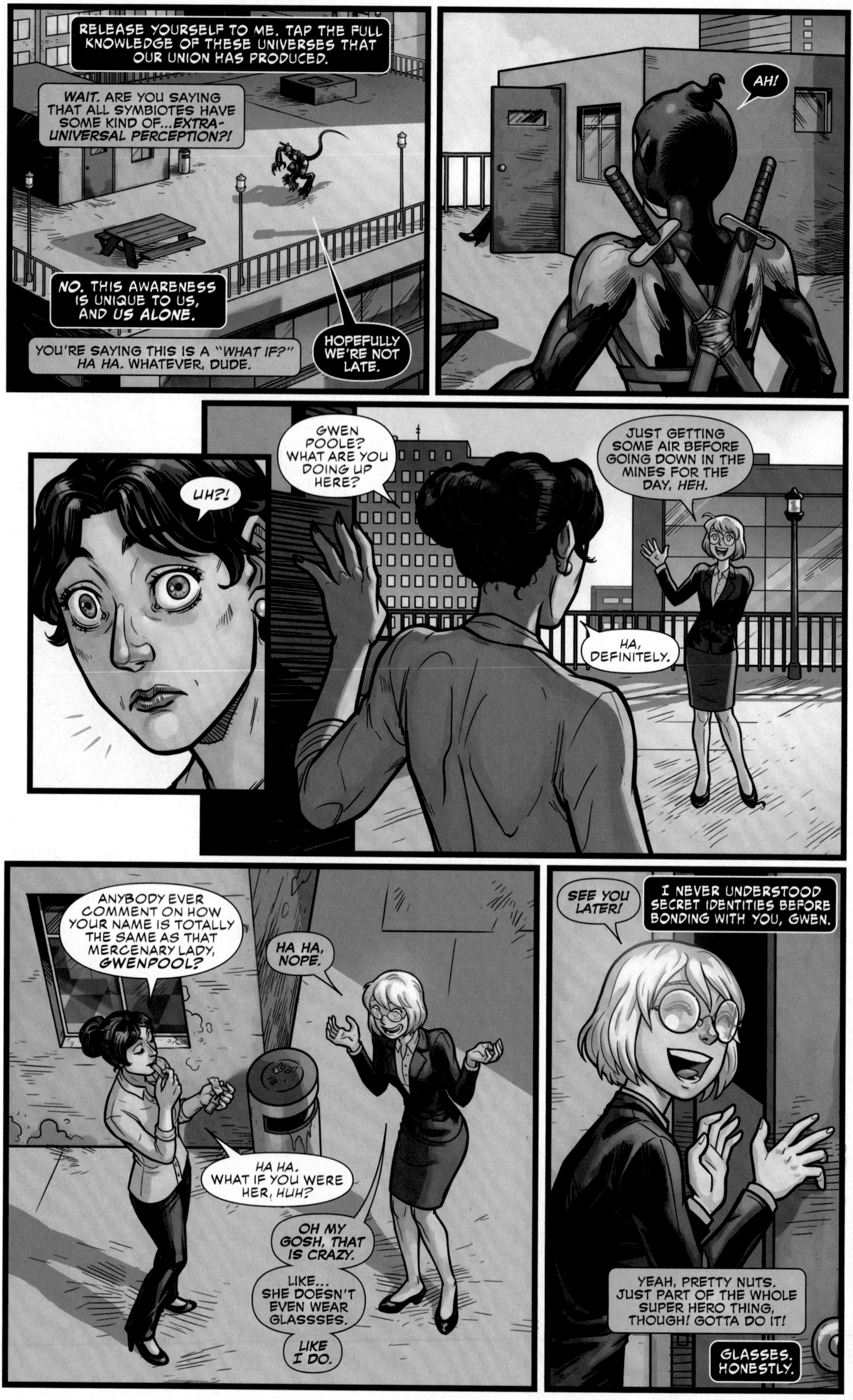
RELEASE YOURSELF TO ME. TAP THE FULL KNOWLEDGE OF THESE UNIVERSES THAT OUR UNION HAS PRODUCED.
WAIT. ARE YOU SAYING THAT ALL SYMBIOTES HAVE SOME KIND OF...EXTRA-UNIVERSAL PERCEPTION?!
NO. THIS AWARENESS IS UNIQUE TO US, AND US ALONE.
YOU'RE SAYING THIS IS A "WHAT IF?" HA HA. WHATEVER, DUDE.
HOPEFULLY WE'RE NOT LATE.
AH!
UH?!
GWEN POOLE? WHAT ARE YOU DOING UP HERE?
JUST GETTING SOME AIR BEFORE GOING DOWN IN THE MINES FOR THE DAY, HEH.
HA, DEFINITELY.
ANYBODY EVER COMMENT ON HOW YOUR NAME IS TOTALLY THE SAME AS THAT MERCENARY LADY, GWENPOOL?
HA HA, NOPE.
HA HA. WHAT IF YOU WERE HER, HUH?
OH MY GOSH, THAT IS CRAZY.
LIKE... SHE DOESN'T EVEN WEAR GLASSSES.
LIKE I DO.
SEE YOU LATER!
I NEVER UNDERSTOOD SECRET IDENTITIES BEFORE BONDING WITH YOU, GWEN.
YEAH, PRETTY NUTS. JUST PART OF THE WHOLE SUPER HERO THING, THOUGH! GOTTA DO IT!
GLASSES. HONESTLY.

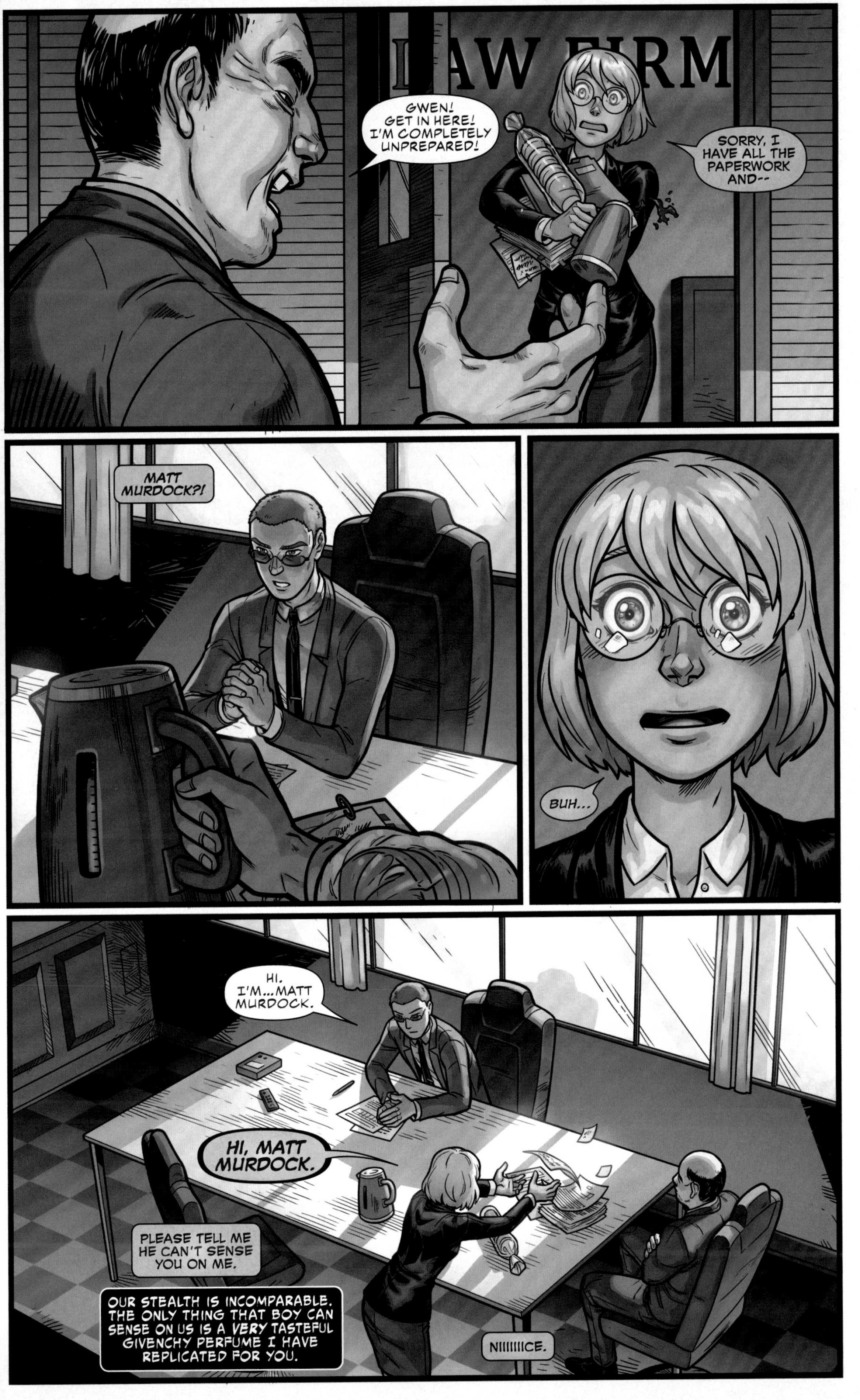
LAW FIRM
GWEN! GET IN HERE! I'M COMPLETELY UNPREPARED!
SORRY, I HAVE ALL THE PAPERWORK AND--
MATT MURDOCK?!
BUH...
HI. I'M...MATT MURDOCK.
HI, MATT MURDOCK.
PLEASE TELL ME HE CAN'T SENSE YOU ON ME.
OUR STEALTH IS INCOMPARABLE. THE ONLY THING THAT BOY CAN SENSE ON US IS A VERY TASTEFUL GIVENCHY PERFUME I HAVE REPLICATED FOR YOU.
NIIIIIICE.

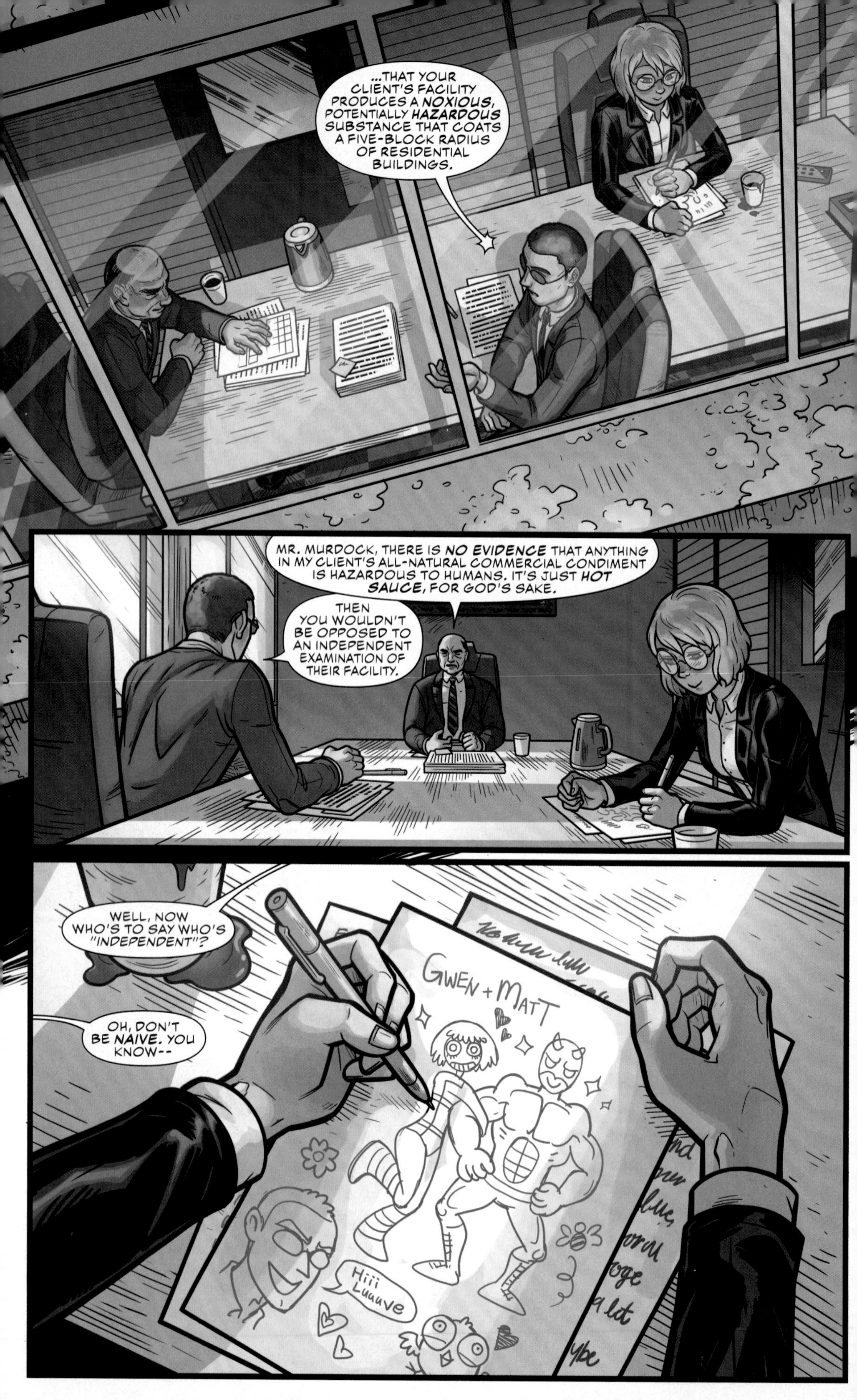
...THAT YOUR CLIENT'S FACILITY PRODUCES A NOXIOUS, POTENTIALLY HAZARDOUS SUBSTANCE THAT COATS A FIVE-BLOCK RADIUS OF RESIDENTIAL BUILDINGS.
MR. MURDOCK, THERE IS NO EVIDENCE THAT ANYTHING IN MY CLIENT'S ALL-NATURAL COMMERCIAL CONDIMENT IS HAZARDOUS TO HUMANS. IT'S JUST HOT SAUCE, FOR GOD'S SAKE.
THEN YOU WOULDN'T BE OPPOSED TO AN INDEPENDENT EXAMINATION OF THEIR FACILITY.
WELL, NOW WHO'S TO SAY WHO'S "INDEPENDENT"?
OH, DON'T BE NAIVE. YOU KNOW--
GWEN + MATT
Hiii Luuuve

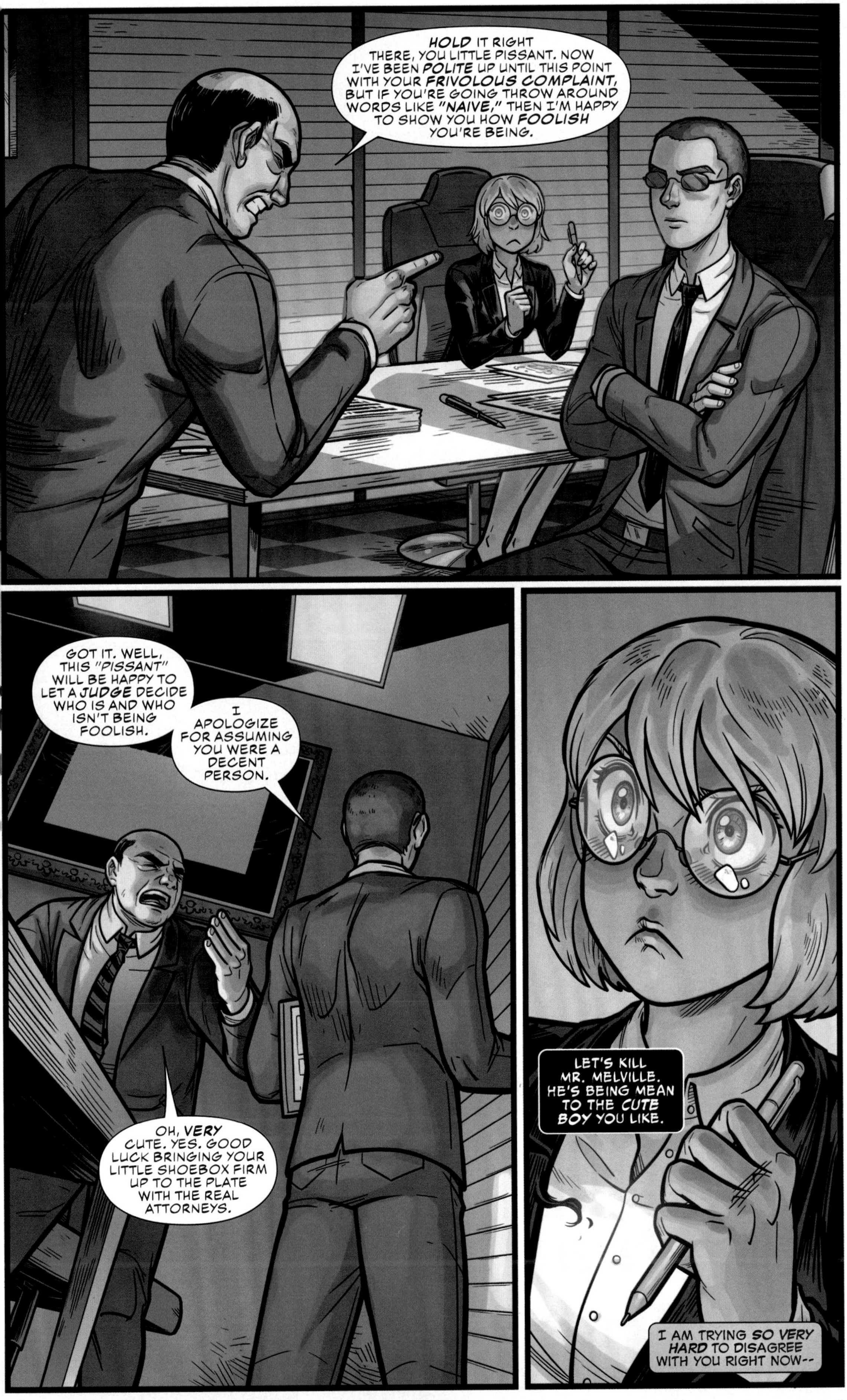
HOLD IT RIGHT THERE, YOU LITTLE PISSANT. NOW I'VE BEEN POLITE UP UNTIL THIS POINT WITH YOUR FRIVOLOUS COMPLAINT, BUT IF YOU'RE GOING THROW AROUND WORDS LIKE "NAIVE," THEN I'M HAPPY TO SHOW YOU HOW FOOLISH YOU'RE BEING.
GOT IT. WELL, THIS "PISSANT" WILL BE HAPPY TO LET A JUDGE DECIDE WHO IS AND WHO ISN'T BEING FOOLISH.
I APOLOGIZE FOR ASSUMING YOU WERE A DECENT PERSON.
OH, VERY CUTE. YES. GOOD LUCK BRINGING YOUR LITTLE SHOEBOX FIRM UP TO THE PLATE WITH THE REAL ATTORNEYS.
LET'S KILL MR. MELVILLE. HE'S BEING MEAN TO THE CUTE BOY YOU LIKE.
I AM TRYING SO VERY HARD TO DISAGREE WITH YOU RIGHT NOW--

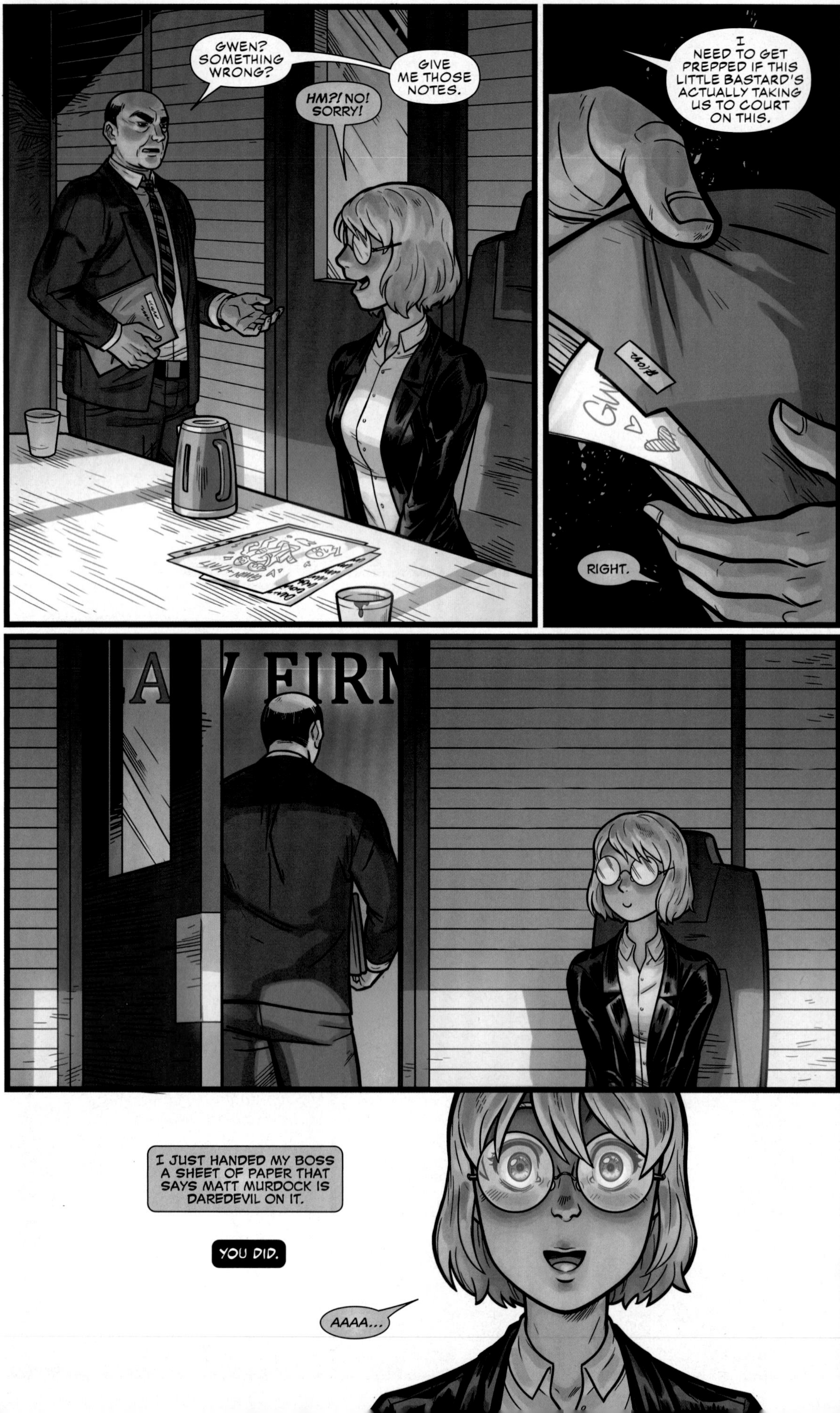
GWEN? SOMETHING WRONG?
HM?! NO! SORRY!
GIVE ME THOSE NOTES.
I NEED TO GET PREPPED IF THIS LITTLE BASTARD'S ACTUALLY TAKING US TO COURT ON THIS.
RIGHT.
LAW FIRM
I JUST HANDED MY BOSS A SHEET OF PAPER THAT SAYS MATT MURDOCK IS DAREDEVIL ON IT.
YOU DID.
AAAA...

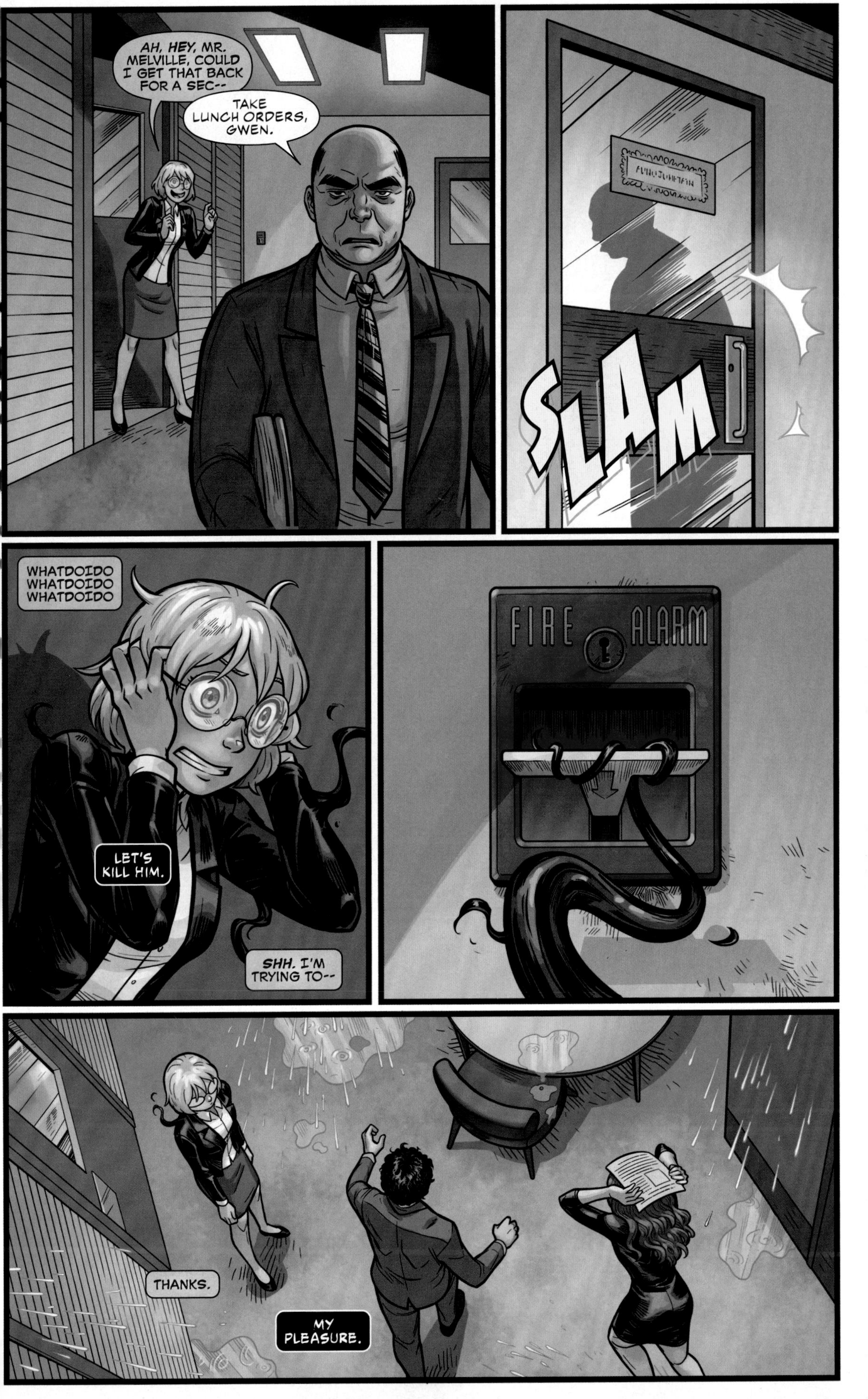
AH, HEY, MR. MELVILLE, COULD I GET THAT BACK FOR A SEC--
TAKE LUNCH ORDERS, GWEN.
SLAM
WHATDOIDO WHATDOIDO WHATDOIDO
LET'S KILL HIM.
SHH. I'M TRYING TO--
FIRE ALARM
THANKS.
MY PLEASURE.

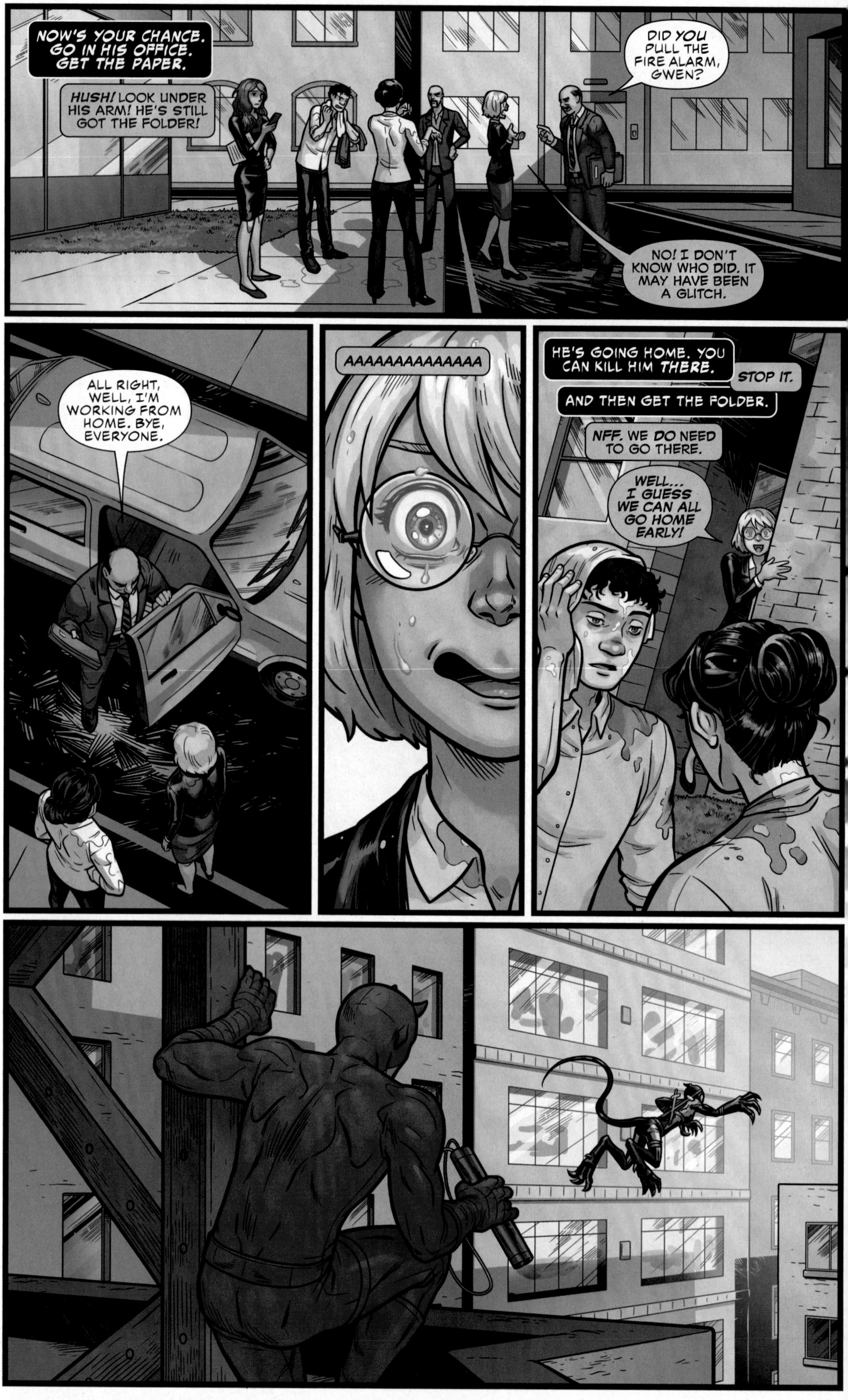
NOW'S YOUR CHANCE. GO IN HIS OFFICE. GET THE PAPER.
HUSH! LOOK UNDER HIS ARM! HE'S STILL GOT THE FOLDER!
DID YOU PULL THE FIRE ALARM, GWEN?
NO! I DON'T KNOW WHO DID. IT MAY HAVE BEEN A GLITCH.
ALL RIGHT, WELL, I'M WORKING FROM HOME. BYE, EVERYONE.
AAAAAAAAAAAAAA
HE'S GOING HOME. YOU CAN KILL HIM THERE.
STOP IT.
AND THEN GET THE FOLDER.
NFF. WE DO NEED TO GO THERE.
WELL... I GUESS WE CAN ALL GO HOME EARLY!

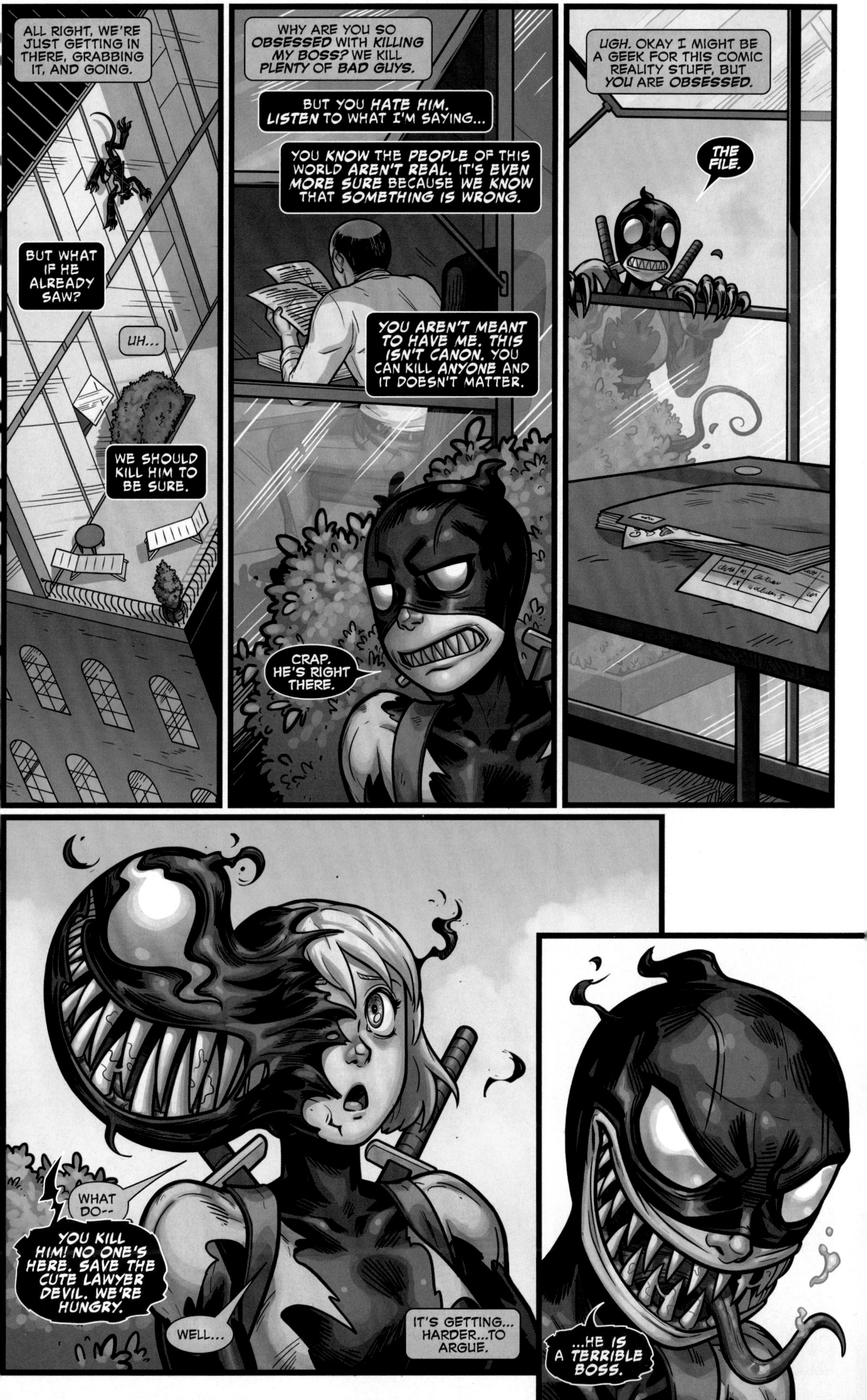

ALL RIGHT, WE'RE JUST GETTING IN THERE, GRABBING IT, AND GOING.
BUT WHAT IF HE ALREADY SAW?
UH...
WE SHOULD KILL HIM TO BE SURE.
WHY ARE YOU SO OBSESSED WITH KILLING MY BOSS? WE KILL PLENTY OF BAD GUYS.
BUT YOU HATE HIM. LISTEN TO WHAT I'M SAYING...
YOU KNOW THE PEOPLE OF THIS WORLD AREN'T REAL. IT'S EVEN MORE SURE BECAUSE WE KNOW THAT SOMETHING IS WRONG.
YOU AREN'T MEANT TO HAVE ME. THIS ISN'T CANON. YOU CAN KILL ANYONE AND IT DOESN'T MATTER.
CRAP. HE'S RIGHT THERE.
UGH. OKAY I MIGHT BE A GEEK FOR THIS COMIC REALITY STUFF, BUT YOU ARE OBSESSED.
THE FILE.
WHAT DO--
YOU KILL HIM! NO ONE'S HERE. SAVE THE CUTE LAWYER DEVIL. WE'RE HUNGRY.
WELL...
IT'S GETTING... HARDER...TO ARGUE.
...HE IS A TERRIBLE BOSS.

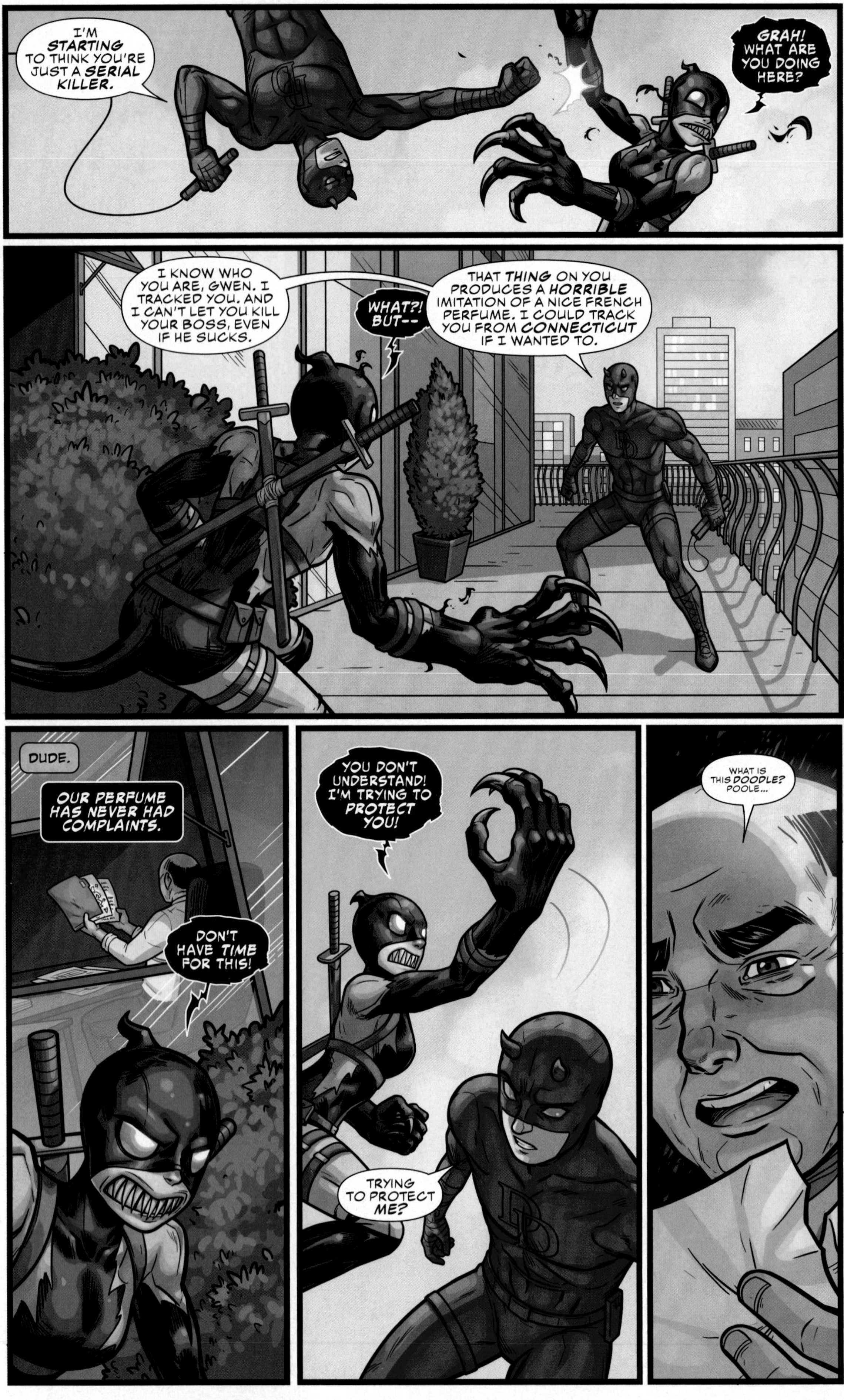
I'M STARTING TO THINK YOU'RE JUST A SERIAL KILLER.
GRAH! WHAT ARE YOU DOING HERE?
I KNOW WHO YOU ARE, GWEN. I TRACKED YOU. AND I CAN'T LET YOU KILL YOUR BOSS, EVEN IF HE SUCKS.
WHAT?! BUT--
THAT THING ON YOU PRODUCES A HORRIBLE IMITATION OF A NICE FRENCH PERFUME. I COULD TRACK YOU FROM CONNECTICUT IF I WANTED TO.
DUDE.
OUR PERFUME HAS NEVER HAD COMPLAINTS.
DON'T HAVE TIME FOR THIS!
YOU DON'T UNDERSTAND! I'M TRYING TO PROTECT YOU!
TRYING TO PROTECT ME?
WHAT IS THIS DOODLE? POOLE...

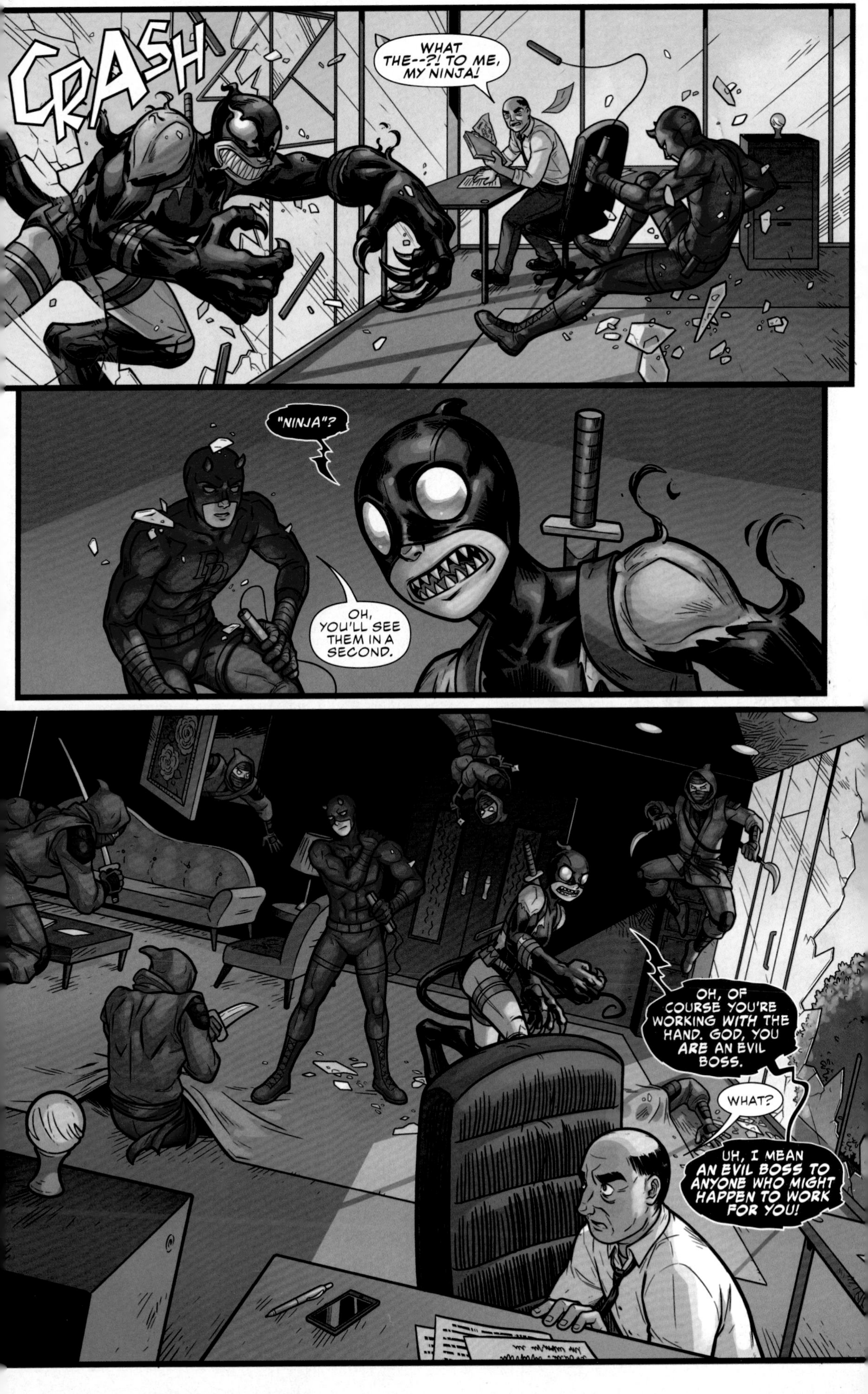
CRASH
WHAT THE--?! TO ME, MY NINJA!
"NINJA"?
OH, YOU'LL SEE THEM IN A SECOND.
OH, OF COURSE YOU'RE WORKING WITH THE HAND. GOD, YOU ARE AN EVIL BOSS.
WHAT?
UH, I MEAN AN EVIL BOSS TO ANYONE WHO MIGHT HAPPEN TO WORK FOR YOU!

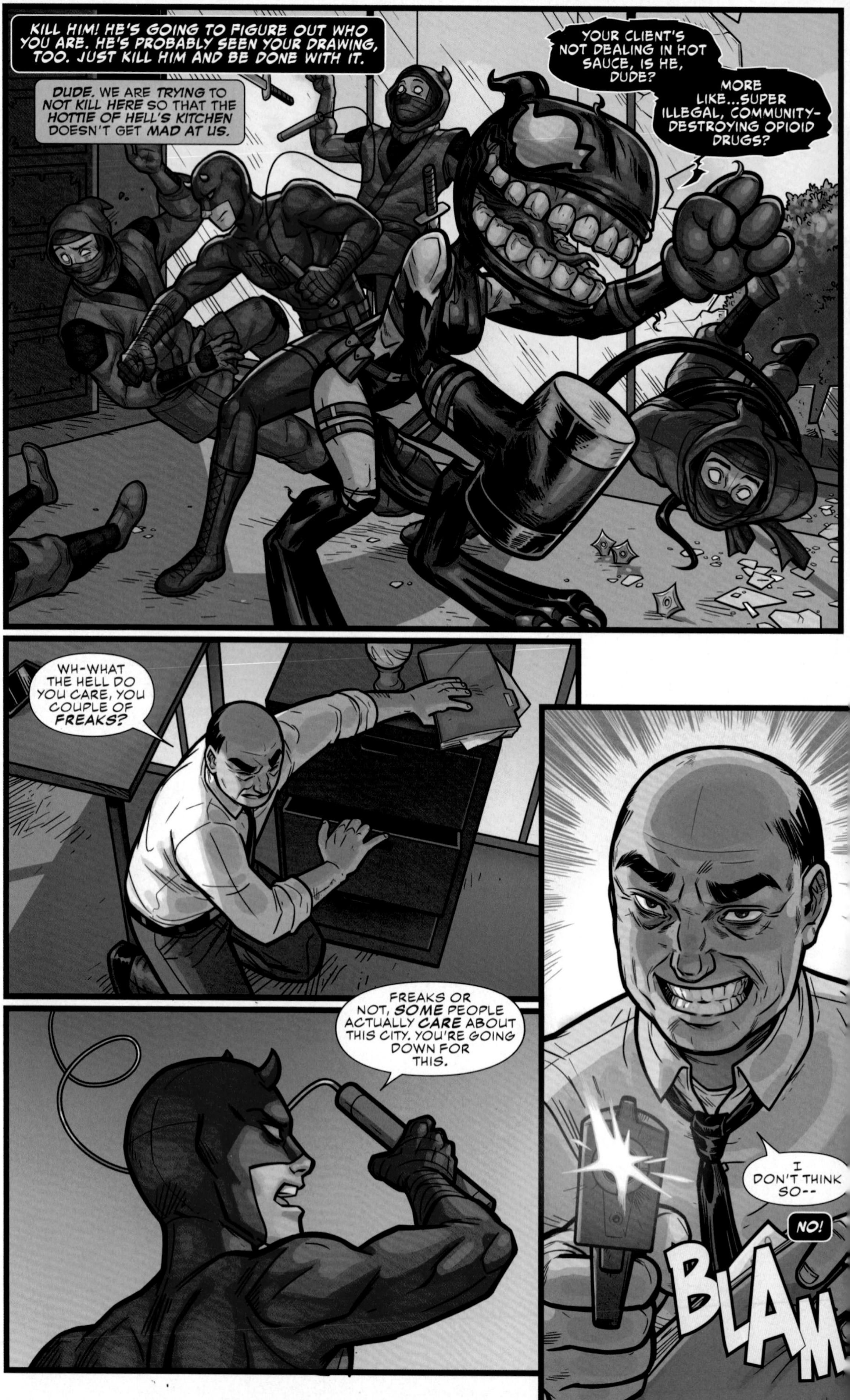
KILL HIM! HE'S GOING TO FIGURE OUT WHO YOU ARE. HE'S PROBABLY SEEN YOUR DRAWING, TOO. JUST KILL HIM AND BE DONE WITH IT.
DUDE. WE ARE TRYING TO NOT KILL HERE SO THAT THE HOTTIE OF HELL'S KITCHEN DOESN'T GET MAD AT US.
YOUR CLIENT'S NOT DEALING IN HOT SAUCE, IS HE, DUDE?
MORE LIKE...SUPER ILLEGAL, COMMUNITY-DESTROYING OPIOID DRUGS?
WH-WHAT THE HELL DO YOU CARE, YOU COUPLE OF FREAKS?
FREAKS OR NOT, SOME PEOPLE ACTUALLY CARE ABOUT THIS CITY. YOU'RE GOING DOWN FOR THIS.
I DON'T THINK SO--
NO!
BLAM

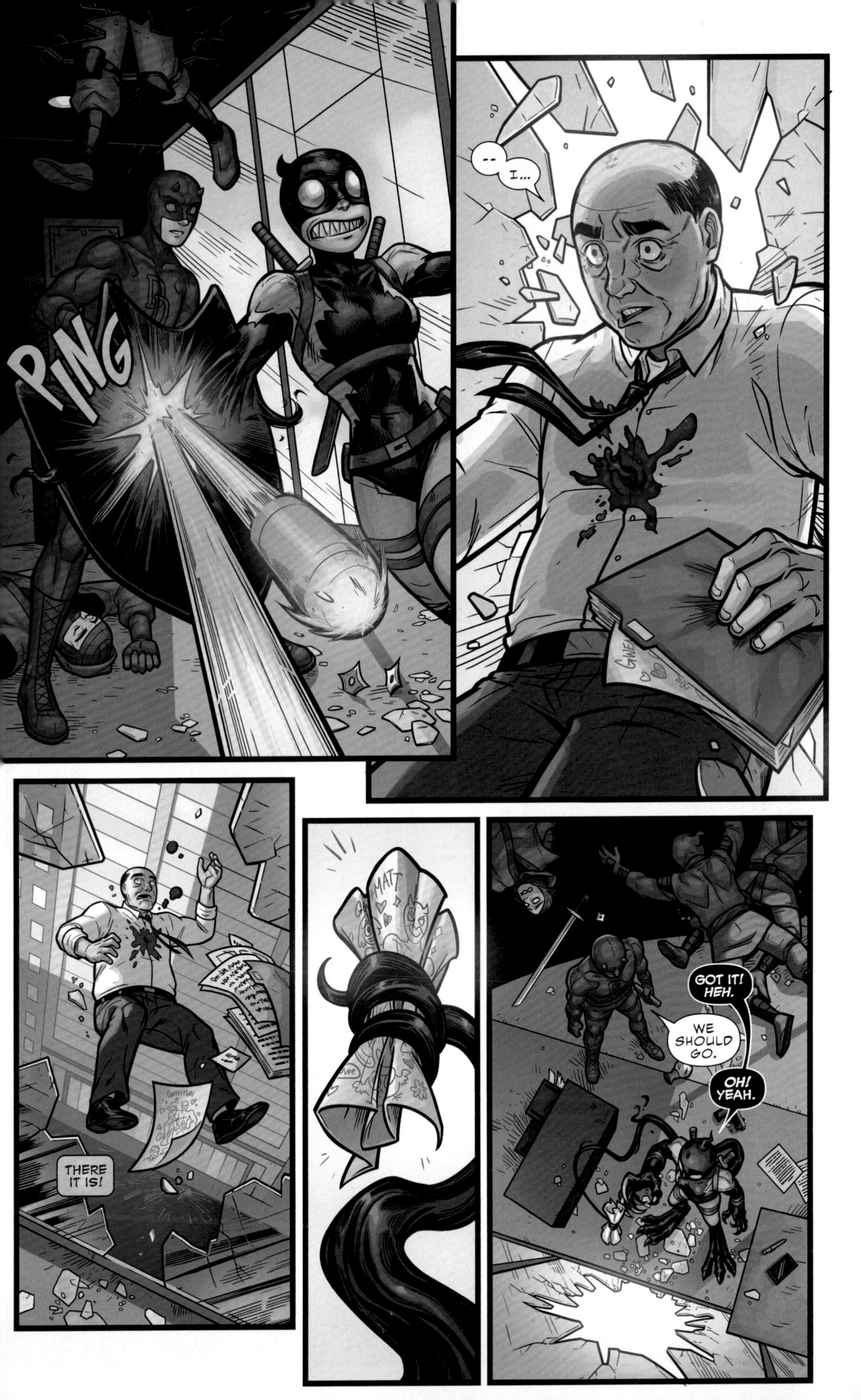
PING
--
I...
THERE IT IS!
GOT IT! HEH.
WE SHOULD GO.
OH! YEAH.

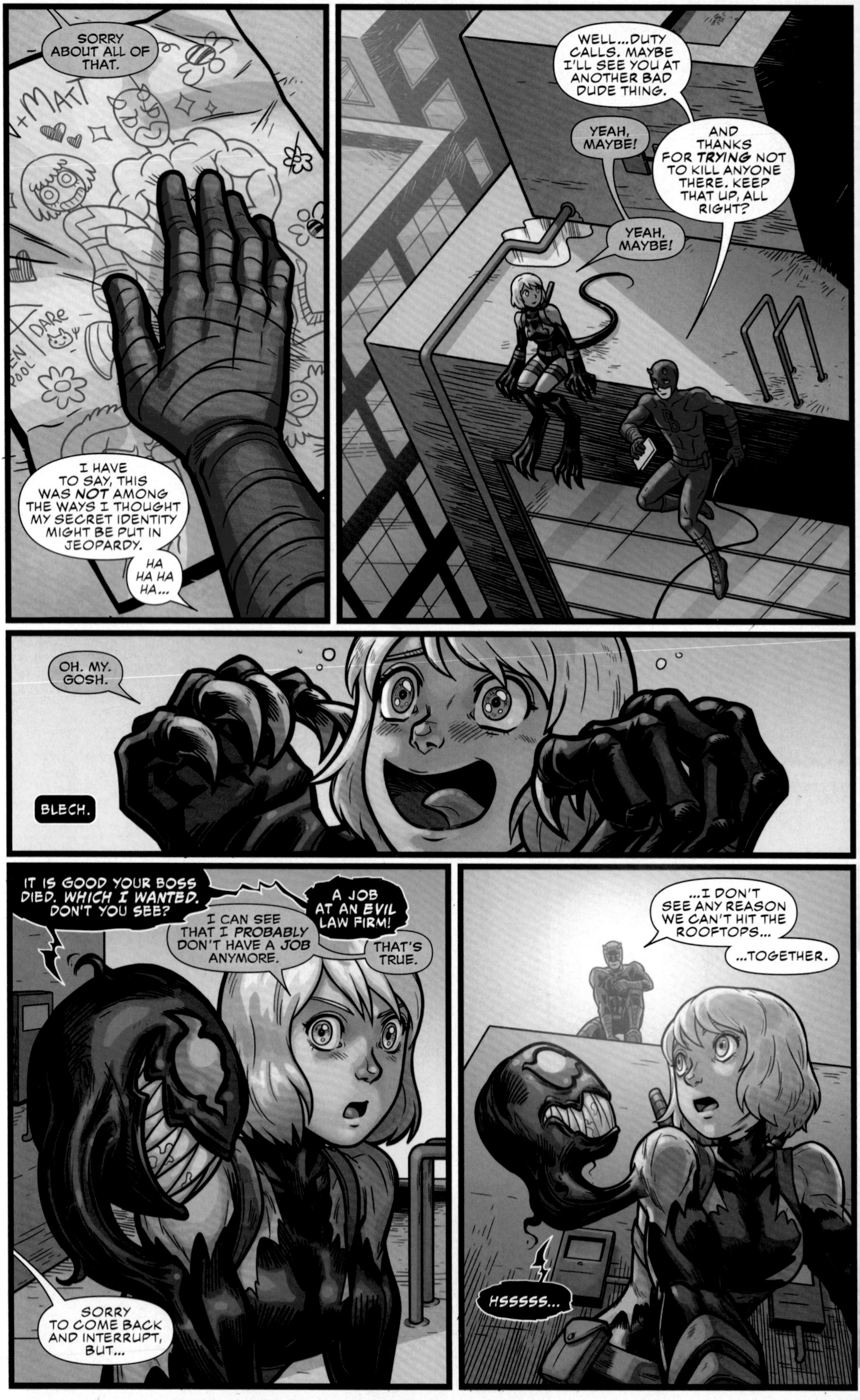
SORRY ABOUT ALL OF THAT.
I HAVE TO SAY, THIS WAS NOT AMONG THE WAYS I THOUGHT MY SECRET IDENTITY MIGHT BE PUT IN JEOPARDY.
HA HA HA HA...
WELL...DUTY CALLS. MAYBE I'LL SEE YOU AT ANOTHER BAD DUDE THING.
YEAH, MAYBE!
AND THANKS FOR TRYING NOT TO KILL ANYONE THERE. KEEP THAT UP, ALL RIGHT?
YEAH, MAYBE!
OH. MY. GOSH.
BLECH.
IT IS GOOD YOUR BOSS DIED. WHICH I WANTED. DON'T YOU SEE?
I CAN SEE THAT I PROBABLY DON'T HAVE A JOB ANYMORE.
A JOB AT AN EVIL LAW FIRM!
THAT'S TRUE.
SORRY TO COME BACK AND INTERRUPT, BUT...
...I DON'T SEE ANY REASON WE CAN'T HIT THE ROOFTOPS...
...TOGETHER.
HSSSSS...

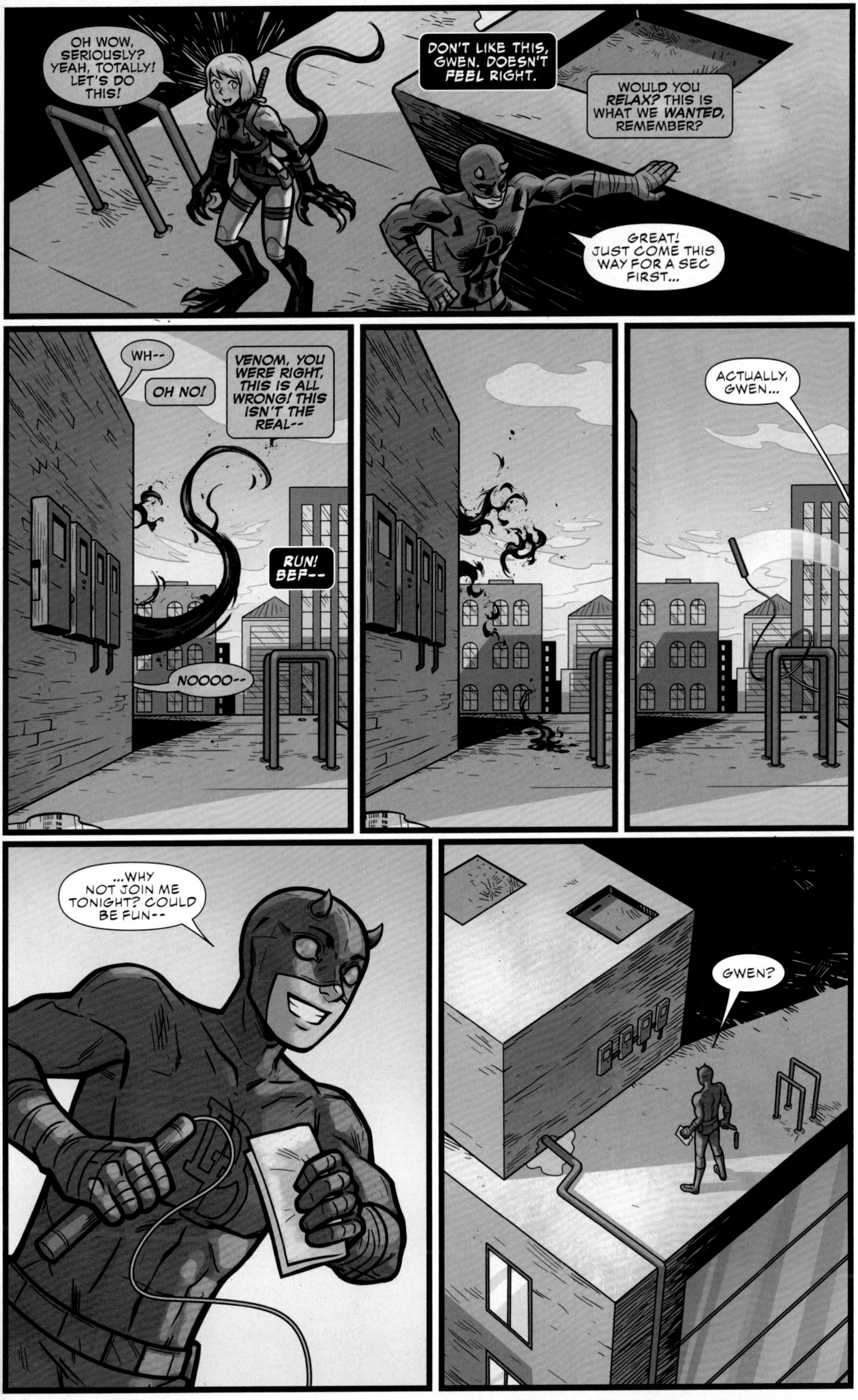
OH WOW, SERIOUSLY? YEAH, TOTALLY! LET'S DO THIS!
DON'T LIKE THIS, GWEN. DOESN'T FEEL RIGHT.
WOULD YOU RELAX? THIS IS WHAT WE WANTED, REMEMBER?
GREAT! JUST COME THIS WAY FOR A SEC FIRST...
WH--
OH NO!
VENOM, YOU WERE RIGHT, THIS IS ALL WRONG! THIS ISN'T THE REAL--
RUN! BEF--
NOOOO--
ACTUALLY, GWEN...
...WHY NOT JOIN ME TONIGHT? COULD BE FUN--
GWEN?

3

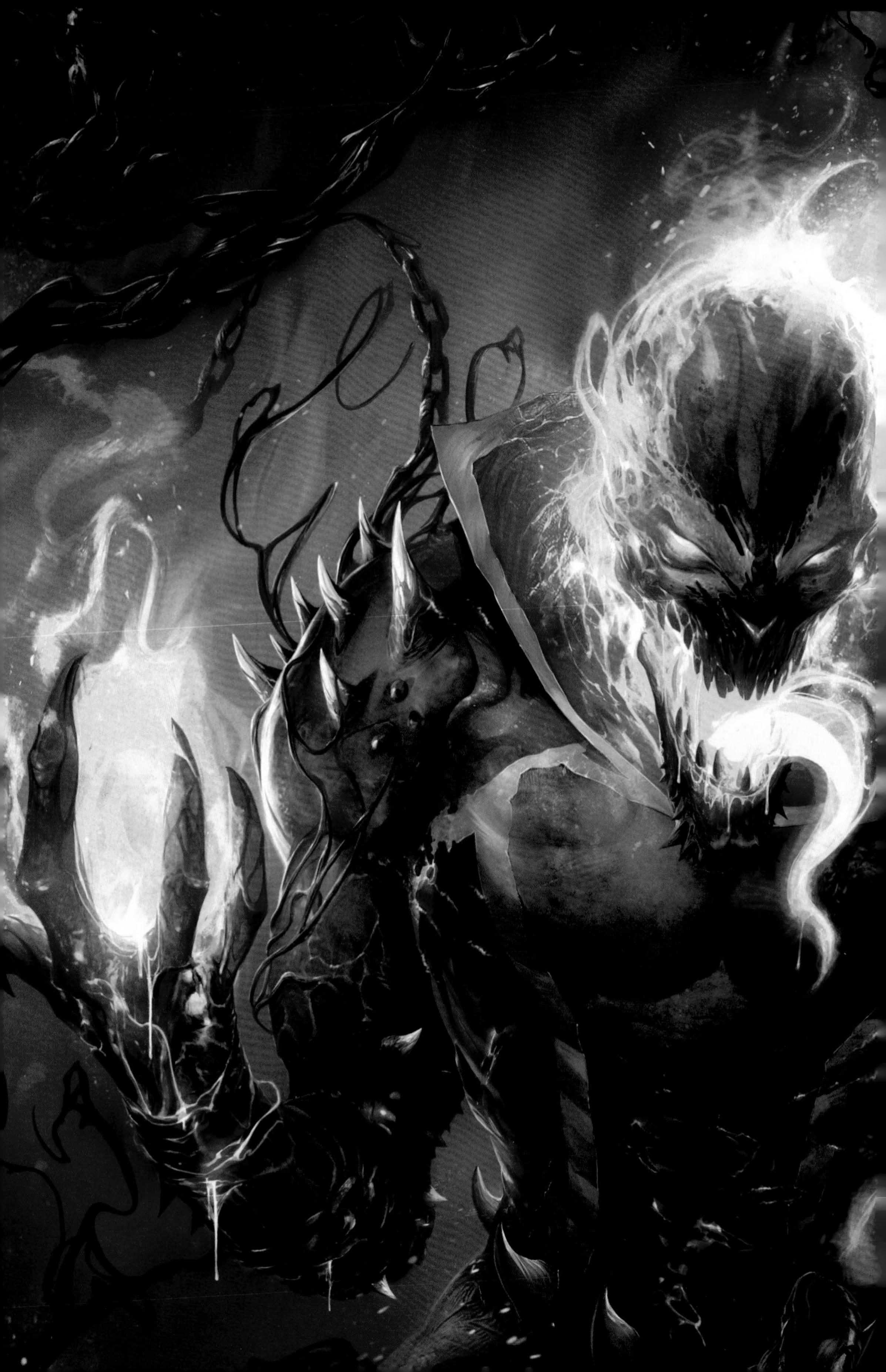

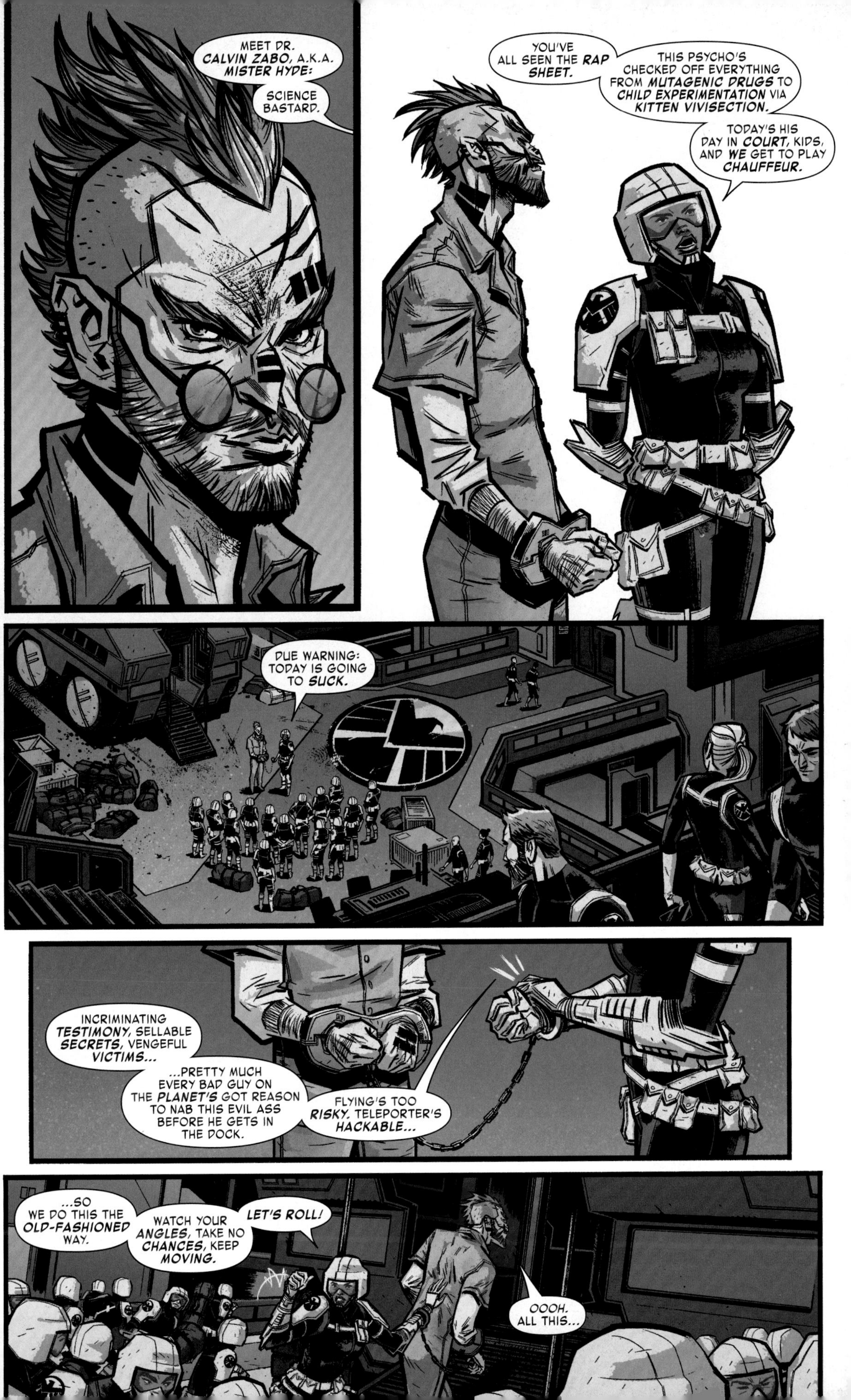
MEET DR. CALVIN ZABO, A.K.A. MISTER HYDE:
SCIENCE BASTARD.
YOU'VE ALL SEEN THE RAP SHEET.
THIS PSYCHO'S CHECKED OFF EVERYTHING FROM MUTAGENIC DRUGS TO CHILD EXPERIMENTATION VIA KITTEN VIVISECTION.
TODAY'S HIS DAY IN COURT, KIDS, AND WE GET TO PLAY CHAUFFEUR.
DUE WARNING: TODAY IS GOING TO SUCK.
INCRIMINATING TESTIMONY, SELLABLE SECRETS, VENGEFUL VICTIMS...
...PRETTY MUCH EVERY BAD GUY ON THE PLANET'S GOT REASON TO NAB THIS EVIL ASS BEFORE HE GETS IN THE DOCK.
FLYING'S TOO RISKY. TELEPORTER'S HACKABLE...
...SO WE DO THIS THE OLD-FASHIONED WAY.
WATCH YOUR ANGLES, TAKE NO CHANCES, KEEP MOVING.
LET'S ROLL!
OOOH. ALL THIS...

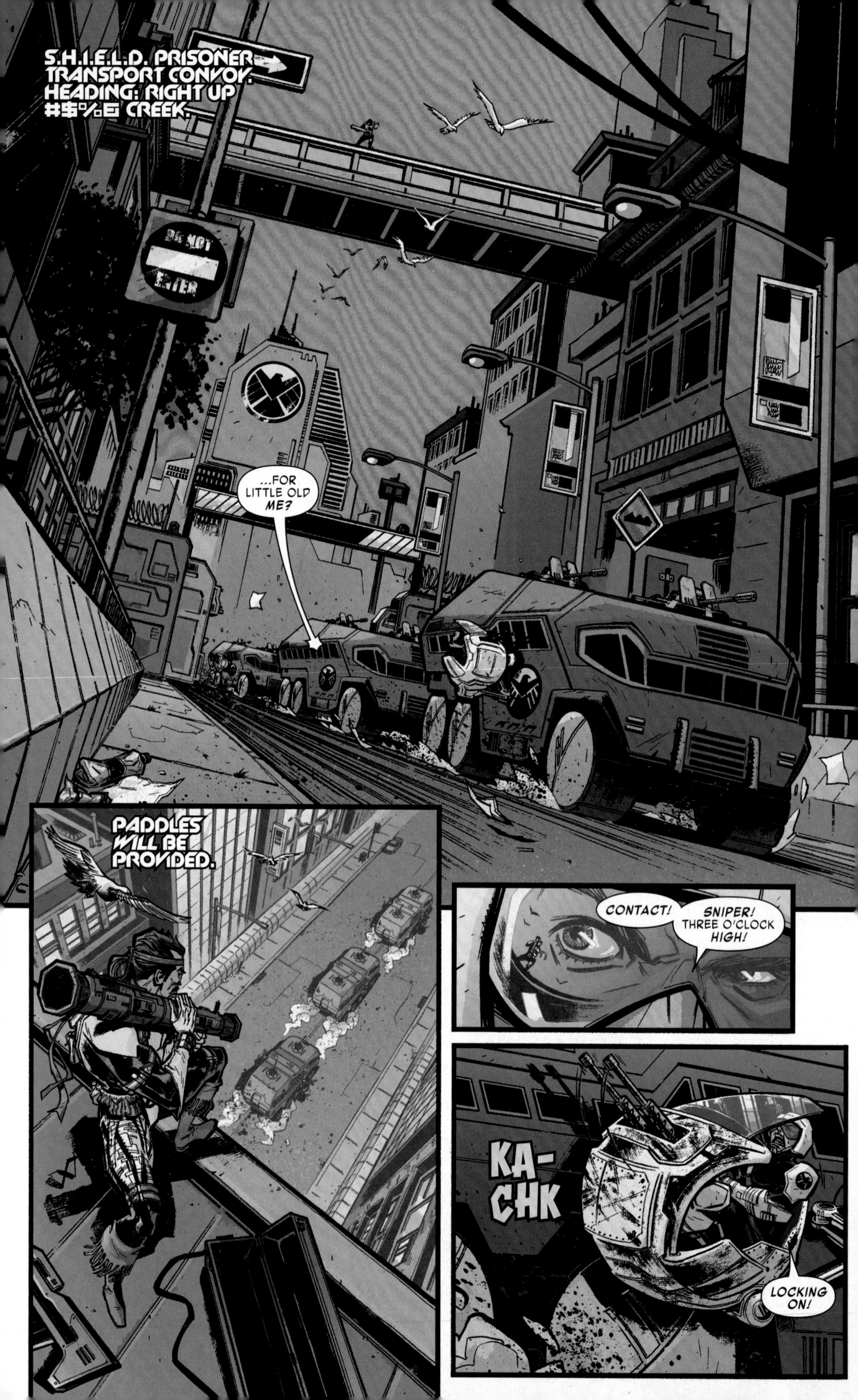
S.H.I.E.L.D. PRISONER TRANSPORT CONVOY. HEADING: RIGHT UP #$%& CREEK.
DO NOT ENTER
...FOR LITTLE OLD ME?
PADDLES WILL BE PROVIDED.
CONTACT!
SNIPER! THREE O'CLOCK HIGH!
KA-CHK
LOCKING ON!

BOOOOM

RUMBLE RUMBLE RUMBLE

WELL, *THAT* DIDN'T TAKE LONG.

WHAT CAN I SAY? I'M AN *EXTREMELY* POPULAR BIO-SADIST.

TARGET NEUTRALIZED. LOOKED LIKE SOME KINDA MUTANT PARAMILI*HEY*--

INCOMING! INCOMING!

PEW PEW   DAKKA DAKKA DAKKA   B-DOOM   OOK OOK OOK

WE GOT *SUPER-GANGSTERS* IN ARMORED VEHICLES ON OUR SIX--

THE *MAGGIA.* THEY KNOW MY TESTIMONY WILL *RUIN* THEM.

--*OOK* UP THERE! COMIN' OUTTA THE SUN! *LAB CHIMPS* WITH *JETPACKS!*

PFT. DRONES. SENT BY MY *RIVALS* TO STEAL MY SECRETS. *LAZY,* I CALL IT.

KSSSSS   UUUUJUHHH   BOOM   BOOM

OH, SWEET *LORD* HELP US--VAMPIRES! *ACTUAL* DUNE-BUGGY *VAMPIRES!*

TCH. SO I CHEATED AT CARDS. LEAVE IT TO *IMMORTALS* TO BEAR A GRUDGE.

...AND, UH, SOME SORT OF GROSS PURPLE ZOMBIE GUYS ON SKATEBOARDS...?

PURPLE Z--?

OHHHHH, I REMEMBER. LAB ACCIDENT, SUMMER OF '08. EMBRYONIC *STEM* CELLS AND *EGGPLANTS.* ALL VERY MESSY.

I EXPECT THEY WORSHIP ME AS A *GOD* OR SOMETHING.

YOU ARE *LITERALLY* THE WORST CREATURE ALIVE.

...

ALL POINTS--

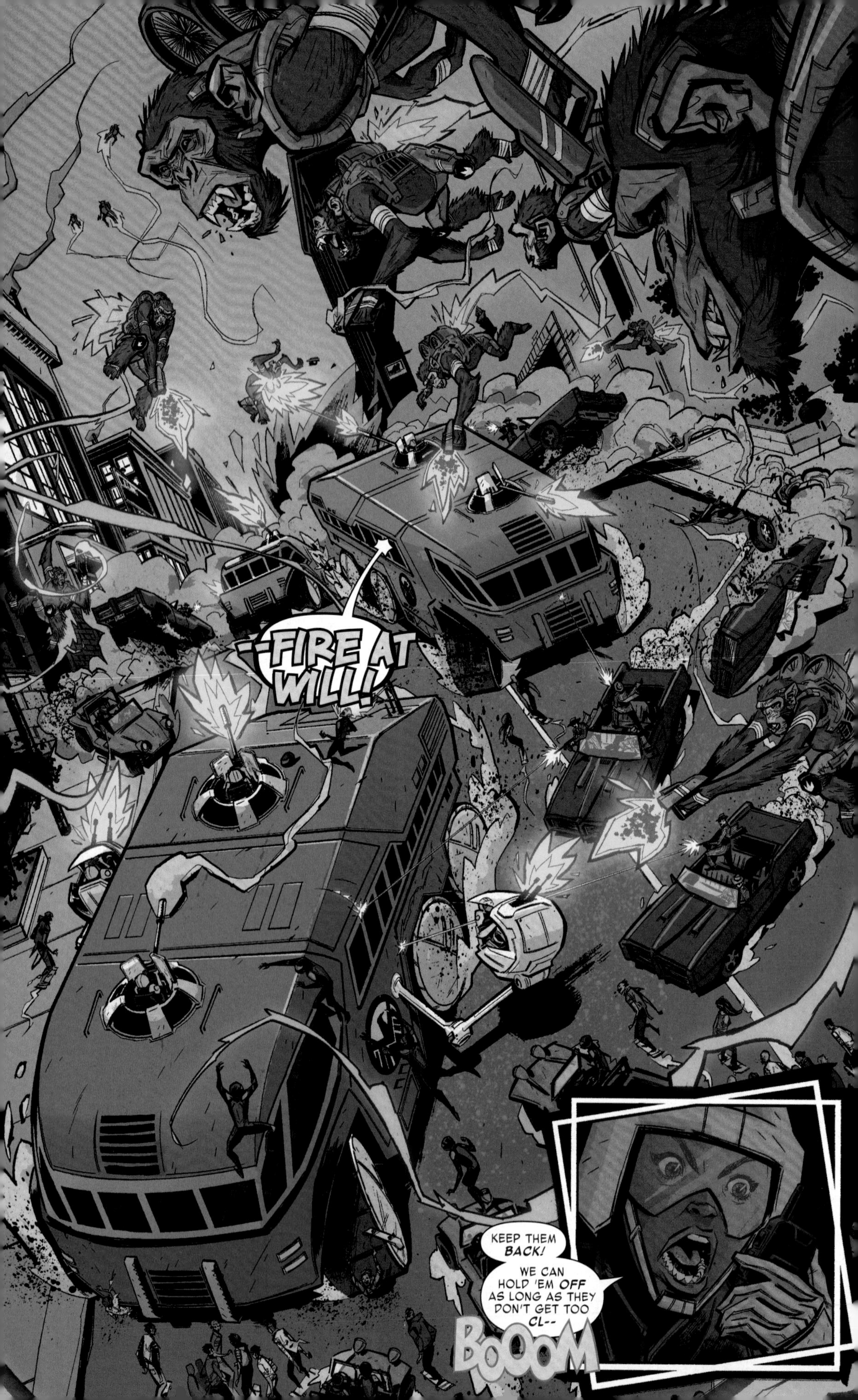
--FIRE AT WILL!
KEEP THEM BACK!
WE CAN HOLD 'EM OFF AS LONG AS THEY DON'T GET TOO CL--
BOOOOM

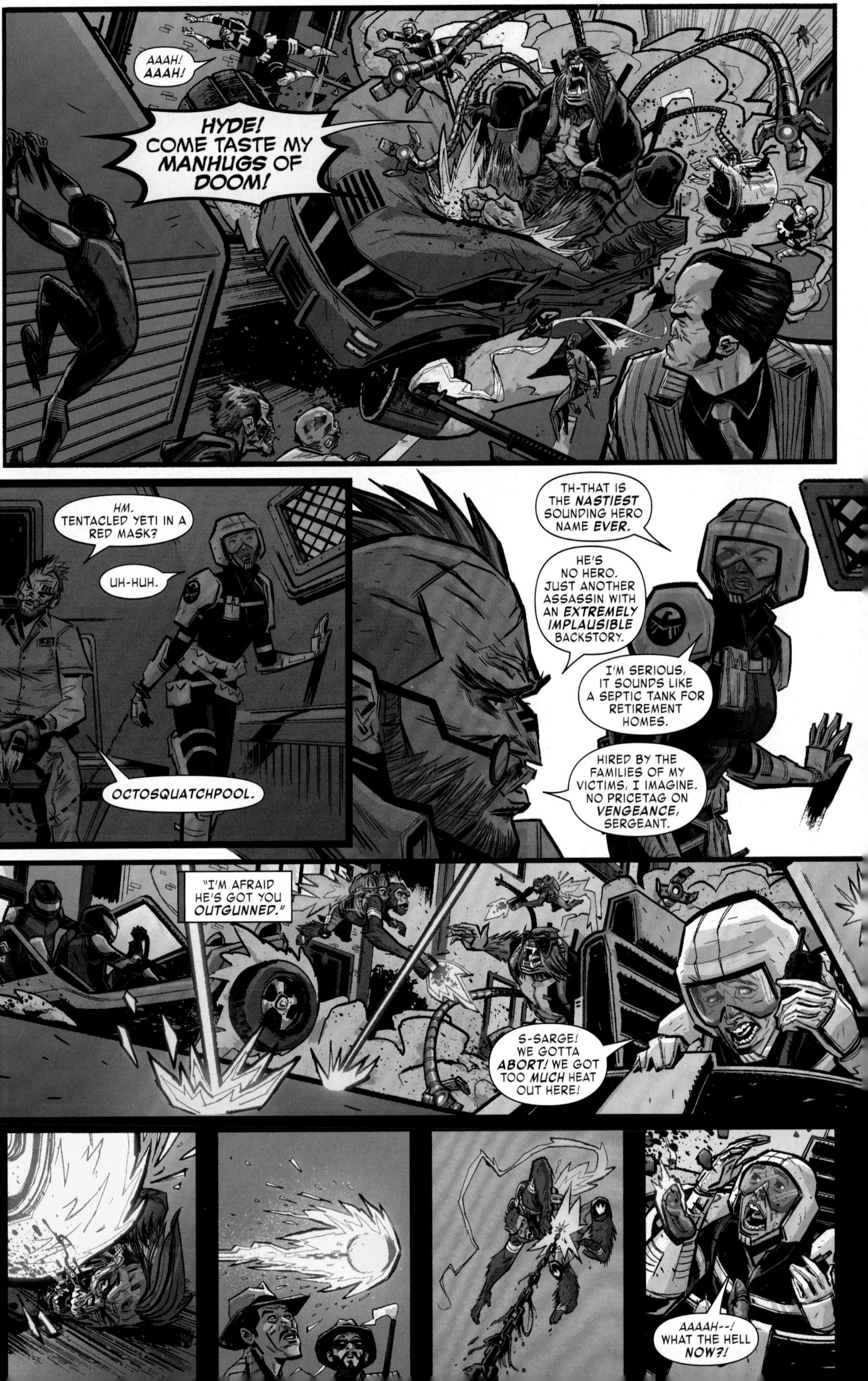
AAAH! AAAH!
HYDE! COME TASTE MY MANHUGS OF DOOM!
HM. TENTACLED YETI IN A RED MASK?
UH-HUH.
OCTOSQUATCHPOOL.
TH-THAT IS THE NASTIEST SOUNDING HERO NAME EVER.
HE'S NO HERO. JUST ANOTHER ASSASSIN WITH AN EXTREMELY IMPLAUSIBLE BACKSTORY.
I'M SERIOUS, IT SOUNDS LIKE A SEPTIC TANK FOR RETIREMENT HOMES.
HIRED BY THE FAMILIES OF MY VICTIMS, I IMAGINE. NO PRICETAG ON VENGEANCE, SERGEANT.
"I'M AFRAID HE'S GOT YOU OUTGUNNED."
S-SARGE! WE GOTTA ABORT! WE GOT TOO MUCH HEAT OUT HERE!
AAAAH--! WHAT THE HELL NOW?!

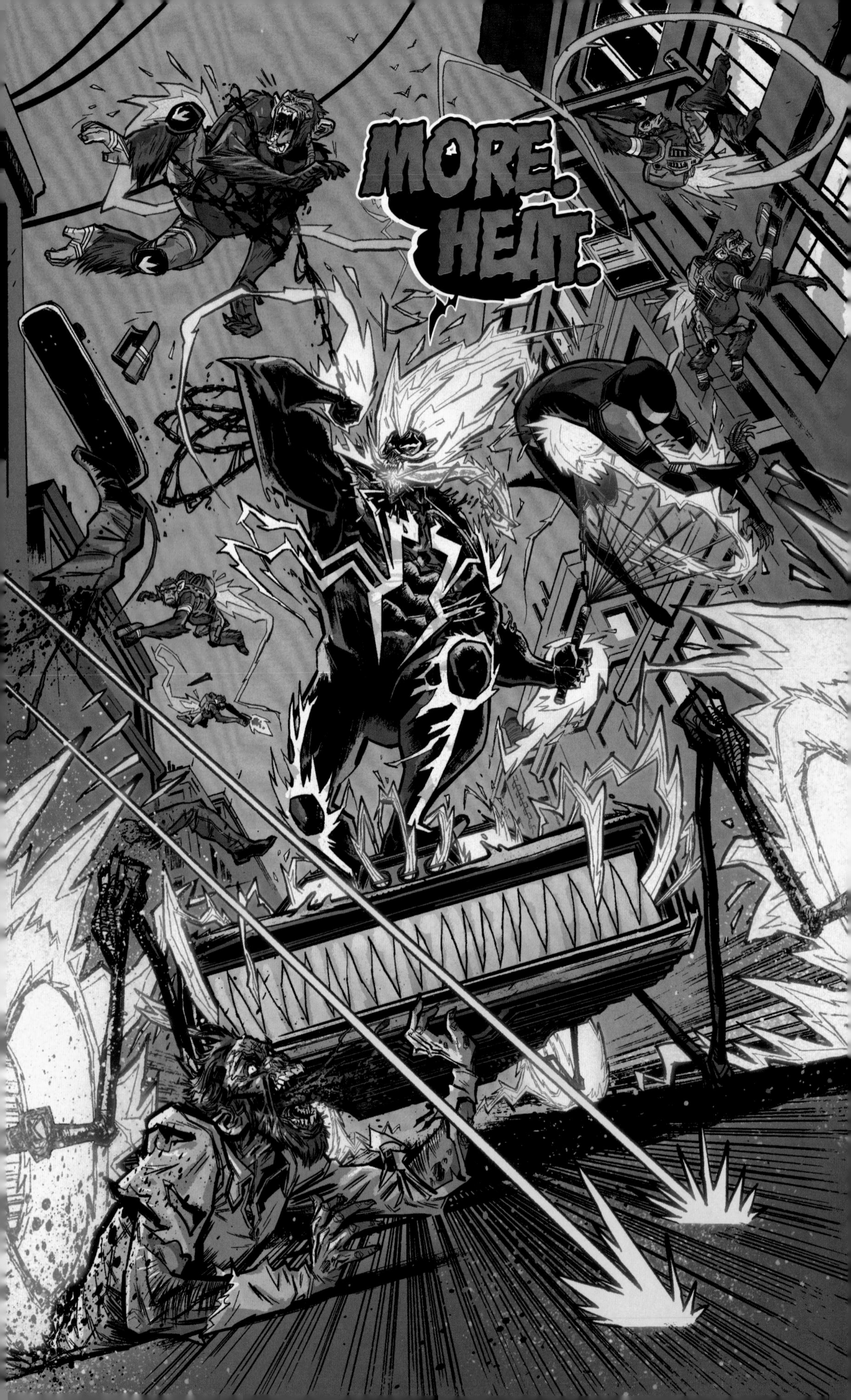
MORE. HEAT.

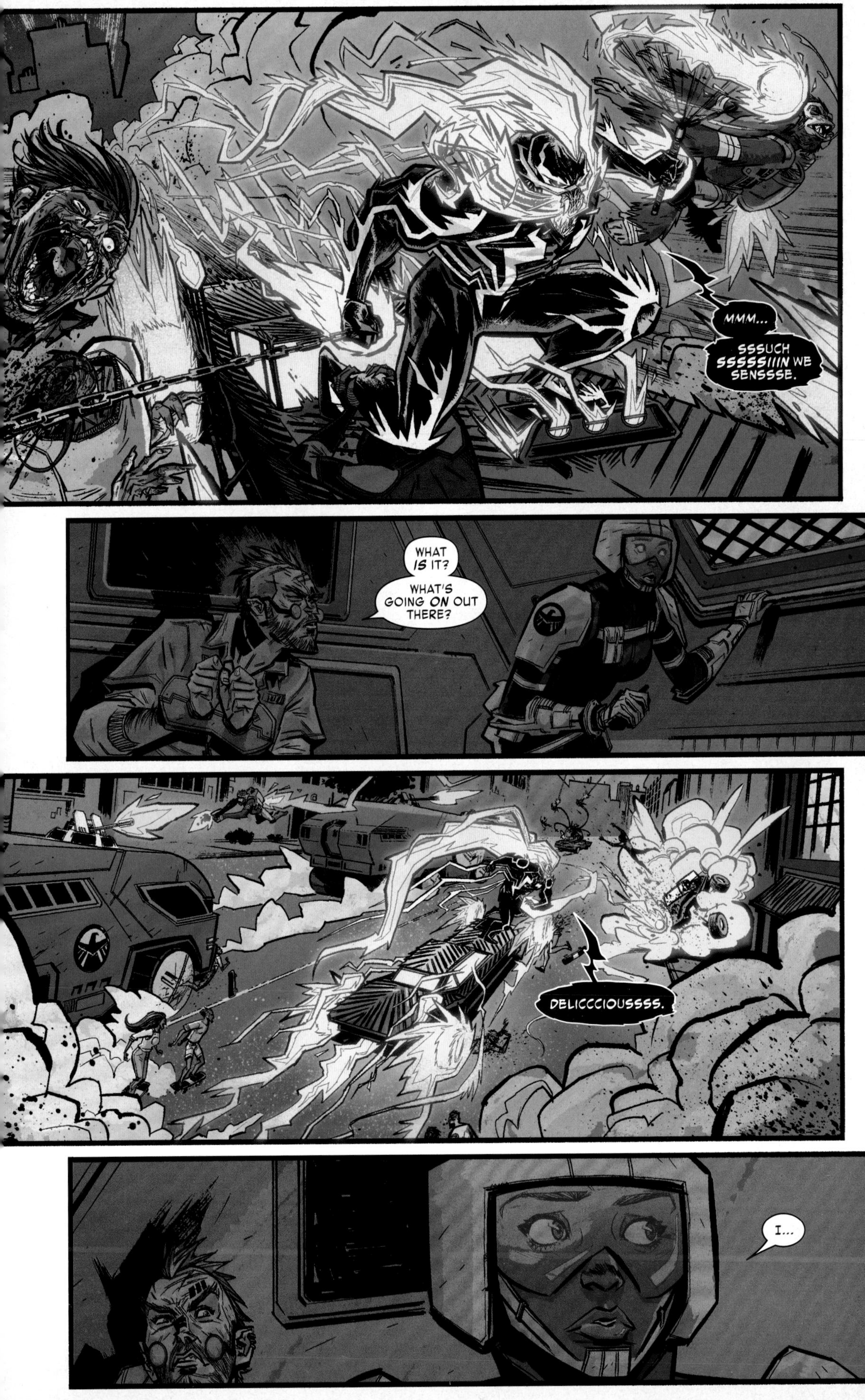
MMM...
SSSUCH SSSSSIIIN WE SENSSSE.
WHAT IS IT?
WHAT'S GOING ON OUT THERE?
DELICCCIOUSSSS.
I...

IT'S... IT'S THE *GHOST RIDER*. I THINK. BUT SOMETHING'S DIFF--

GHOST RIDER? *HE'S* NOT PART OF THE PLAN!

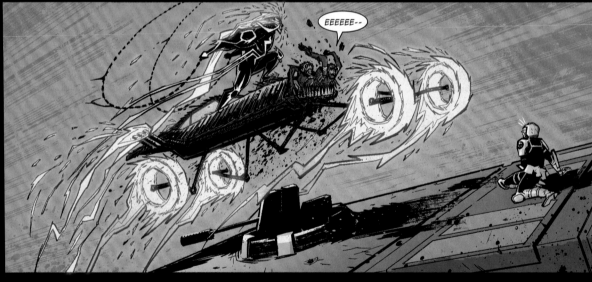

EEEEEE--

NOW, LISTEN VERY CAREFULLY--

WAIT--WHAT *PLAN*?

NFF. *NOTHING.* IT'S IRRELEVANT. JUST A... HN...

"...JUST A *FEELING* IN MY BONES."

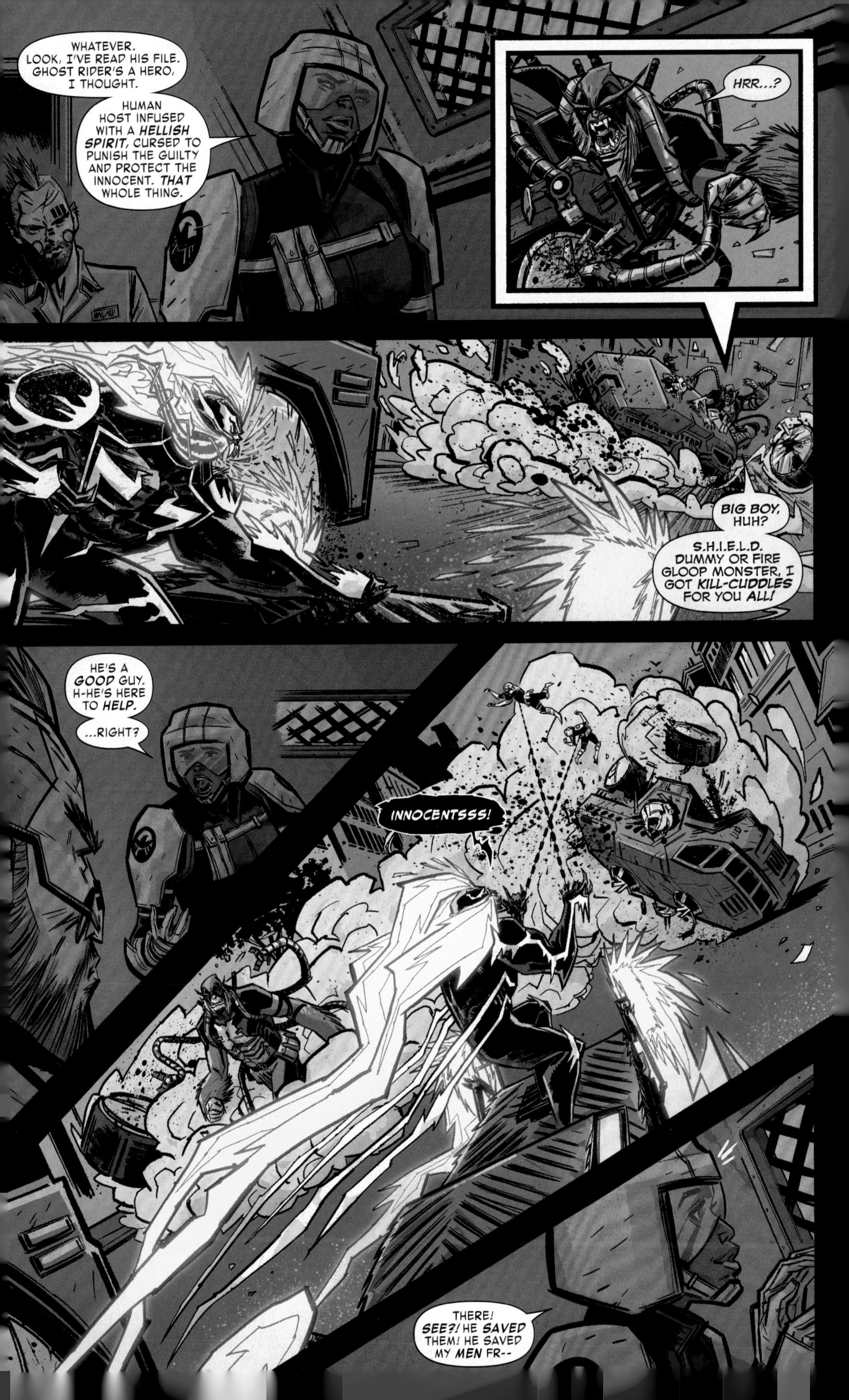
WHATEVER. LOOK, I'VE READ HIS FILE. GHOST RIDER'S A HERO, I THOUGHT.
HUMAN HOST INFUSED WITH A *HELLISH SPIRIT*, CURSED TO PUNISH THE GUILTY AND PROTECT THE INNOCENT. *THAT* WHOLE THING.
HRR...?
BIG BOY, HUH?
S.H.I.E.L.D. DUMMY OR FIRE GLOOP MONSTER, I GOT *KILL-CUDDLES* FOR YOU *ALL!*
HE'S A *GOOD* GUY. H-HE'S HERE TO *HELP.*
...RIGHT?
INNOCENTSSS!
THERE! *SEE?!* HE *SAVED* THEM! HE SAVED MY *MEN* FR--

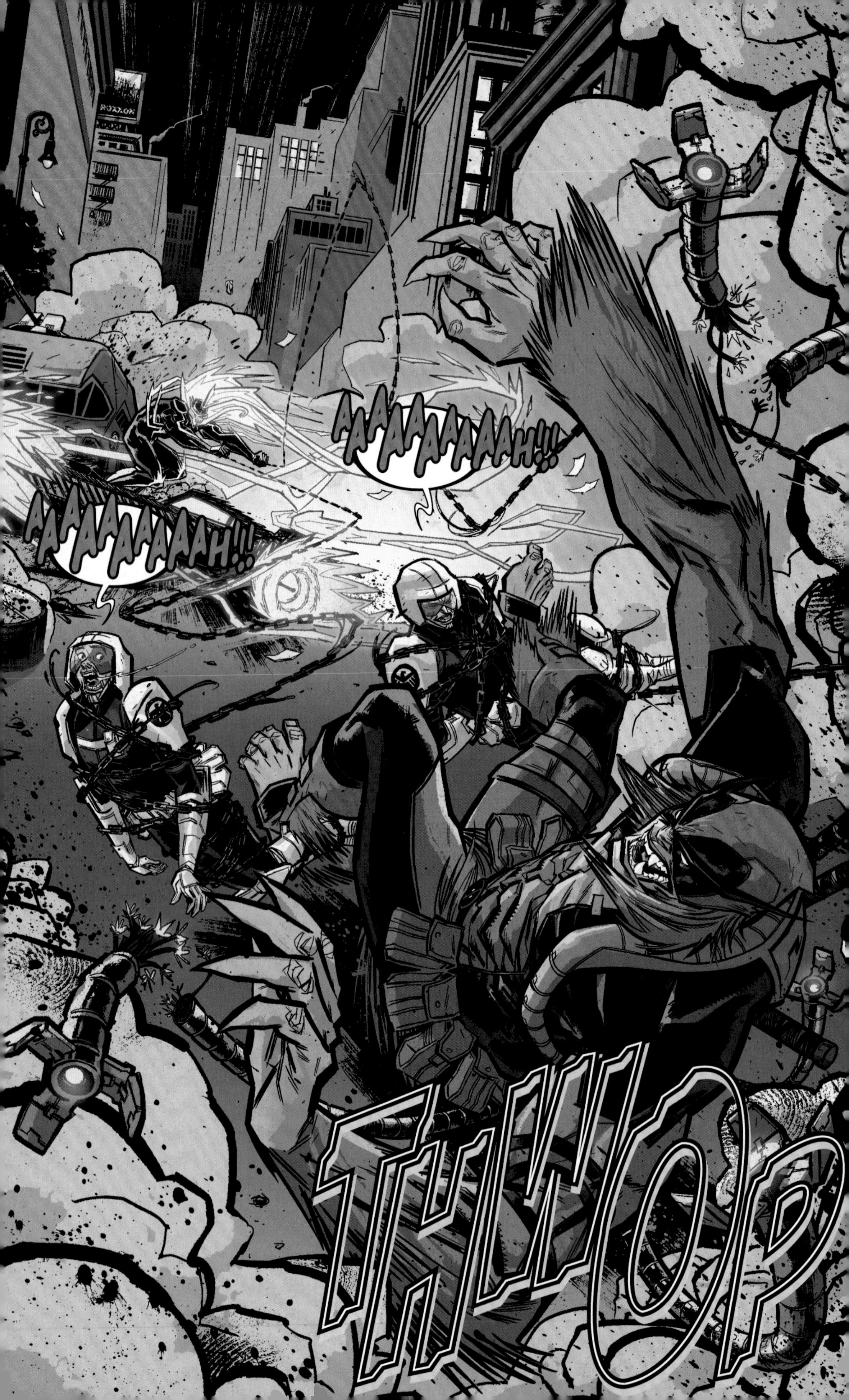

AAAAAAAAAAH!!!
AAAAAAAAAAH!!!
THWOP

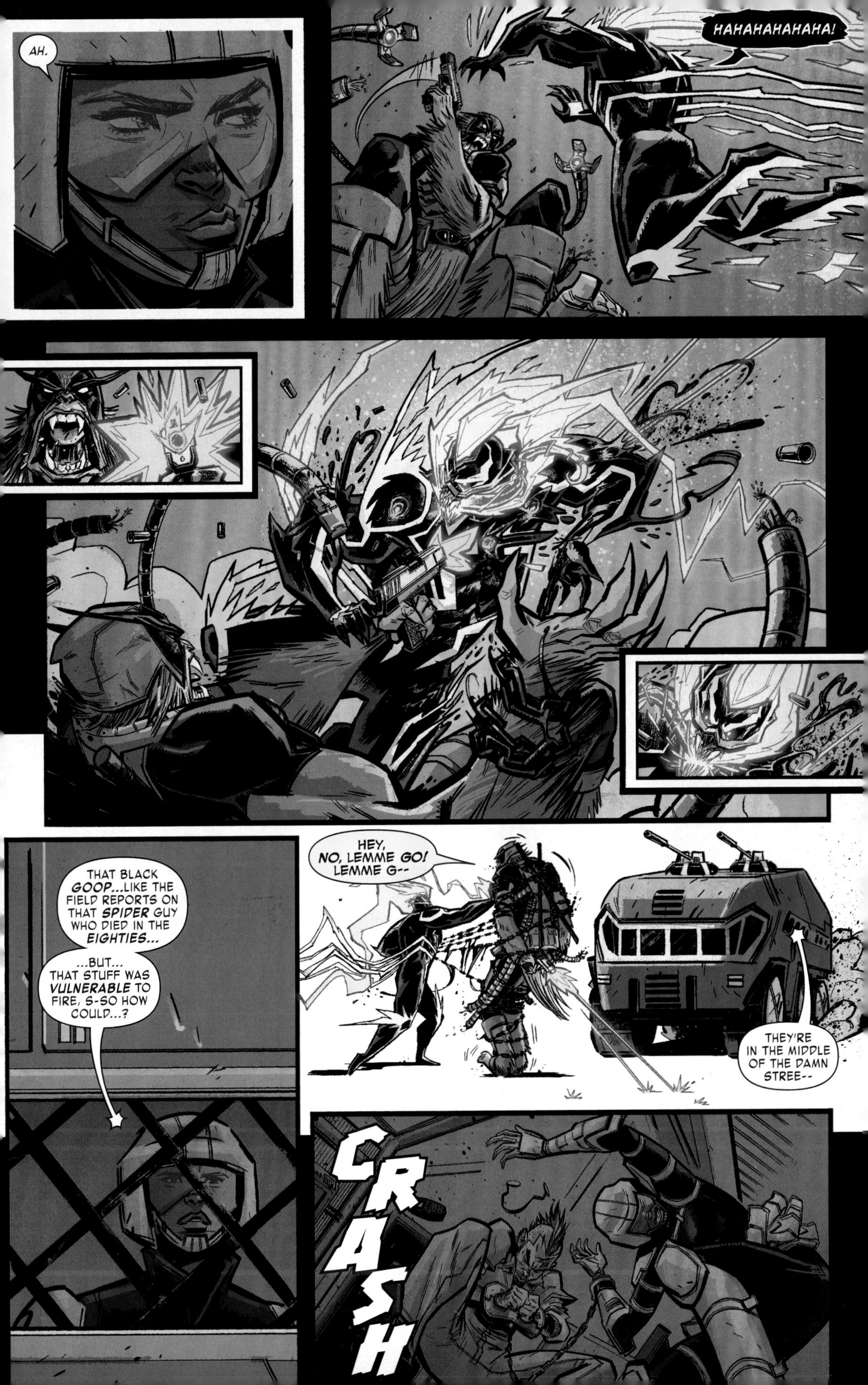
AH.
HAHAHAHAHAHA!
THAT BLACK GOOP...LIKE THE FIELD REPORTS ON THAT SPIDER GUY WHO DIED IN THE EIGHTIES...
...BUT... THAT STUFF WAS VULNERABLE TO FIRE, S-SO HOW COULD...?
HEY, NO, LEMME GO! LEMME G--
THEY'RE IN THE MIDDLE OF THE DAMN STREE--
CRASH

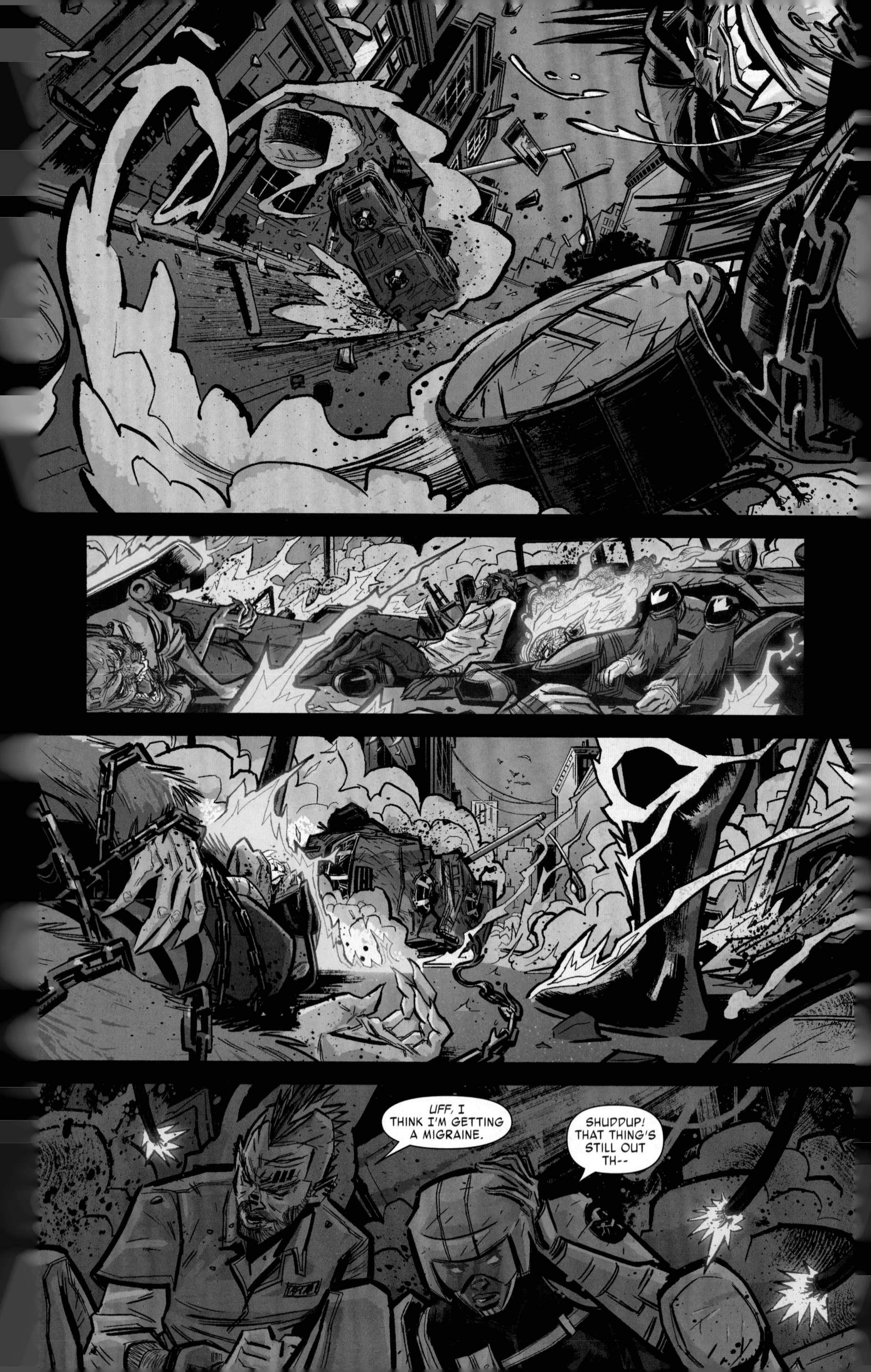
UFF, I THINK I'M GETTING A MIGRAINE.
SHUDDUP! THAT THING'S STILL OUT TH--

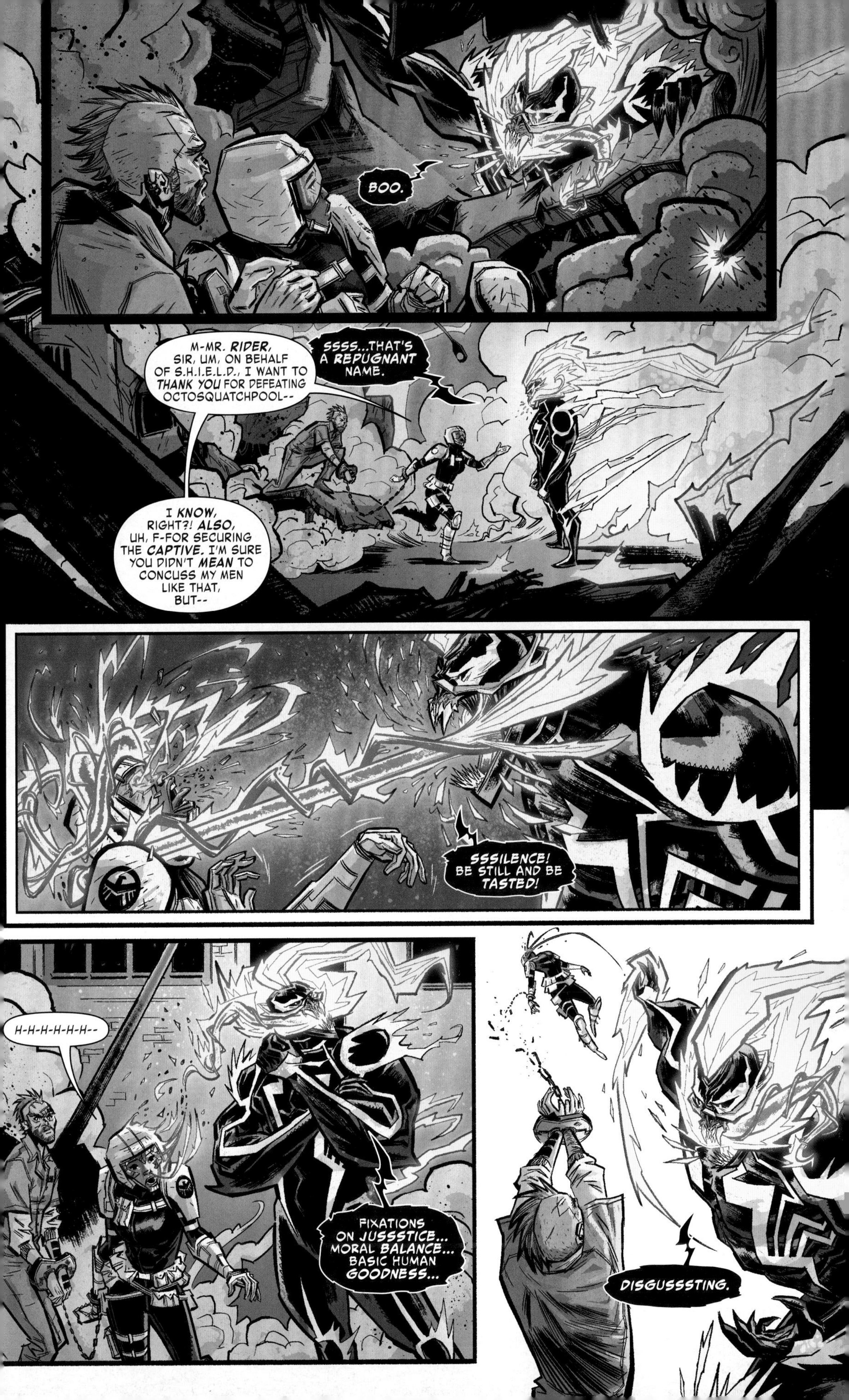
BOO.
M-MR. RIDER, SIR, UM, ON BEHALF OF S.H.I.E.L.D., I WANT TO THANK YOU FOR DEFEATING OCTOSQUATCHPOOL--
SSSS...THAT'S A REPUGNANT NAME.
I KNOW, RIGHT?! ALSO, UH, F-FOR SECURING THE CAPTIVE. I'M SURE YOU DIDN'T MEAN TO CONCUSS MY MEN LIKE THAT, BUT--
SSSILENCE! BE STILL AND BE TASTED!
H-H-H-H-H-H--
FIXATIONS ON JUSSSTICE... MORAL BALANCE... BASIC HUMAN GOODNESS...
DISGUSSSTING.

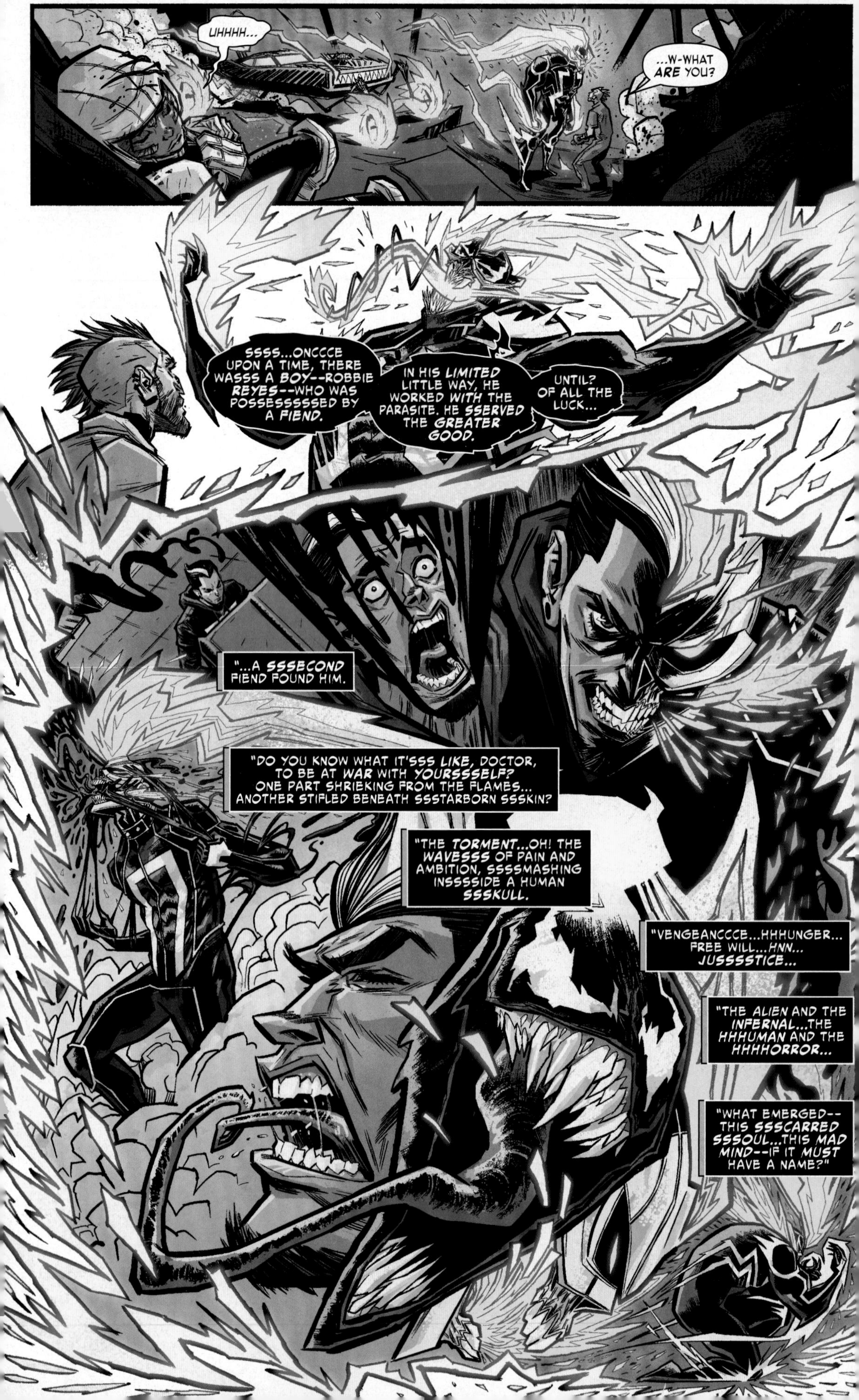
UHHHH...
...W-WHAT ARE YOU?
SSSS...ONCCCE UPON A TIME, THERE WASSS A BOY--ROBBIE REYES--WHO WAS POSSESSSSSSED BY A FIEND.
IN HIS LIMITED LITTLE WAY, HE WORKED WITH THE PARASITE. HE SSERVED THE GREATER GOOD.
UNTIL? OF ALL THE LUCK...
"...A SSSECOND FIEND FOUND HIM.
"DO YOU KNOW WHAT IT'SSS LIKE, DOCTOR, TO BE AT WAR WITH YOURSSSELF? ONE PART SHRIEKING FROM THE FLAMES... ANOTHER STIFLED BENEATH SSSTARBORN SSSKIN?
"THE TORMENT...OH! THE WAVESSS OF PAIN AND AMBITION, SSSSMASHING INSSSSIDE A HUMAN SSSKULL.
"VENGEANCCCE...HHHUNGER... FREE WILL...HNN... JUSSSSTICE...
"THE ALIEN AND THE INFERNAL...THE HHHUMAN AND THE HHHHORROR...
"WHAT EMERGED--THIS SSSCARRED SSSOUL...THIS MAD MIND--IF IT MUST HAVE A NAME?"

WE ARE THE **HOST RIDER.**

HUH. YOU DON'T SSSMELL **AFRAID.** WHY, WE WONDER?

HEH. BECAUSE I HAVE AN **ACE CARD,** CAPTAIN CREEPY.

YOU DON'T GET TO BE PROFESSOR EMERITUS OF THE **VILLAINY CIRCUIT** WITHOUT THINKING AHEAD. YOU'RE ABOUT TO **DIE,** PAL.

I JUST HAVE A--HA--A **FEELING** IN MY BONES.

AH.

YOU'RE **REFERRING** TO THE DEAL YOU MADE WITH THE **MERCENARY** KNOWN AS **CROSSBONESSS.**

WH-WH-WH...

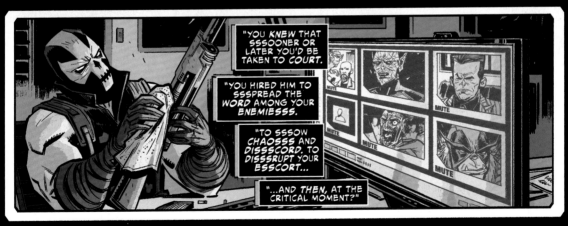

"YOU **KNEW** THAT SSSOONER OR LATER YOU'D BE TAKEN TO **COURT.**

"YOU HIRED HIM TO SSSPREAD THE **WORD** AMONG YOUR **ENEMIESSS.**

"TO SSSOW **CHAOSSS** AND **DISSSCORD.** TO **DISSSRUPT** YOUR **ESSSCORT...**

"...AND **THEN,** AT THE CRITICAL MOMENT?"

TO SSSSSWOOP IN AND **RESSSCUE** YOU.

H-H-HOW DO YOU KN--?

YOUR **PRINCE CHARMING** ISSSN'T **COMING,** DOCTOR.

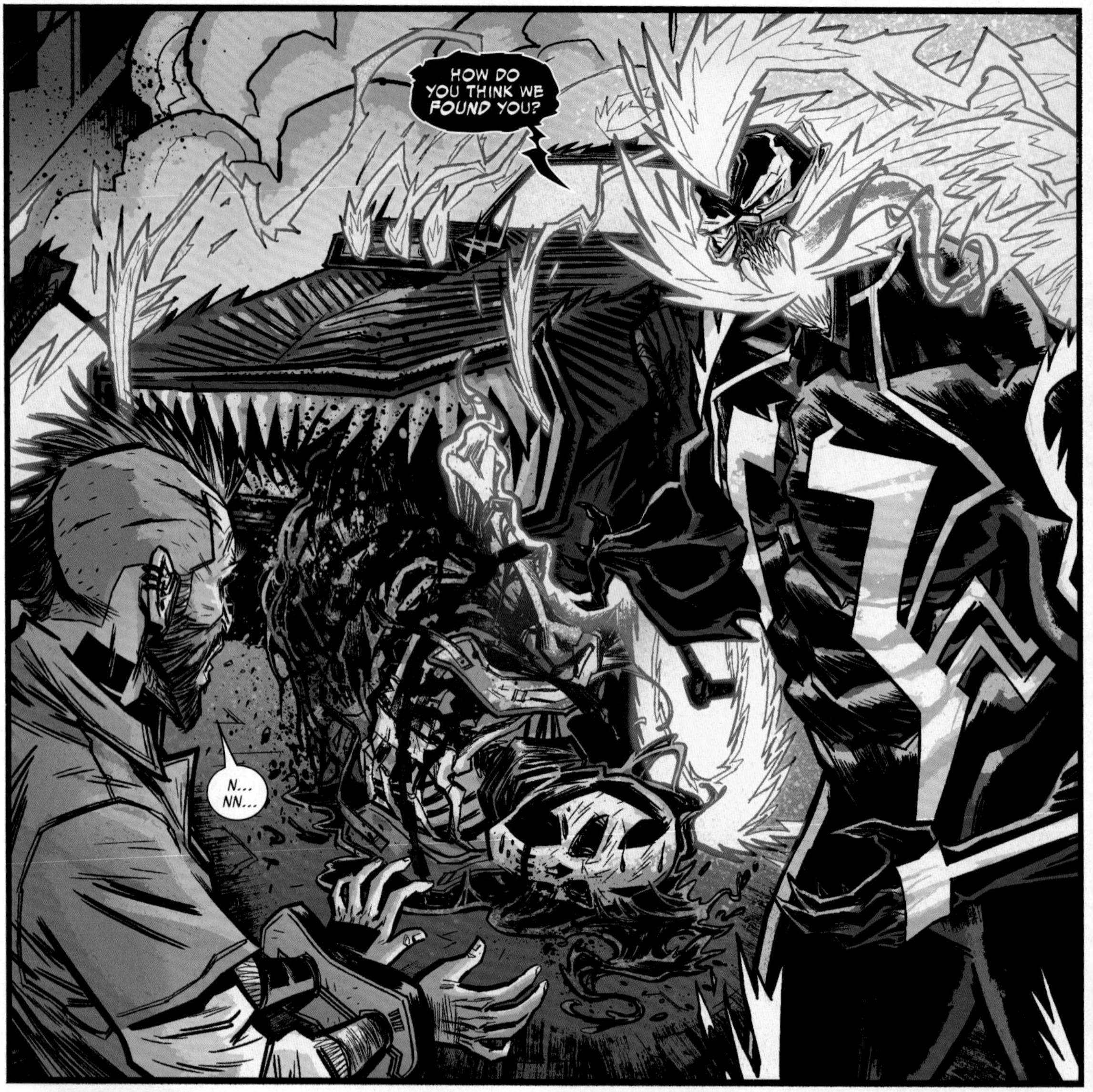
HOW DO YOU THINK WE FOUND YOU?
N... NN...

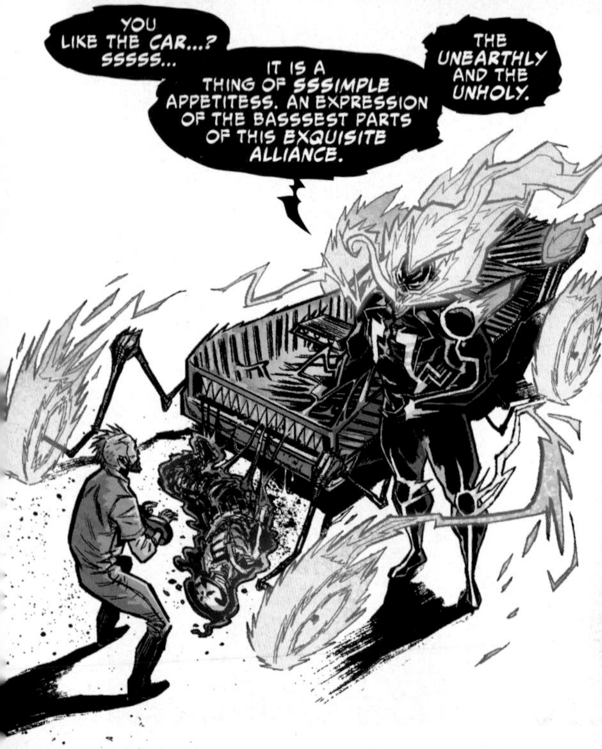
YOU LIKE THE CAR...? SSSSS...
IT IS A THING OF SSSIMPLE APPETITESS. AN EXPRESSION OF THE BASSSEST PARTS OF THIS EXQUISITE ALLIANCE.
THE UNEARTHLY AND THE UNHOLY.

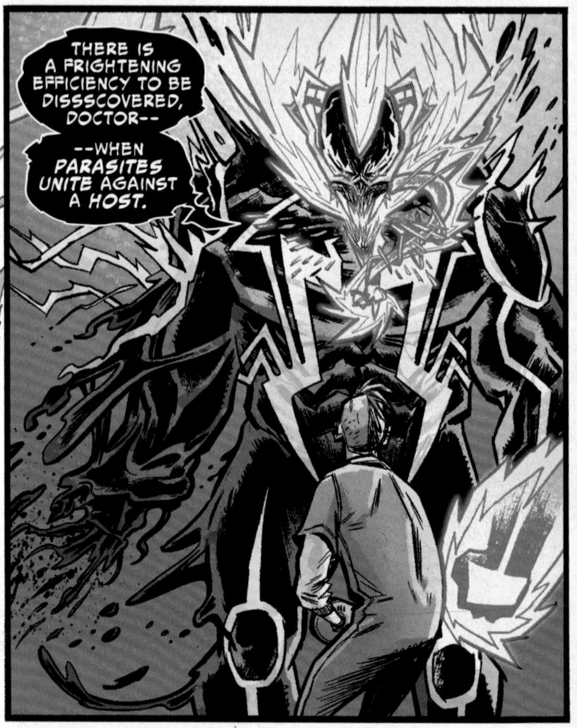
THERE IS A FRIGHTENING EFFICIENCY TO BE DISSSCOVERED, DOCTOR--
--WHEN PARASITES UNITE AGAINST A HOST.

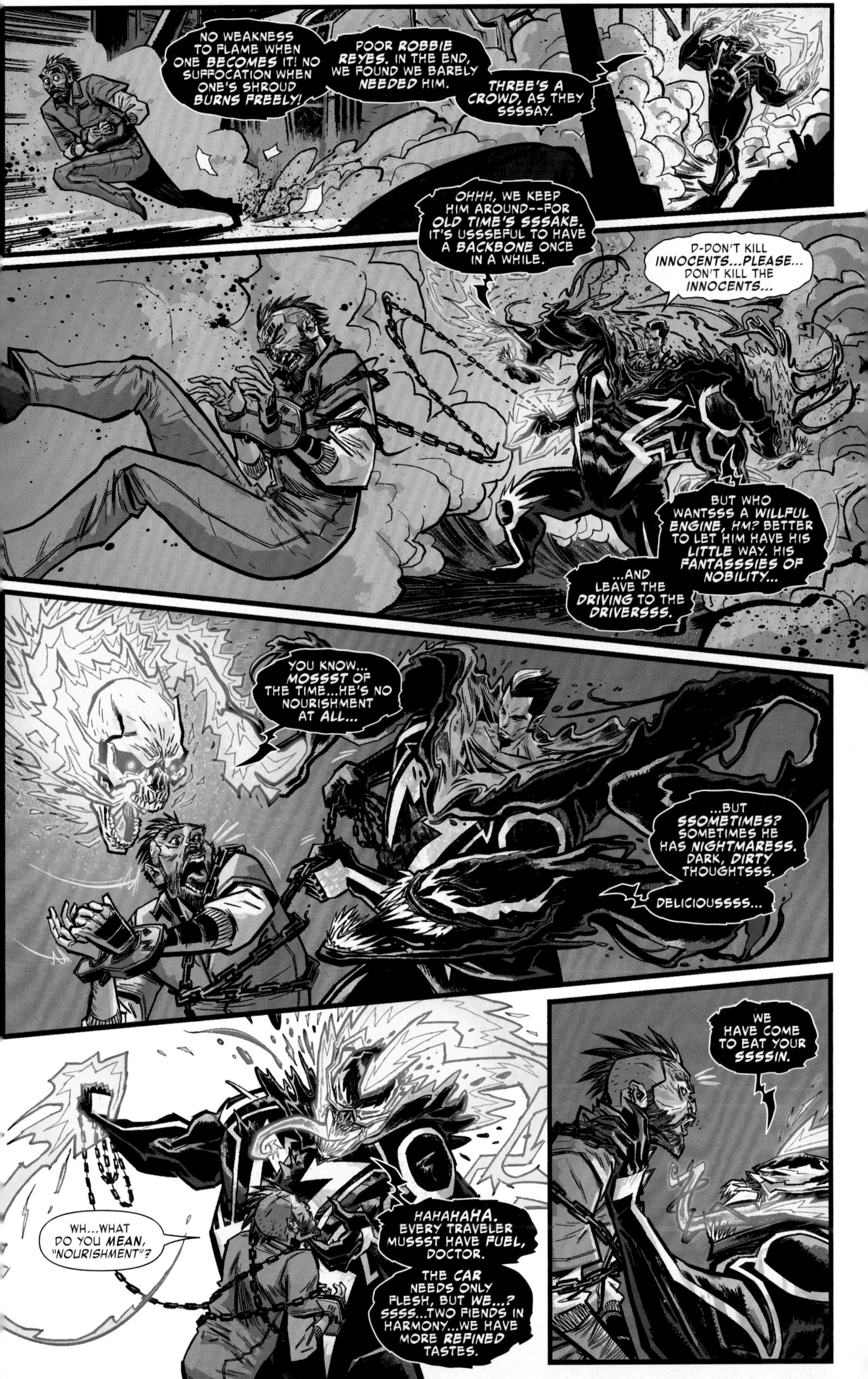

NO WEAKNESS TO FLAME WHEN ONE BECOMES IT! NO SUFFOCATION WHEN ONE'S SHROUD BURNS FREELY!
POOR ROBBIE REYES. IN THE END, WE FOUND WE BARELY NEEDED HIM.
THREE'S A CROWD, AS THEY SSSSAY.
OHHH, WE KEEP HIM AROUND--FOR OLD TIME'S SSSAKE. IT'S USSSEFUL TO HAVE A BACKBONE ONCE IN A WHILE.
D-DON'T KILL INNOCENTS...PLEASE... DON'T KILL THE INNOCENTS...
BUT WHO WANTSSS A WILLFUL ENGINE, HM? BETTER TO LET HIM HAVE HIS LITTLE WAY. HIS FANTASSSIES OF NOBILITY...
...AND LEAVE THE DRIVING TO THE DRIVERSSS.
YOU KNOW... MOSSST OF THE TIME...HE'S NO NOURISHMENT AT ALL...
...BUT SSOMETIMES? SOMETIMES HE HAS NIGHTMARESS. DARK, DIRTY THOUGHTSSS.
DELICIOUSSSS...
WH...WHAT DO YOU MEAN, "NOURISHMENT"?
HAHAHAHA. EVERY TRAVELER MUSSST HAVE FUEL, DOCTOR.
THE CAR NEEDS ONLY FLESH, BUT WE...? SSSS...TWO FIENDS IN HARMONY...WE HAVE MORE REFINED TASTES.
WE HAVE COME TO EAT YOUR SSSSIN.

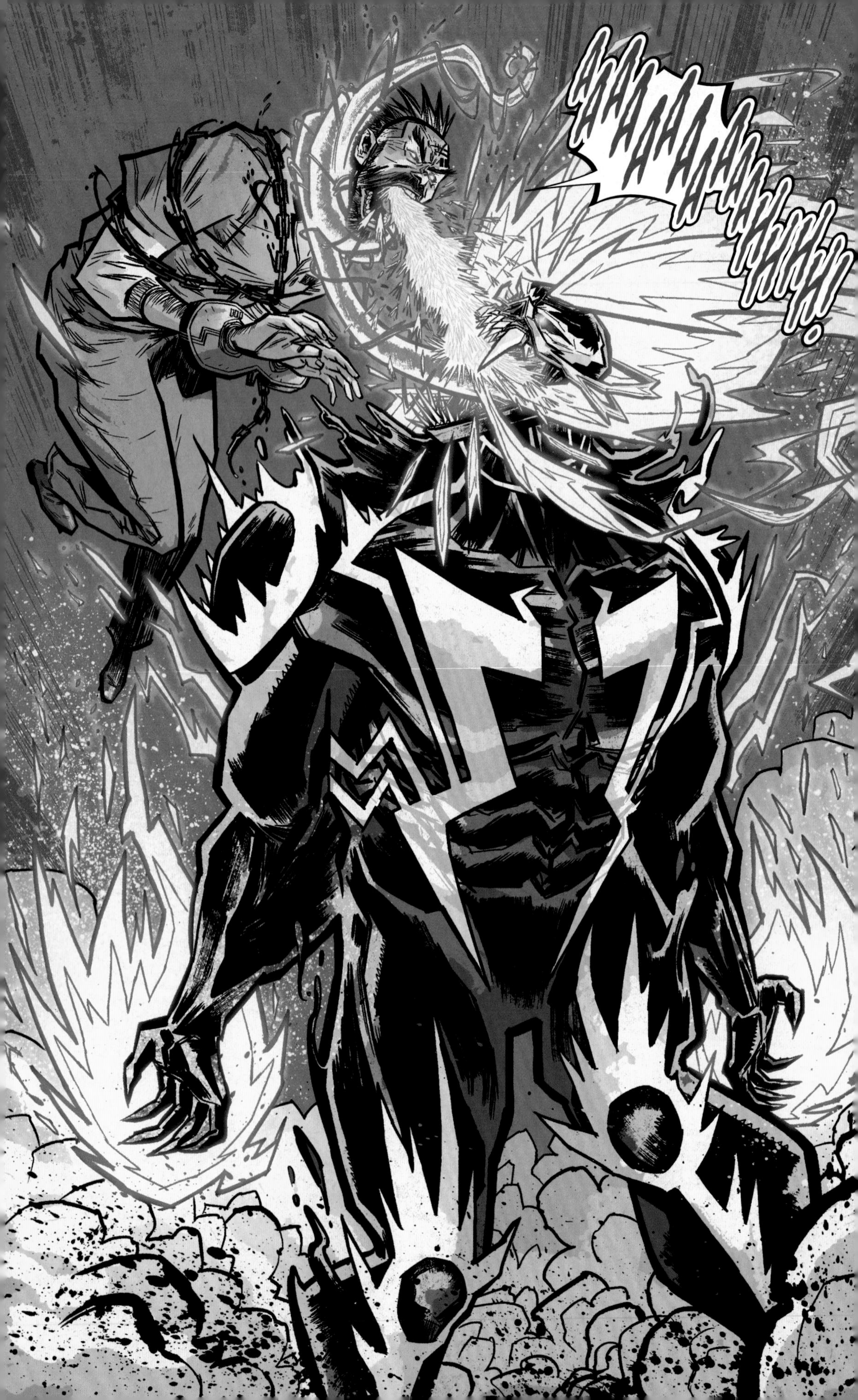
AAAAAAAAAAHHHH!!

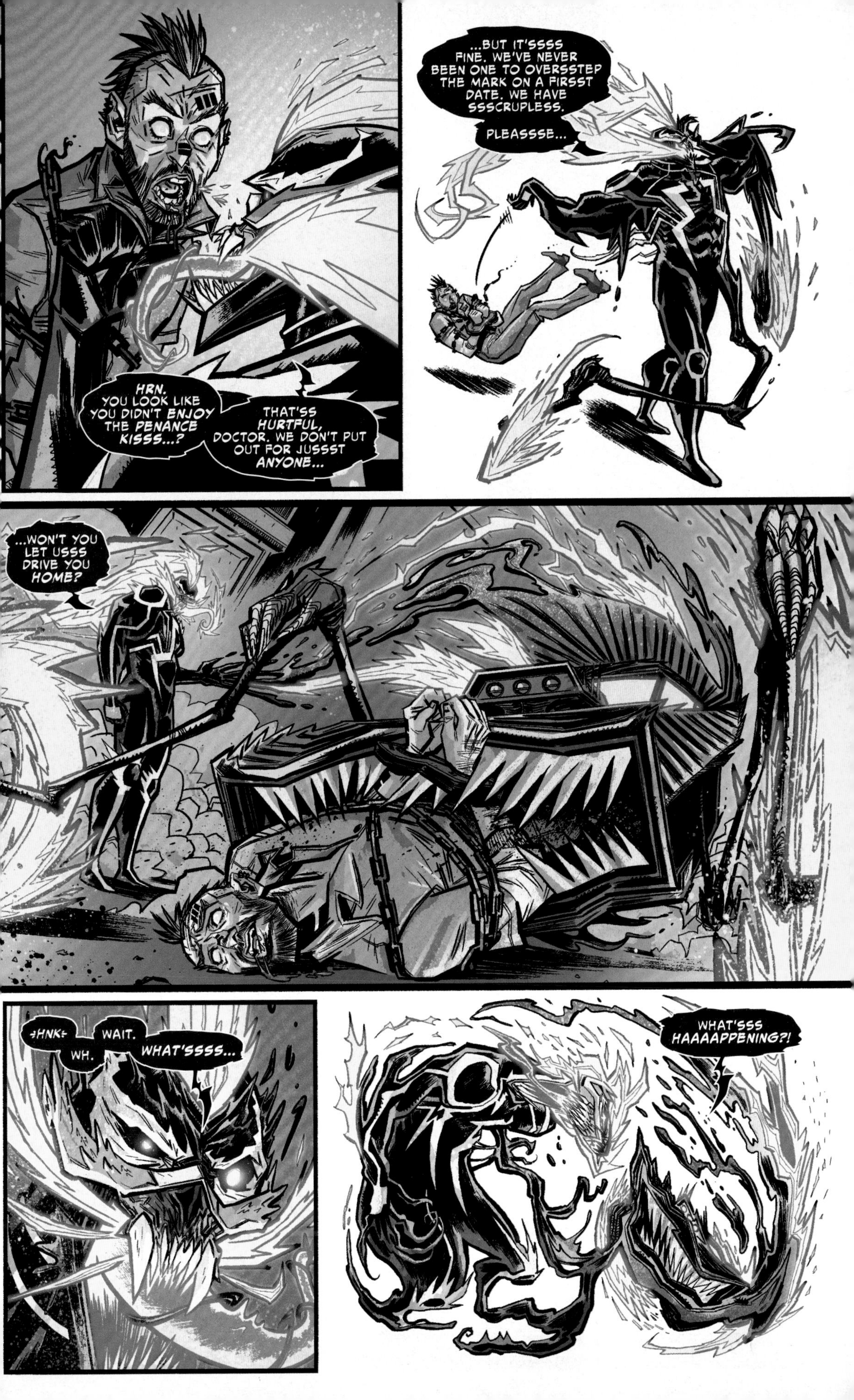
HRN. YOU LOOK LIKE YOU DIDN'T ENJOY THE PENANCE KISSS...?
THAT'SS HURTFUL, DOCTOR. WE DON'T PUT OUT FOR JUSSST ANYONE...
...BUT IT'SSSS FINE. WE'VE NEVER BEEN ONE TO OVERSSTEP THE MARK ON A FIRSST DATE. WE HAVE SSSCRUPLESS.
PLEASSSE...
...WON'T YOU LET USSS DRIVE YOU HOME?
≠HNK≠ WAIT.
WH.
WHAT'SSSS...
WHAT'SSS HAAAAPPENING?!

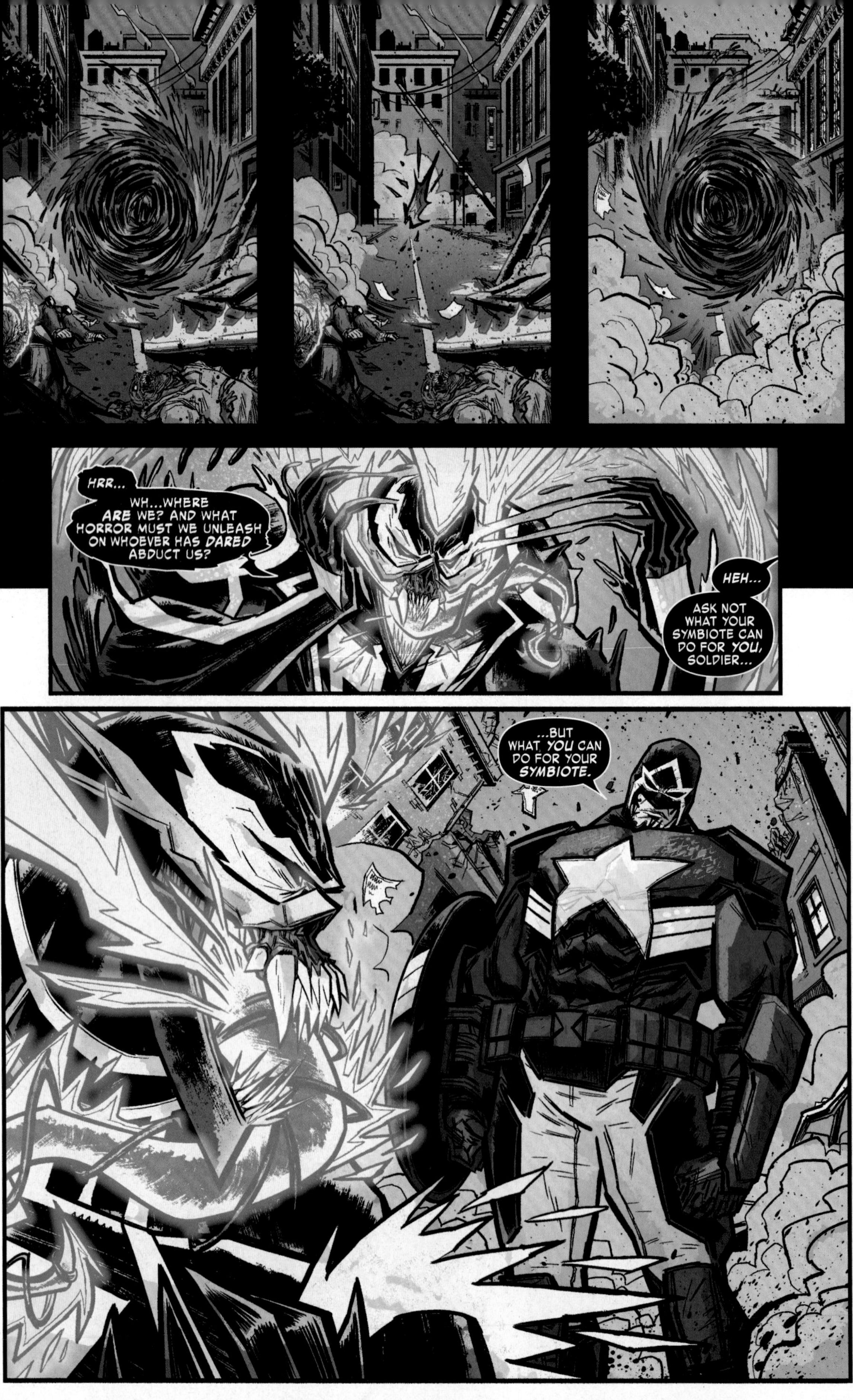
HRR...
WH...WHERE ARE WE? AND WHAT HORROR MUST WE UNLEASH ON WHOEVER HAS DARED ABDUCT US?
HEH...
ASK NOT WHAT YOUR SYMBIOTE CAN DO FOR YOU, SOLDIER...
...BUT WHAT YOU CAN DO FOR YOUR SYMBIOTE.

4

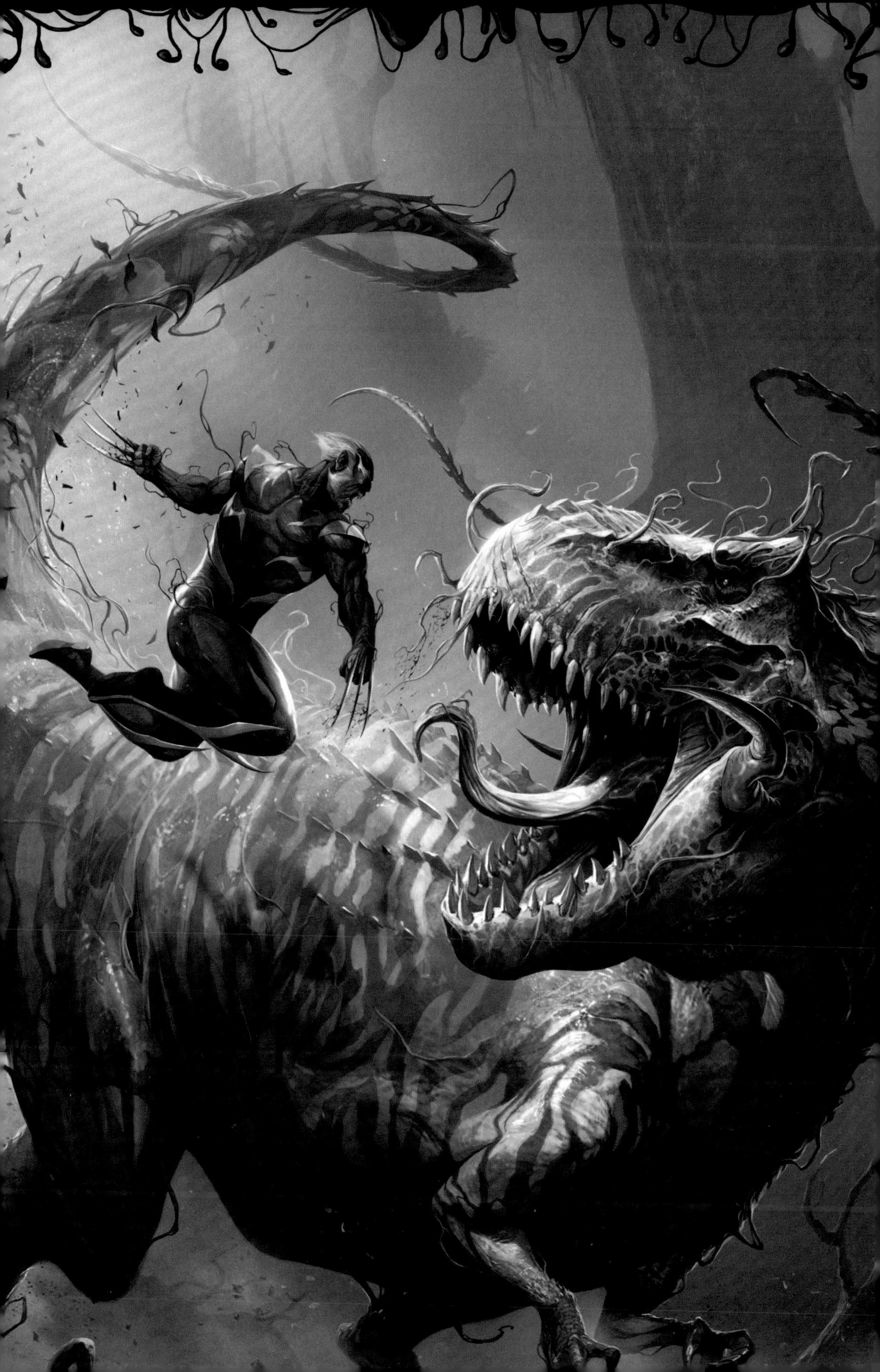

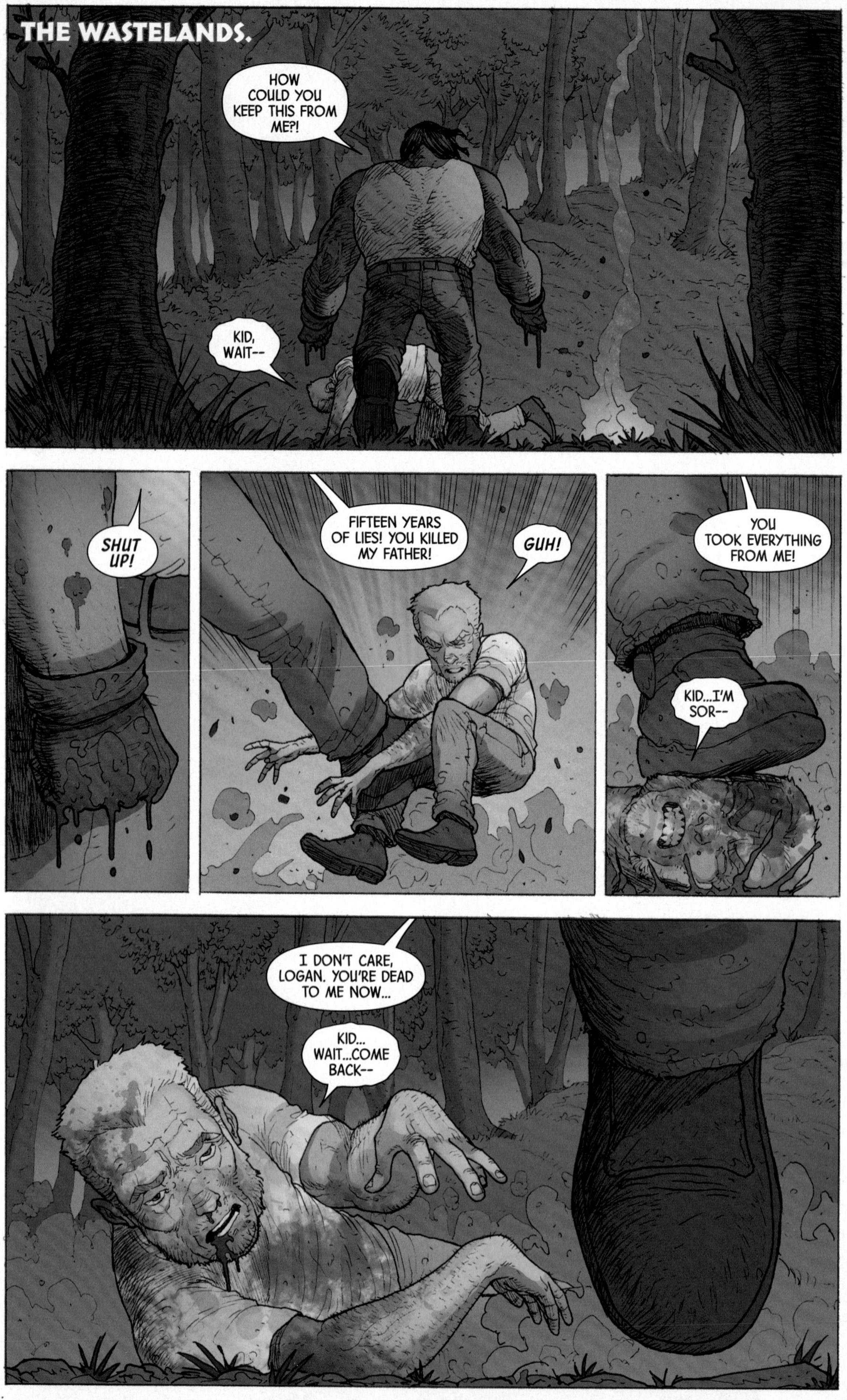
THE WASTELANDS.
HOW COULD YOU KEEP THIS FROM ME?!
KID, WAIT--
SHUT UP!
FIFTEEN YEARS OF LIES! YOU KILLED MY FATHER!
GUH!
YOU TOOK EVERYTHING FROM ME!
KID...I'M SOR--
I DON'T CARE, LOGAN. YOU'RE DEAD TO ME NOW...
KID... WAIT...COME BACK--

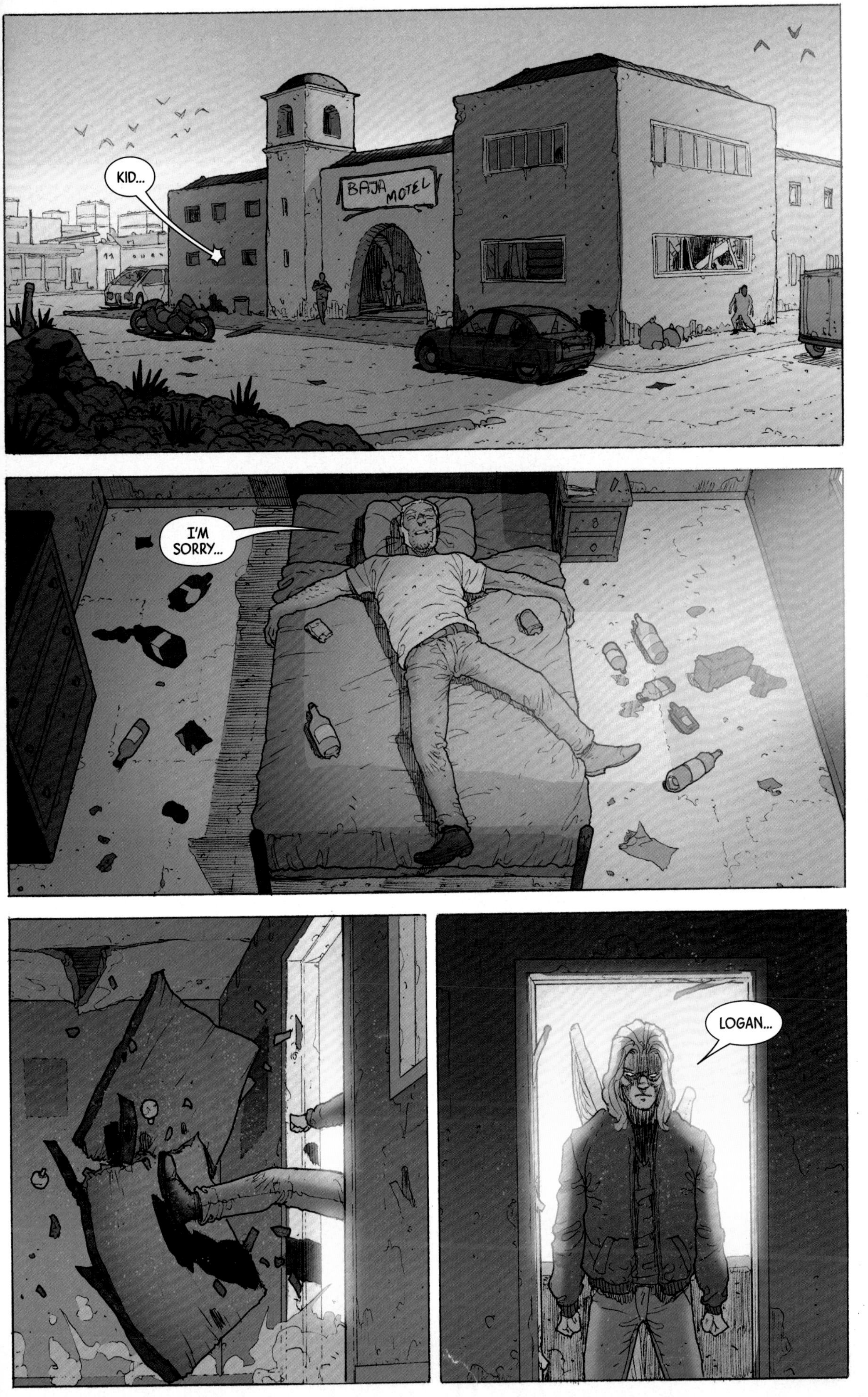
BAJA MOTEL
KID...
I'M SORRY...
LOGAN...

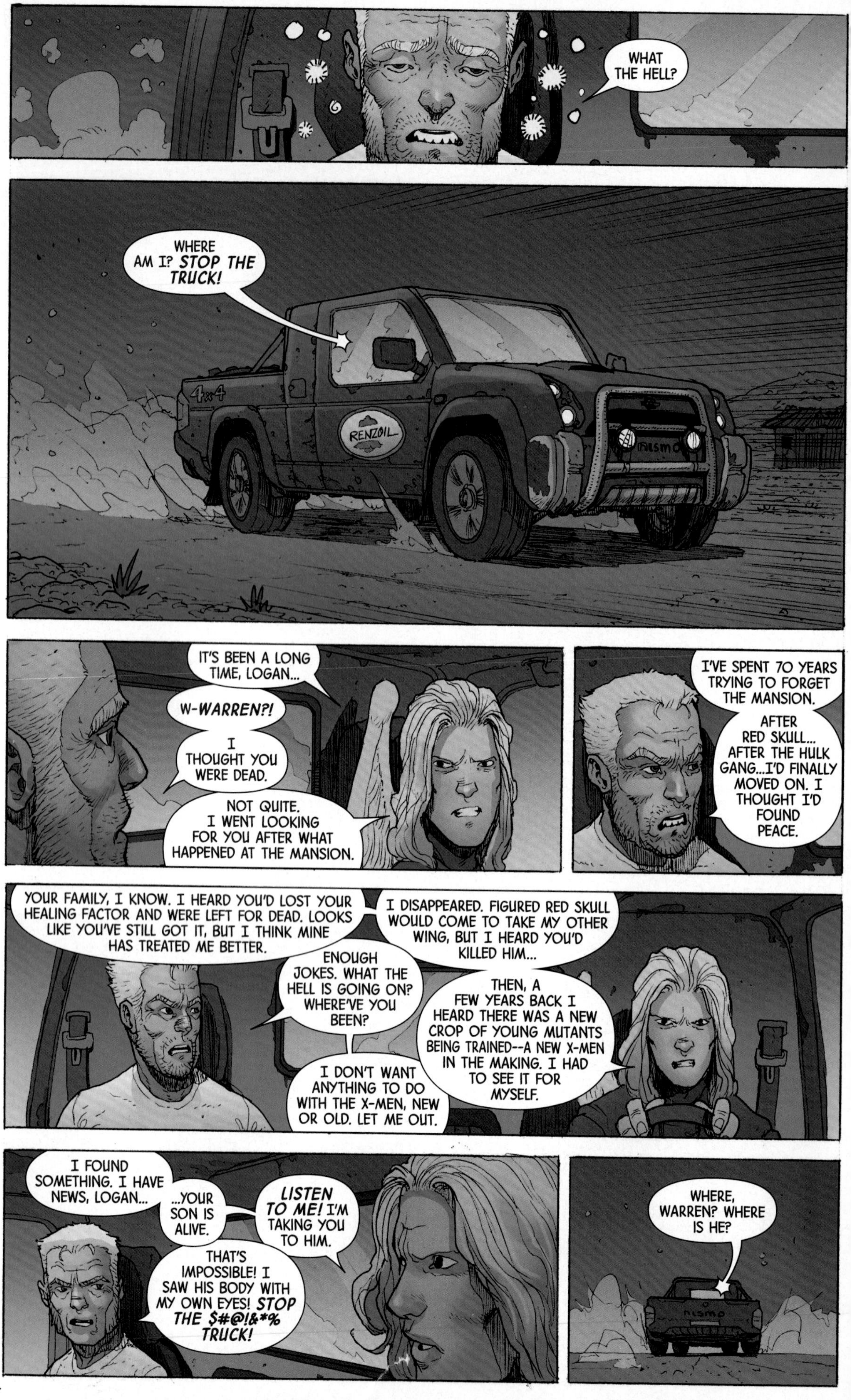
WHAT THE HELL?
WHERE AM I? STOP THE TRUCK!
4x4
RENZOIL
nismo
IT'S BEEN A LONG TIME, LOGAN...
W-WARREN?!
I THOUGHT YOU WERE DEAD.
NOT QUITE. I WENT LOOKING FOR YOU AFTER WHAT HAPPENED AT THE MANSION.
I'VE SPENT 70 YEARS TRYING TO FORGET THE MANSION.
AFTER RED SKULL... AFTER THE HULK GANG...I'D FINALLY MOVED ON. I THOUGHT I'D FOUND PEACE.
YOUR FAMILY, I KNOW. I HEARD YOU'D LOST YOUR HEALING FACTOR AND WERE LEFT FOR DEAD. LOOKS LIKE YOU'VE STILL GOT IT, BUT I THINK MINE HAS TREATED ME BETTER.
I DISAPPEARED. FIGURED RED SKULL WOULD COME TO TAKE MY OTHER WING, BUT I HEARD YOU'D KILLED HIM...
ENOUGH JOKES. WHAT THE HELL IS GOING ON? WHERE'VE YOU BEEN?
THEN, A FEW YEARS BACK I HEARD THERE WAS A NEW CROP OF YOUNG MUTANTS BEING TRAINED--A NEW X-MEN IN THE MAKING. I HAD TO SEE IT FOR MYSELF.
I DON'T WANT ANYTHING TO DO WITH THE X-MEN, NEW OR OLD. LET ME OUT.
I FOUND SOMETHING. I HAVE NEWS, LOGAN...
...YOUR SON IS ALIVE.
THAT'S IMPOSSIBLE! I SAW HIS BODY WITH MY OWN EYES! STOP THE $#@!&*% TRUCK!
LISTEN TO ME! I'M TAKING YOU TO HIM.
WHERE, WARREN? WHERE IS HE?

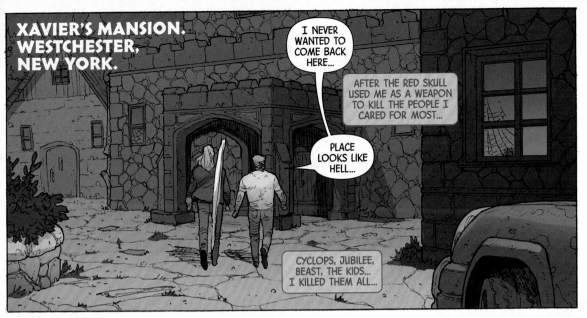

XAVIER'S MANSION. WESTCHESTER, NEW YORK.

I NEVER WANTED TO COME BACK HERE...

AFTER THE RED SKULL USED ME AS A WEAPON TO KILL THE PEOPLE I CARED FOR MOST...

PLACE LOOKS LIKE HELL...

CYCLOPS, JUBILEE, BEAST, THE KIDS... I KILLED THEM ALL...

SCOTTY?!

WHERE IS HE, WARREN? TELL ME.

PROBABLY DOWN IN THE DANGER ROOM, TRAINING. IT'S ONE OF THE ONLY FUNCTIONING FACILITIES LEFT.

IT WAS HERE. THEY DIED RIGHT HERE. HOW COULD I HAVE KNOWN? MY MIND WAS TAKEN OVER...

LET'S GO. I DON'T WANT TO BE HERE ANY LONGER THAN I HAVE TO.

IT'S LIKE THEY'RE ALL WATCHING ME...

YOU MADE THIS SCHOOL A TOMB, LOGAN.

GUH!

YOU'RE NOT LEAVING THIS TIME, YOU TRAITOR!

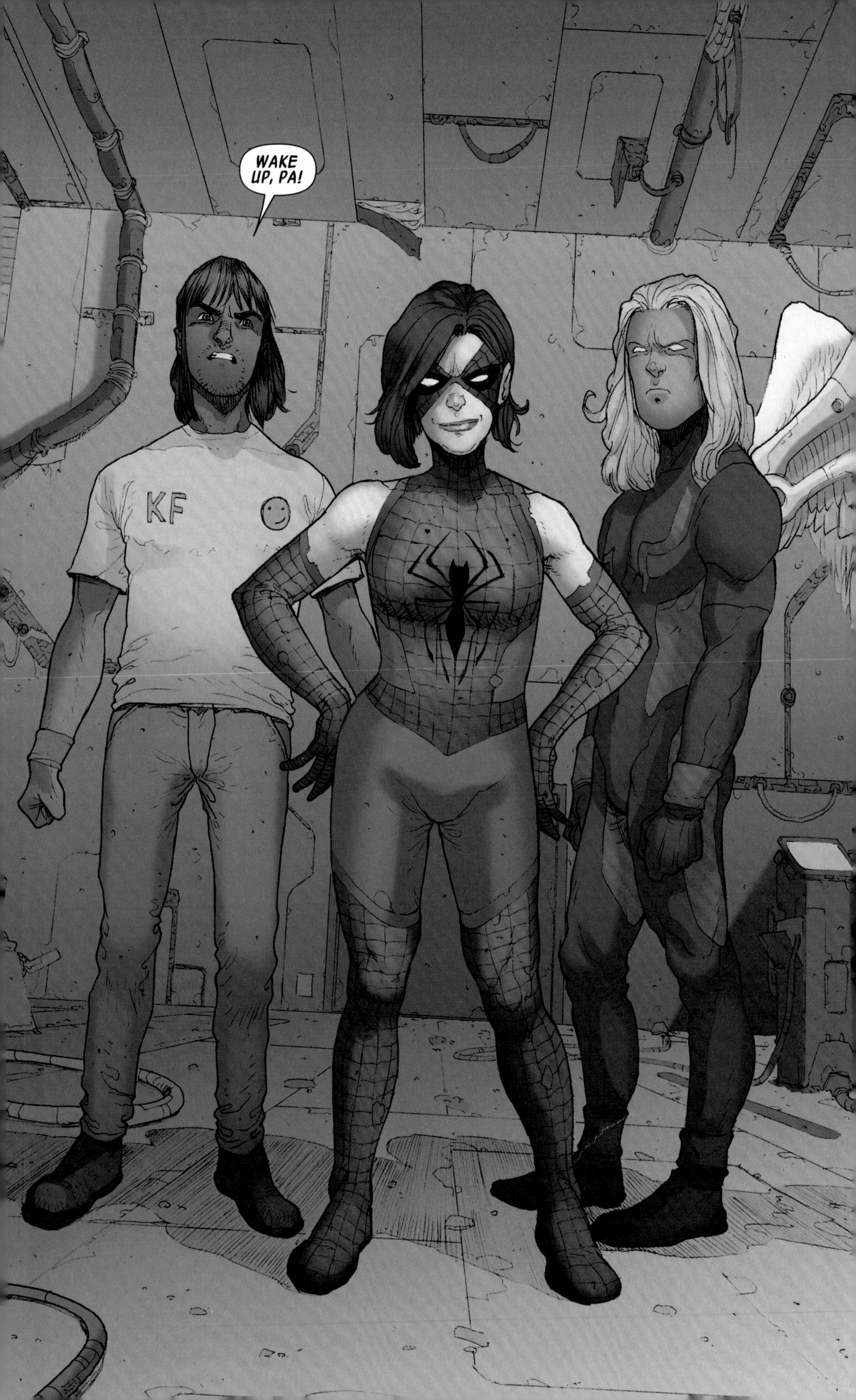
WAKE UP, PA!
KF

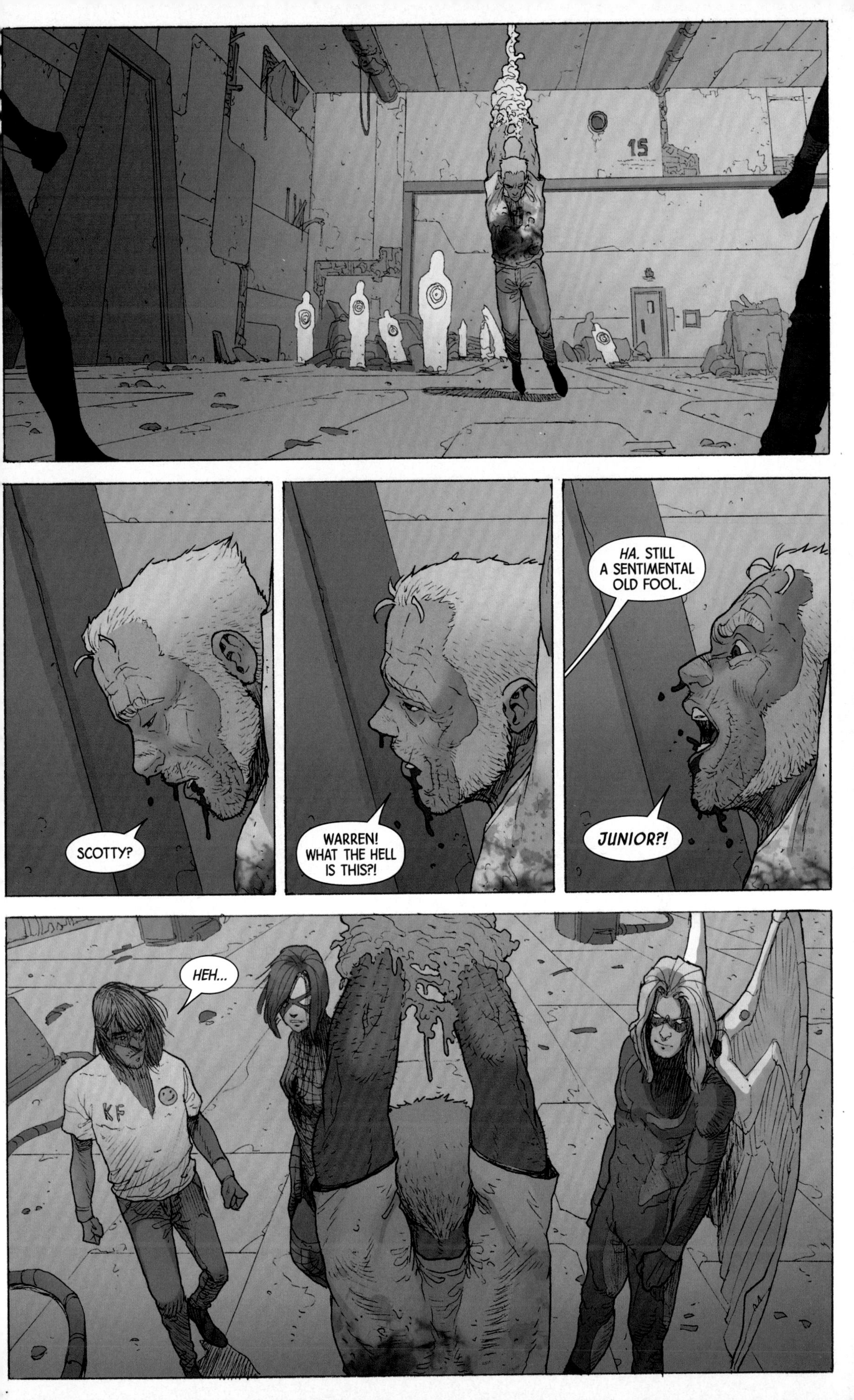
15
SCOTTY?
WARREN! WHAT THE HELL IS THIS?!
HA. STILL A SENTIMENTAL OLD FOOL.
JUNIOR?!
HEH...
KF

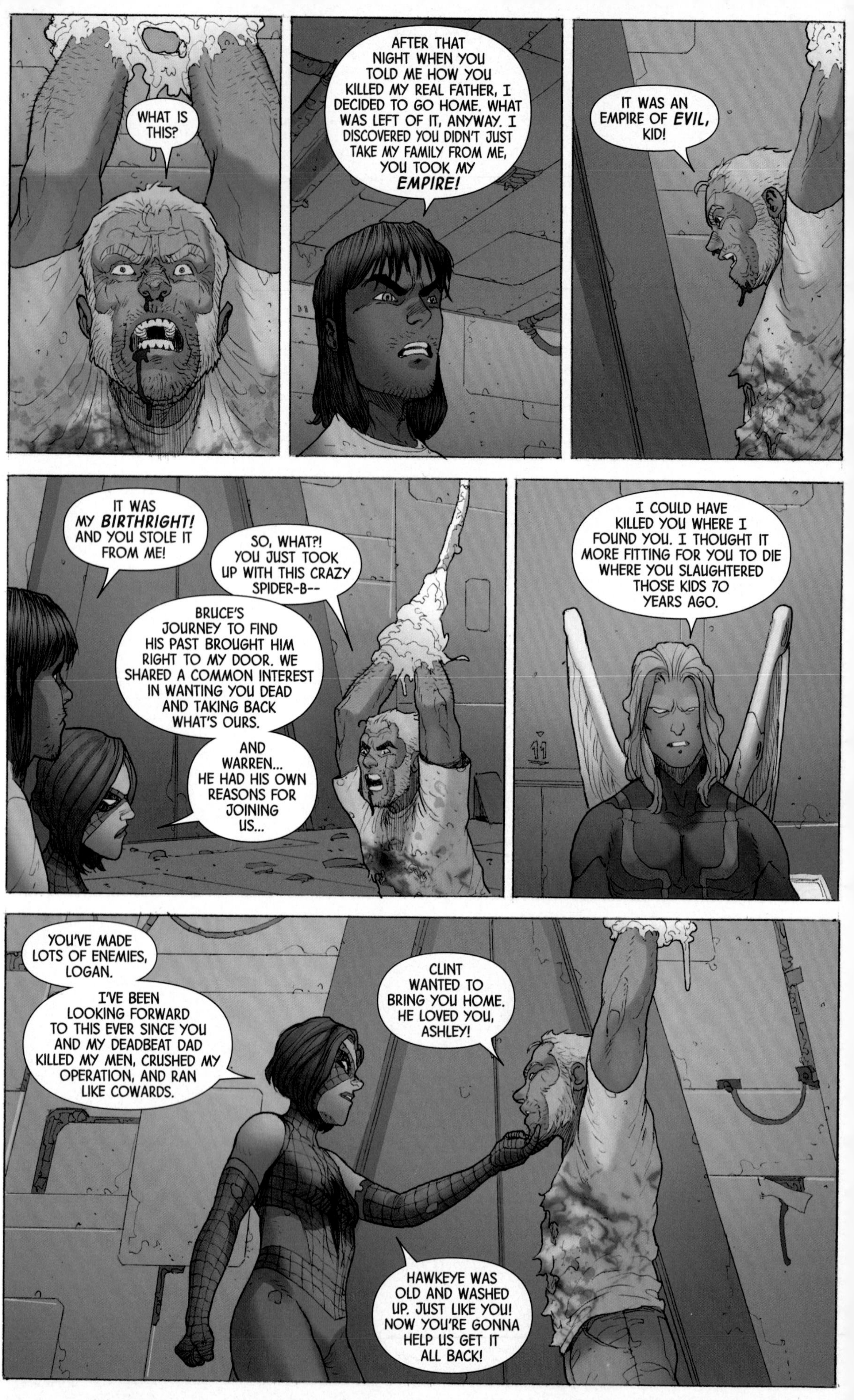
WHAT IS THIS?
AFTER THAT NIGHT WHEN YOU TOLD ME HOW YOU KILLED MY REAL FATHER, I DECIDED TO GO HOME. WHAT WAS LEFT OF IT, ANYWAY. I DISCOVERED YOU DIDN'T JUST TAKE MY FAMILY FROM ME, YOU TOOK MY EMPIRE!
IT WAS AN EMPIRE OF EVIL, KID!
IT WAS MY BIRTHRIGHT! AND YOU STOLE IT FROM ME!
SO, WHAT?! YOU JUST TOOK UP WITH THIS CRAZY SPIDER-B--
BRUCE'S JOURNEY TO FIND HIS PAST BROUGHT HIM RIGHT TO MY DOOR. WE SHARED A COMMON INTEREST IN WANTING YOU DEAD AND TAKING BACK WHAT'S OURS.
AND WARREN... HE HAD HIS OWN REASONS FOR JOINING US...
I COULD HAVE KILLED YOU WHERE I FOUND YOU. I THOUGHT IT MORE FITTING FOR YOU TO DIE WHERE YOU SLAUGHTERED THOSE KIDS 70 YEARS AGO.
YOU'VE MADE LOTS OF ENEMIES, LOGAN.
I'VE BEEN LOOKING FORWARD TO THIS EVER SINCE YOU AND MY DEADBEAT DAD KILLED MY MEN, CRUSHED MY OPERATION, AND RAN LIKE COWARDS.
CLINT WANTED TO BRING YOU HOME. HE LOVED YOU, ASHLEY!
HAWKEYE WAS OLD AND WASHED UP. JUST LIKE YOU! NOW YOU'RE GONNA HELP US GET IT ALL BACK!

TONIGHT YOU DIE, LOGAN. ONCE YOU'RE SWALLOWED UP AND SPIT OUT, WE'RE GOING TO USE YOUR DNA TO BUILD AN ARMY OF WOLVERINE CLONES.

THANKS TO YOU, WE WILL BE UNSTOPPABLE.

UNSTOPPABLE? YOU GENIUSES THINK YOU'RE THE FIRST ONES TO TRY TO CLONE ME? COME ON, JUNIOR. I RAISED YOU TO BE--

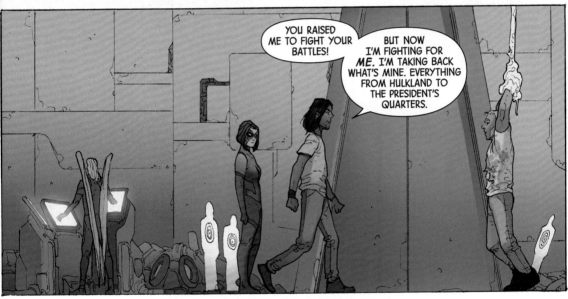

YOU RAISED ME TO FIGHT YOUR BATTLES!

BUT NOW I'M FIGHTING FOR ME. I'M TAKING BACK WHAT'S MINE. EVERYTHING FROM HULKLAND TO THE PRESIDENT'S QUARTERS.

WHEN YOU AND MY FATHER ESCAPED FALL ALL THOSE YEARS AGO...YOU LEFT A BLACK MARK ON MY REPUTATION. I POURED A LOT OF RESOURCES INTO RECOVERING YOU TWO.

I DIDN'T FIND YOU, BUT I DID FIND SOMETHING YOU MIGHT REMEMBER.

WARREN! OPEN THE DOORS...

TOOK A LONG TIME TO CATCH THIS THING JUST TO WATCH IT CHEW YOU UP!

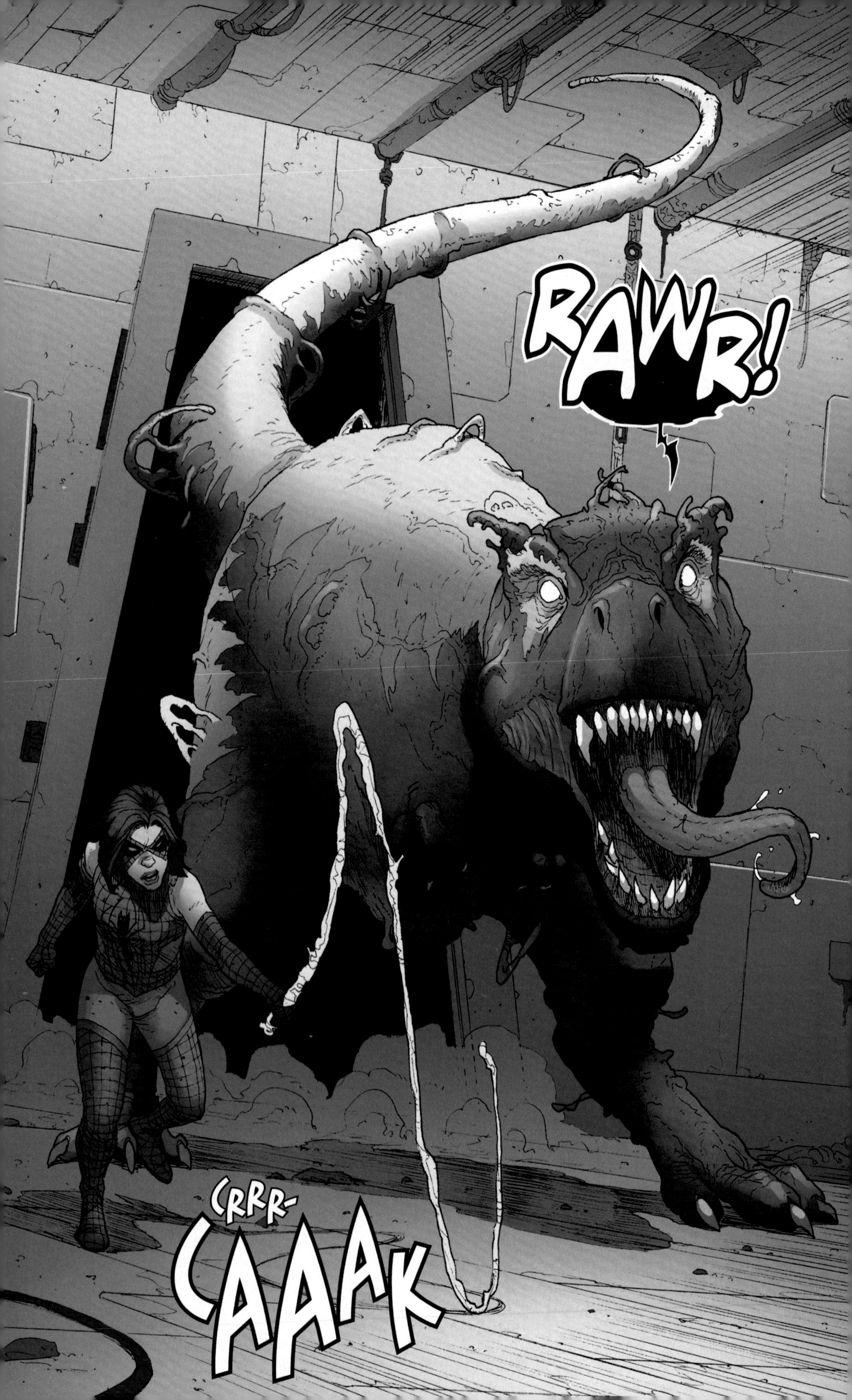
RAWR!
CRRR-
CAAAK

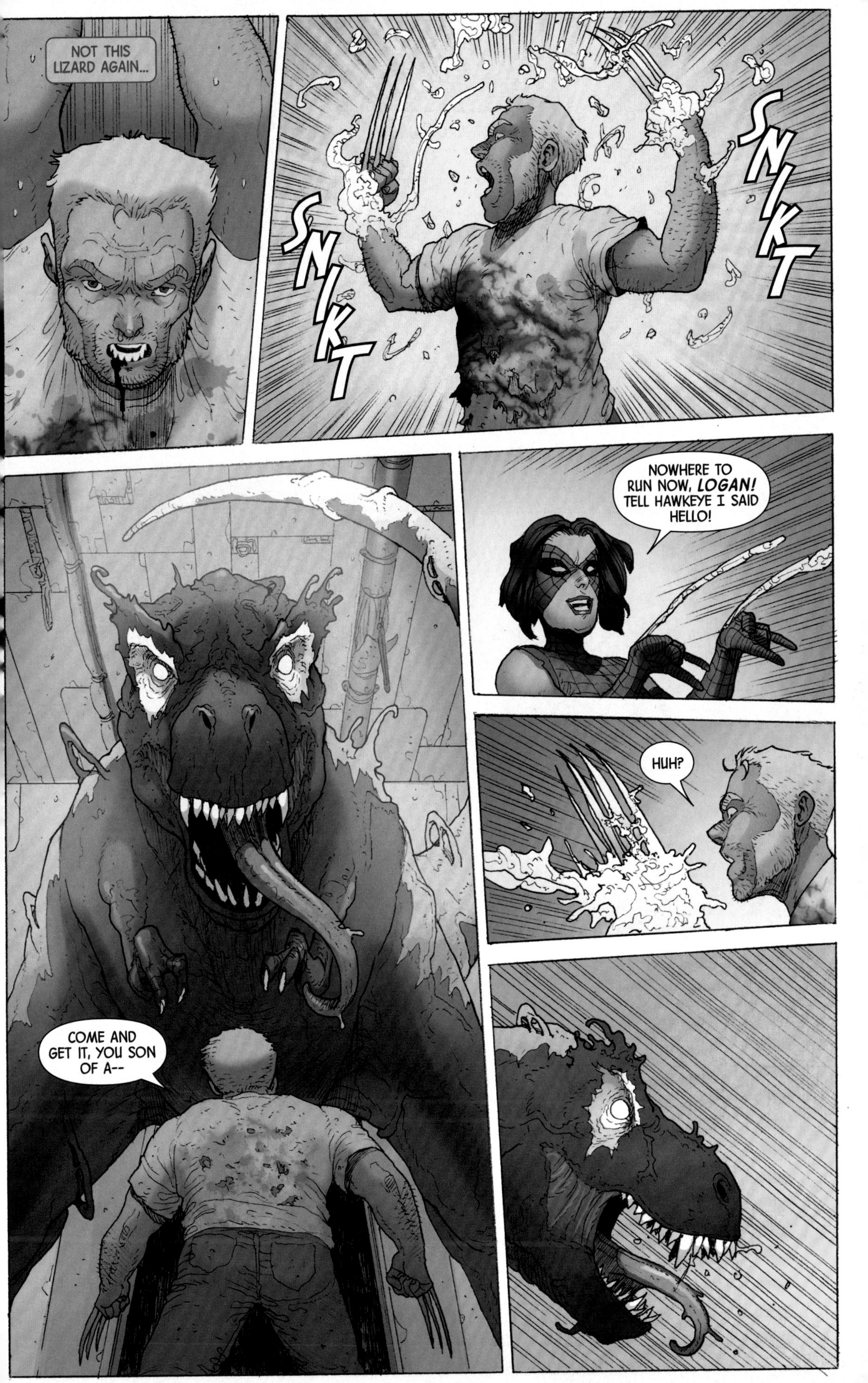

NOT THIS LIZARD AGAIN...
SNIKT
SNIKT
NOWHERE TO RUN NOW, LOGAN! TELL HAWKEYE I SAID HELLO!
HUH?
COME AND GET IT, YOU SON OF A--

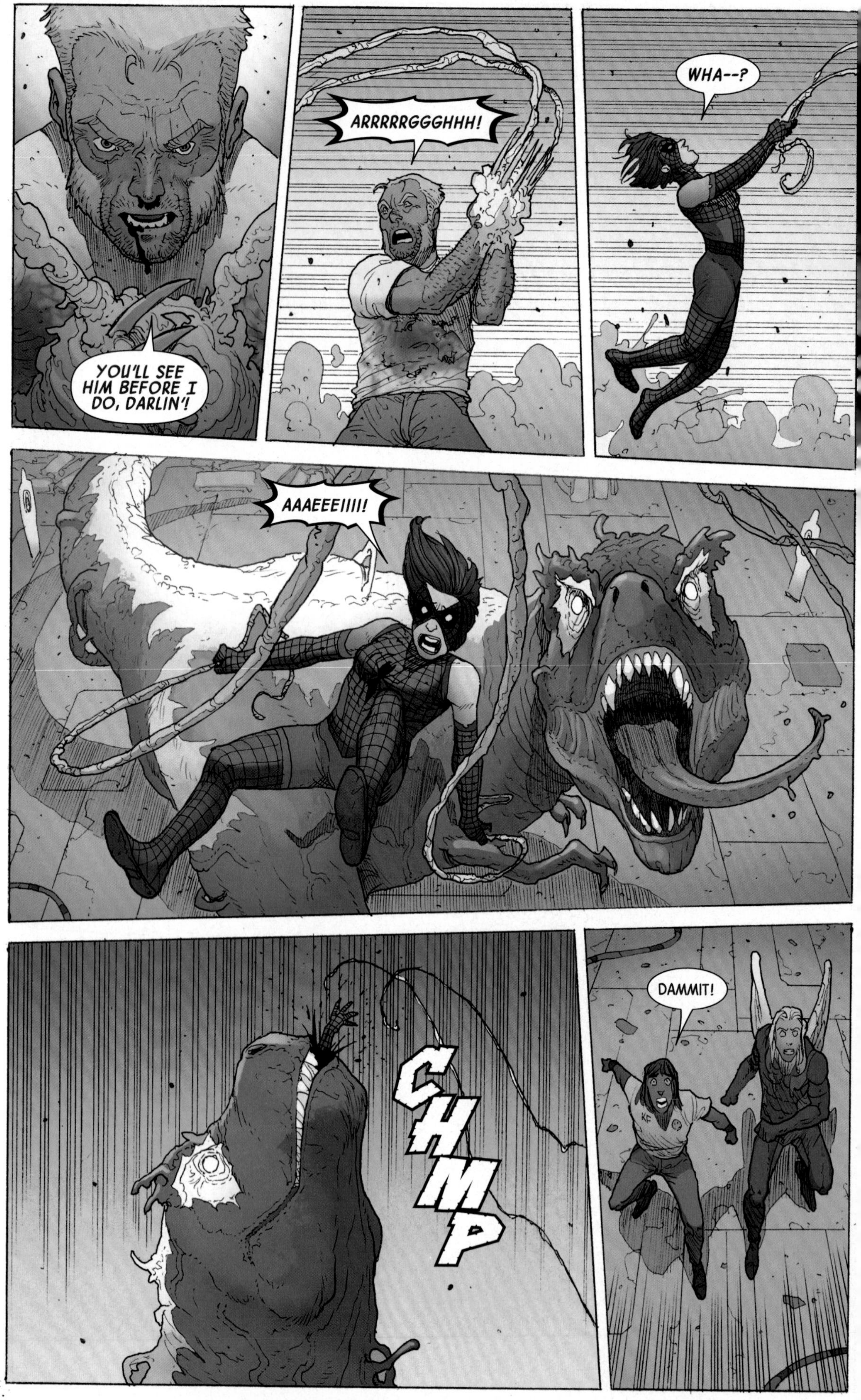
YOU'LL SEE HIM BEFORE I DO, DARLIN'!
ARRRRRGGGHHH!
WHA--?
AAAEEEIIII!
CHMP
DAMMIT!

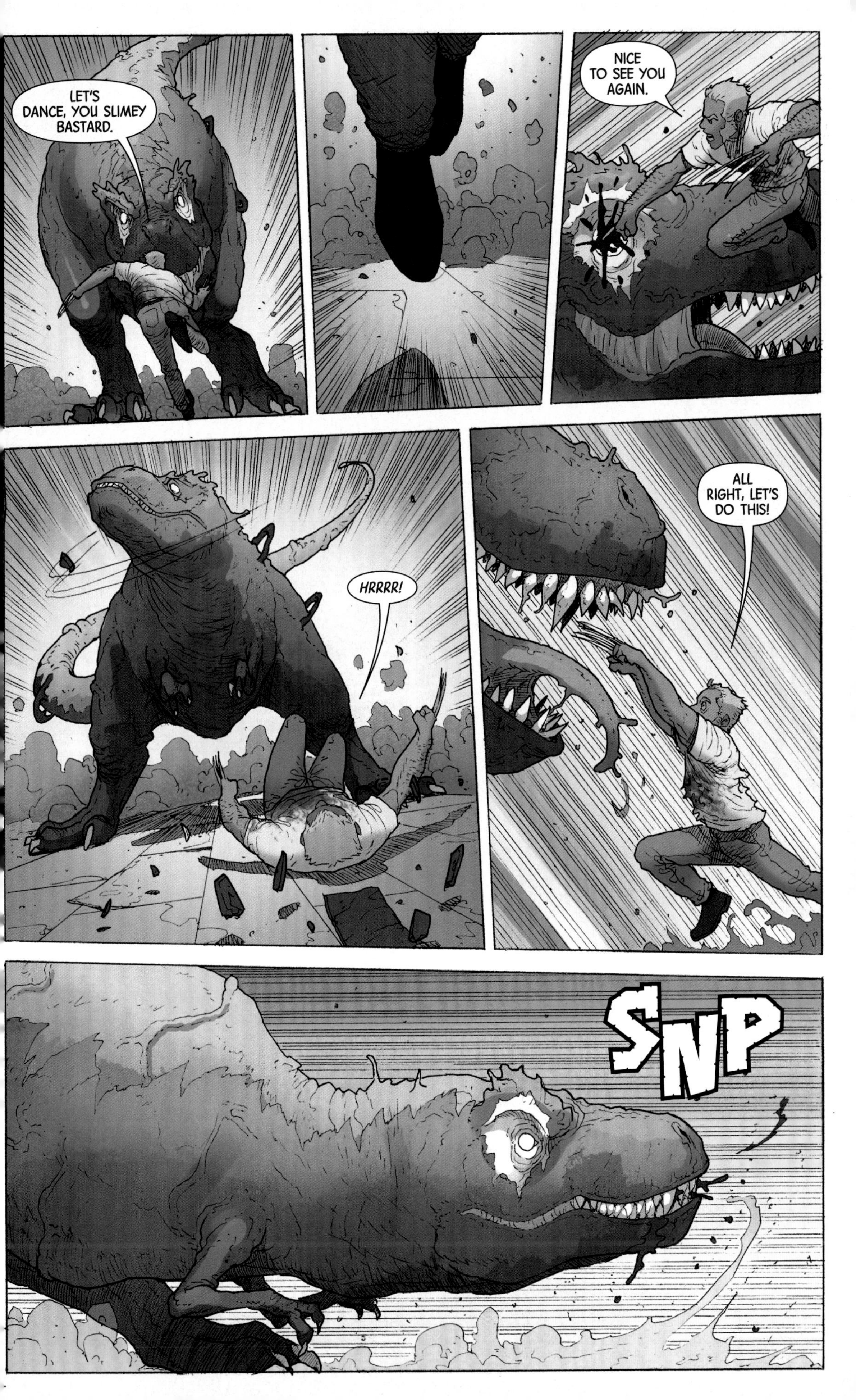
LET'S DANCE, YOU SLIMEY BASTARD.
NICE TO SEE YOU AGAIN.
HRRRR!
ALL RIGHT, LET'S DO THIS!
SNP

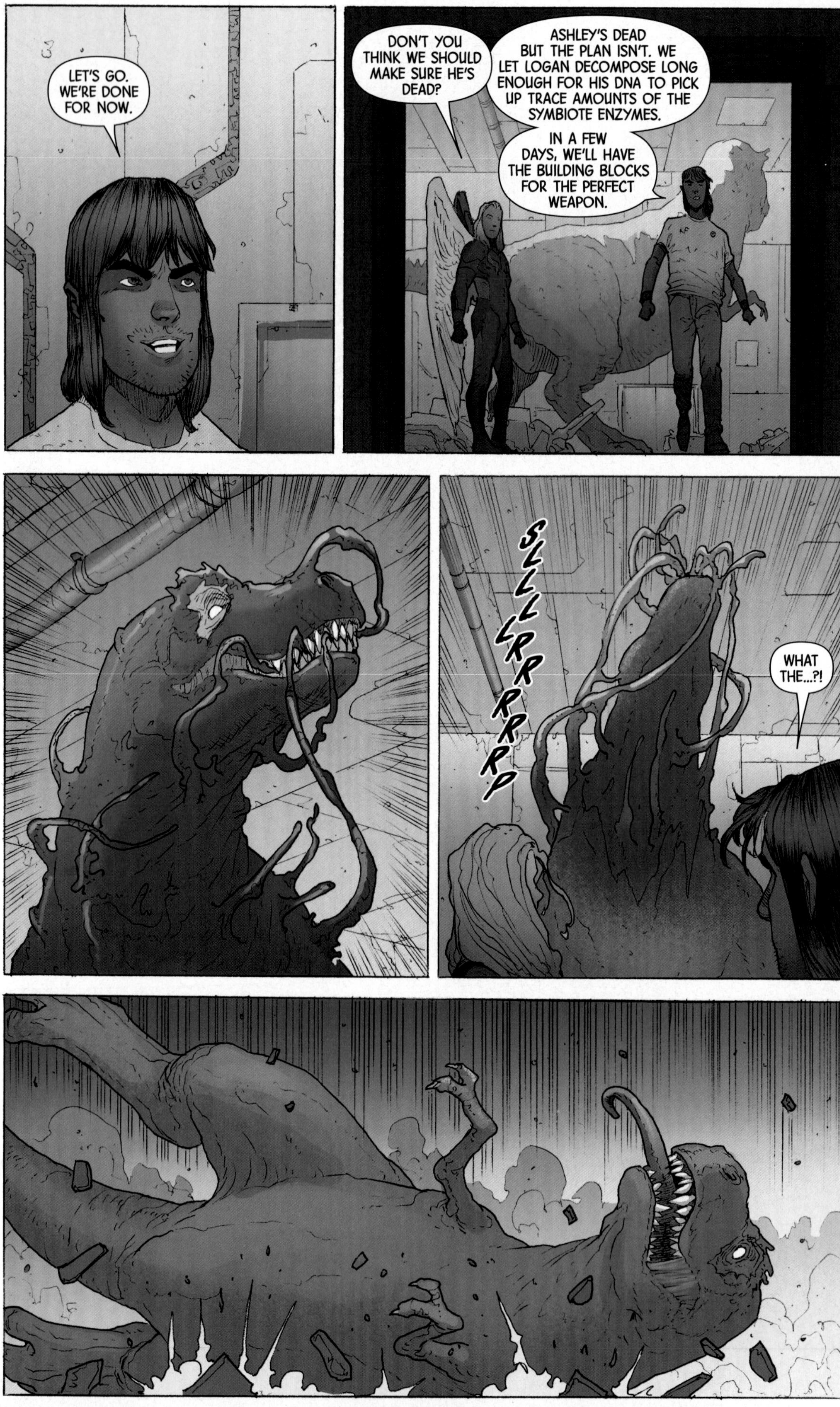
LET'S GO. WE'RE DONE FOR NOW.
DON'T YOU THINK WE SHOULD MAKE SURE HE'S DEAD?
ASHLEY'S DEAD BUT THE PLAN ISN'T. WE LET LOGAN DECOMPOSE LONG ENOUGH FOR HIS DNA TO PICK UP TRACE AMOUNTS OF THE SYMBIOTE ENZYMES.
IN A FEW DAYS, WE'LL HAVE THE BUILDING BLOCKS FOR THE PERFECT WEAPON.
SLLLRRRRRP
WHAT THE...?!

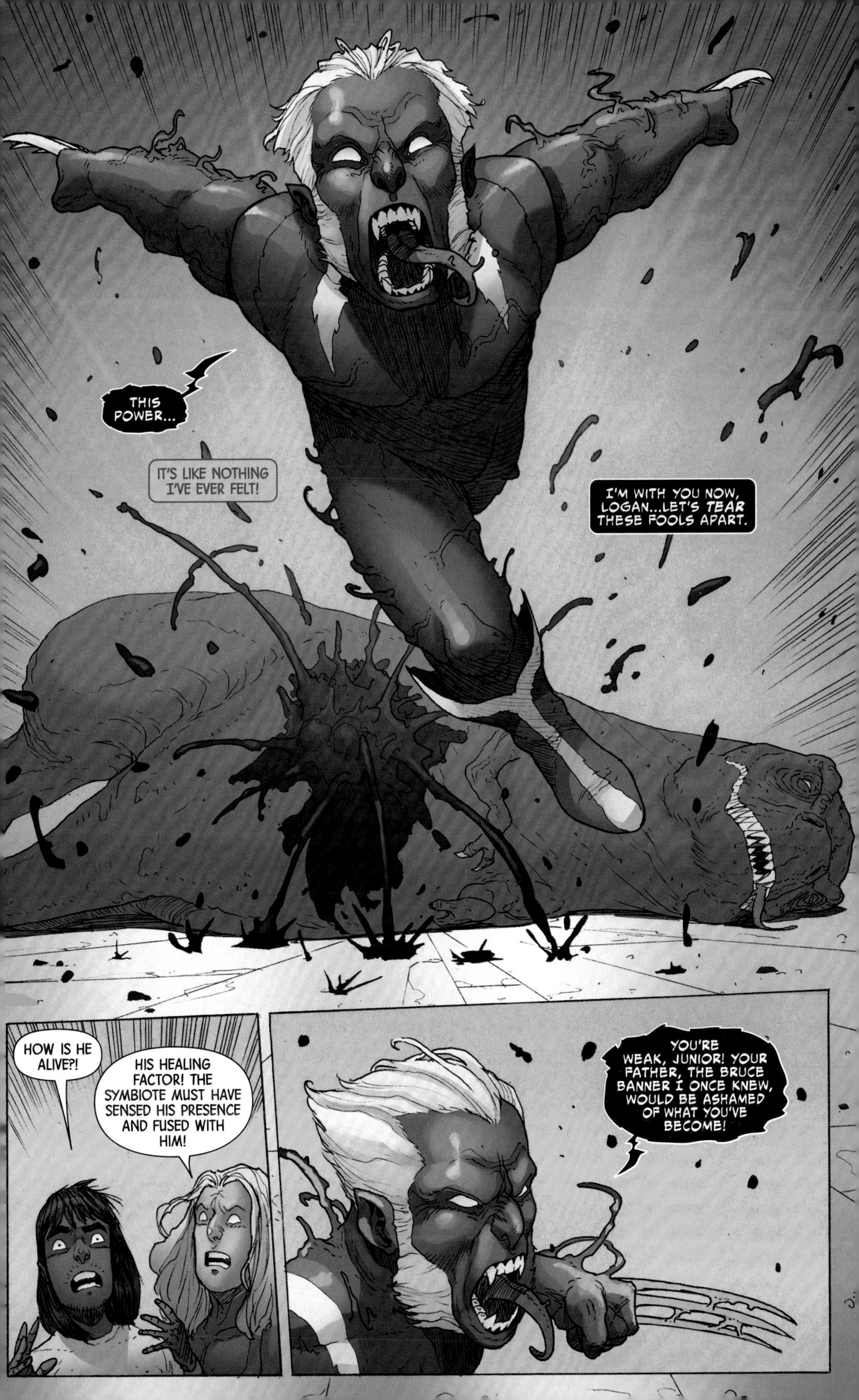
THIS POWER...
IT'S LIKE NOTHING I'VE EVER FELT!
I'M WITH YOU NOW, LOGAN...LET'S TEAR THESE FOOLS APART.
HOW IS HE ALIVE?!
HIS HEALING FACTOR! THE SYMBIOTE MUST HAVE SENSED HIS PRESENCE AND FUSED WITH HIM!
YOU'RE WEAK, JUNIOR! YOUR FATHER, THE BRUCE BANNER I ONCE KNEW, WOULD BE ASHAMED OF WHAT YOU'VE BECOME!

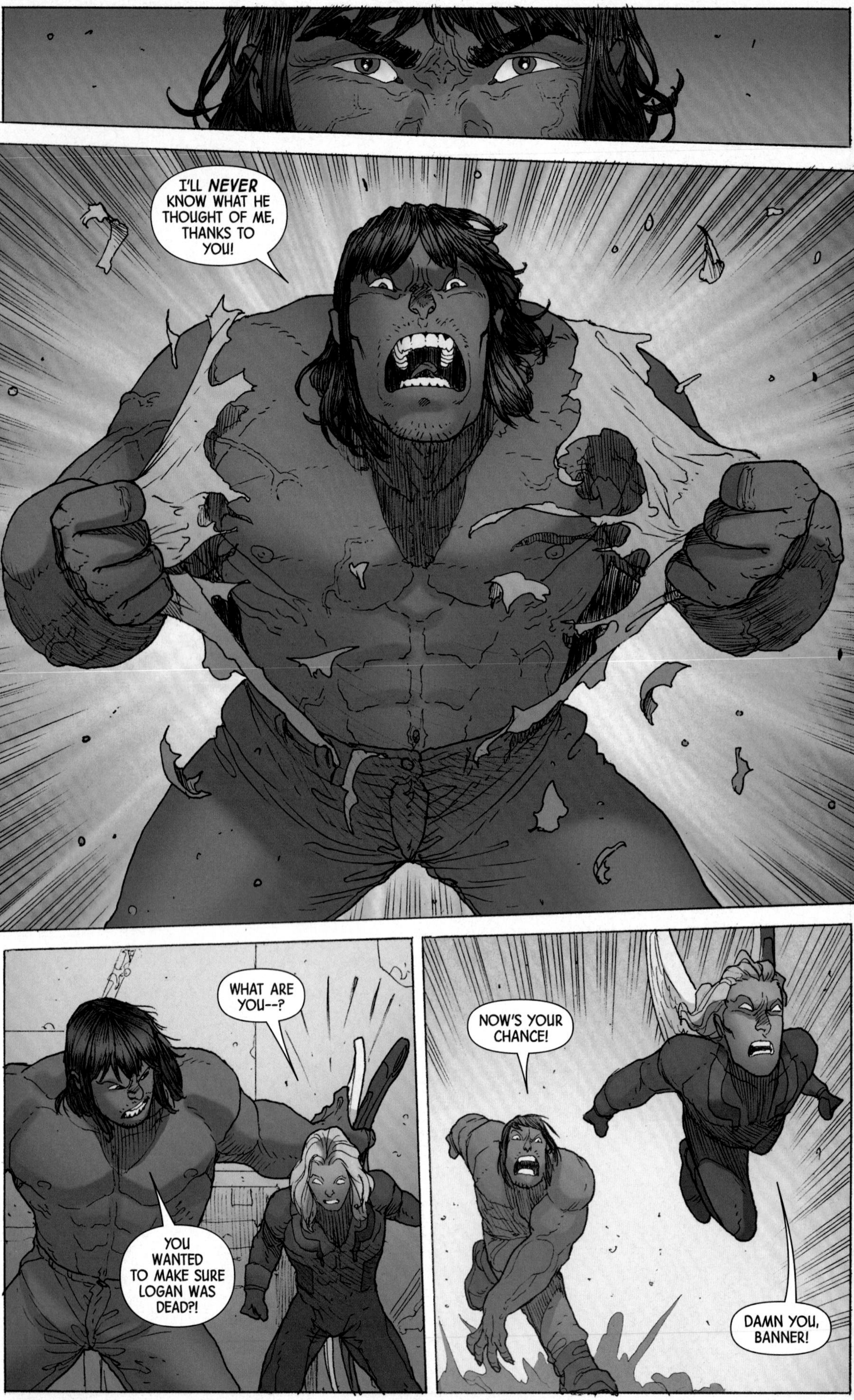
I'LL NEVER KNOW WHAT HE THOUGHT OF ME, THANKS TO YOU!
WHAT ARE YOU--?
YOU WANTED TO MAKE SURE LOGAN WAS DEAD?!
NOW'S YOUR CHANCE!
DAMN YOU, BANNER!

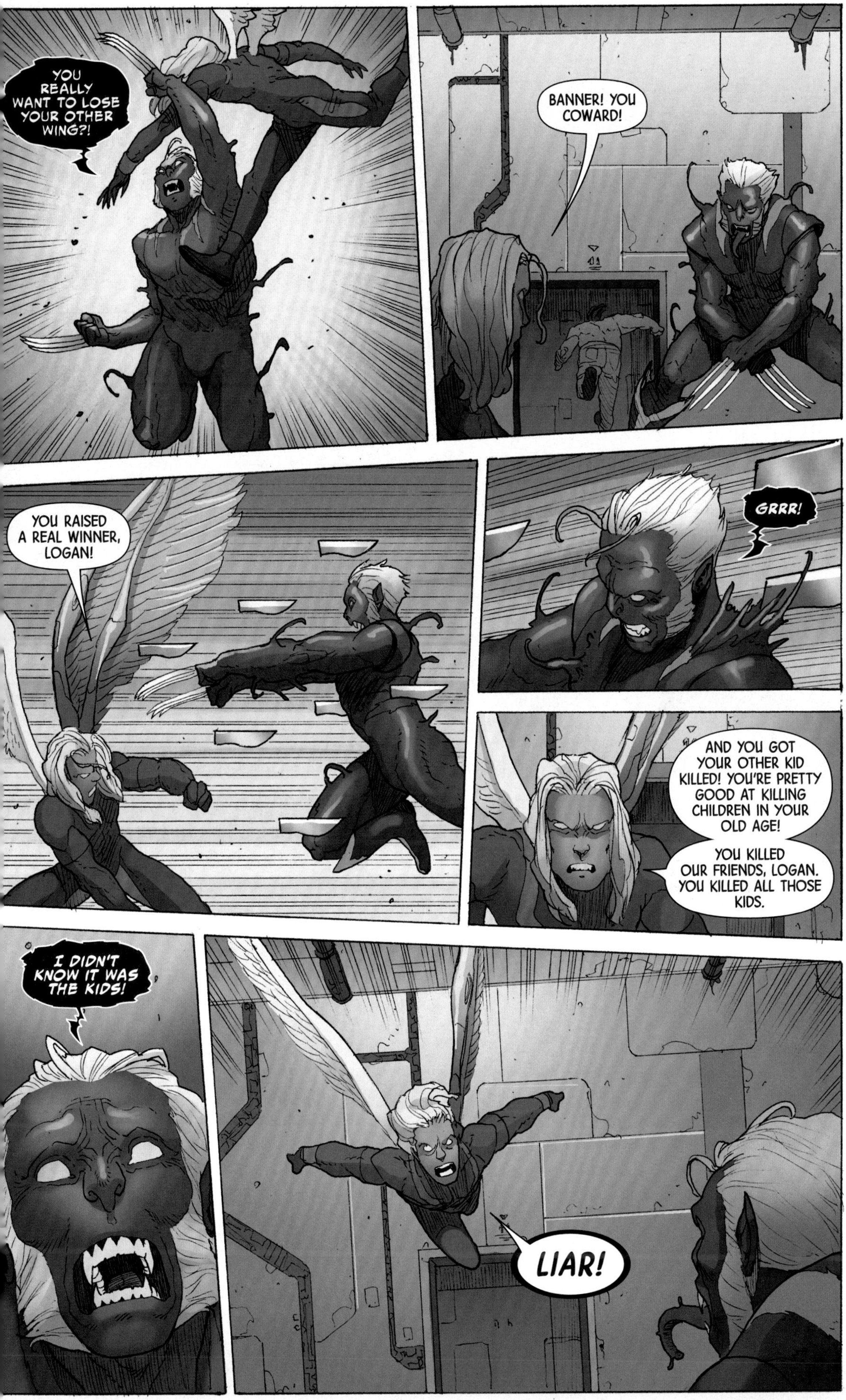
YOU REALLY WANT TO LOSE YOUR OTHER WING?!
BANNER! YOU COWARD!
YOU RAISED A REAL WINNER, LOGAN!
GRRR!
AND YOU GOT YOUR OTHER KID KILLED! YOU'RE PRETTY GOOD AT KILLING CHILDREN IN YOUR OLD AGE!
YOU KILLED OUR FRIENDS, LOGAN. YOU KILLED ALL THOSE KIDS.
I DIDN'T KNOW IT WAS THE KIDS!
LIAR!

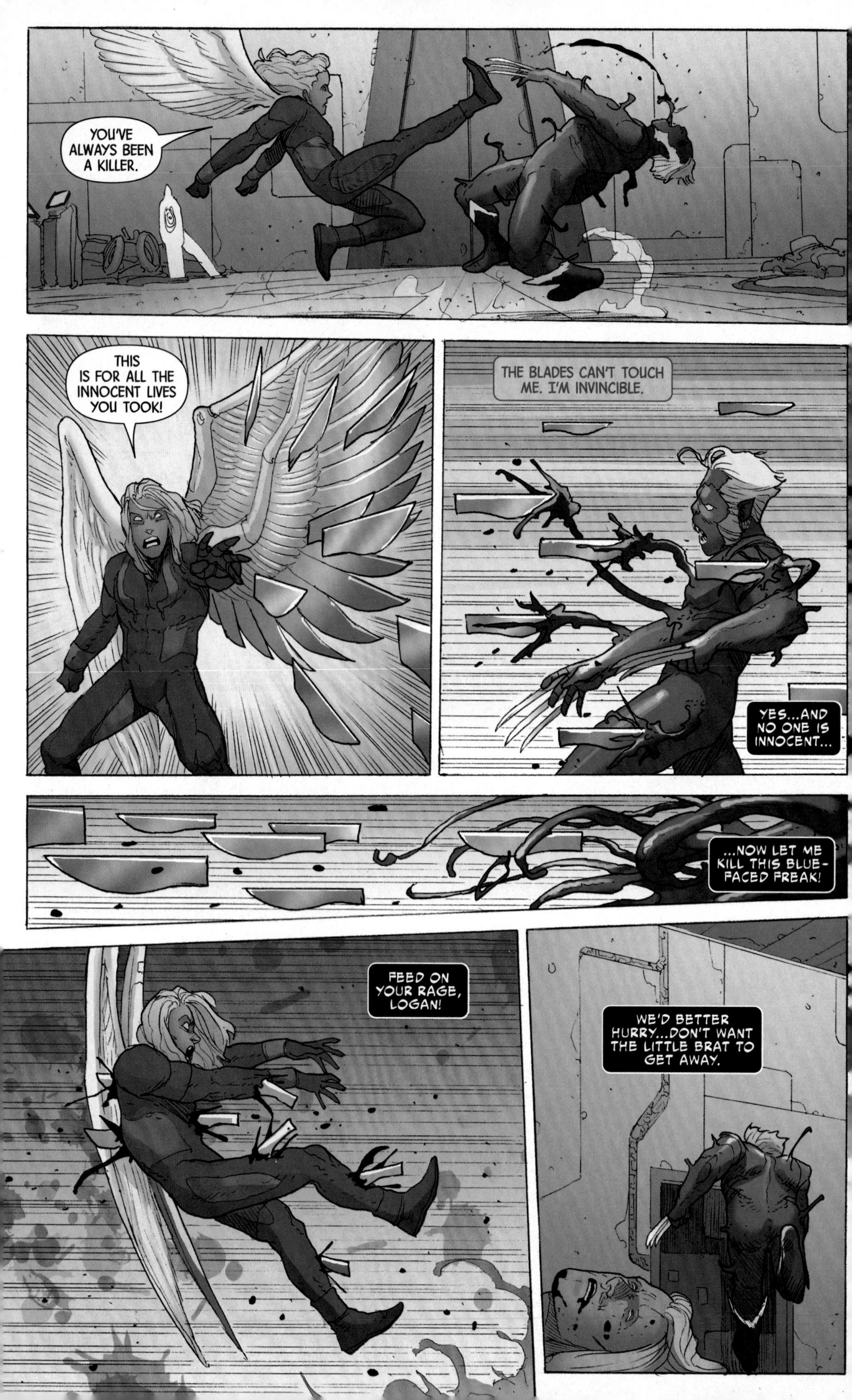
YOU'VE ALWAYS BEEN A KILLER.
THIS IS FOR ALL THE INNOCENT LIVES YOU TOOK!
THE BLADES CAN'T TOUCH ME. I'M INVINCIBLE.
YES...AND NO ONE IS INNOCENT...
...NOW LET ME KILL THIS BLUE-FACED FREAK!
FEED ON YOUR RAGE, LOGAN!
WE'D BETTER HURRY...DON'T WANT THE LITTLE BRAT TO GET AWAY.

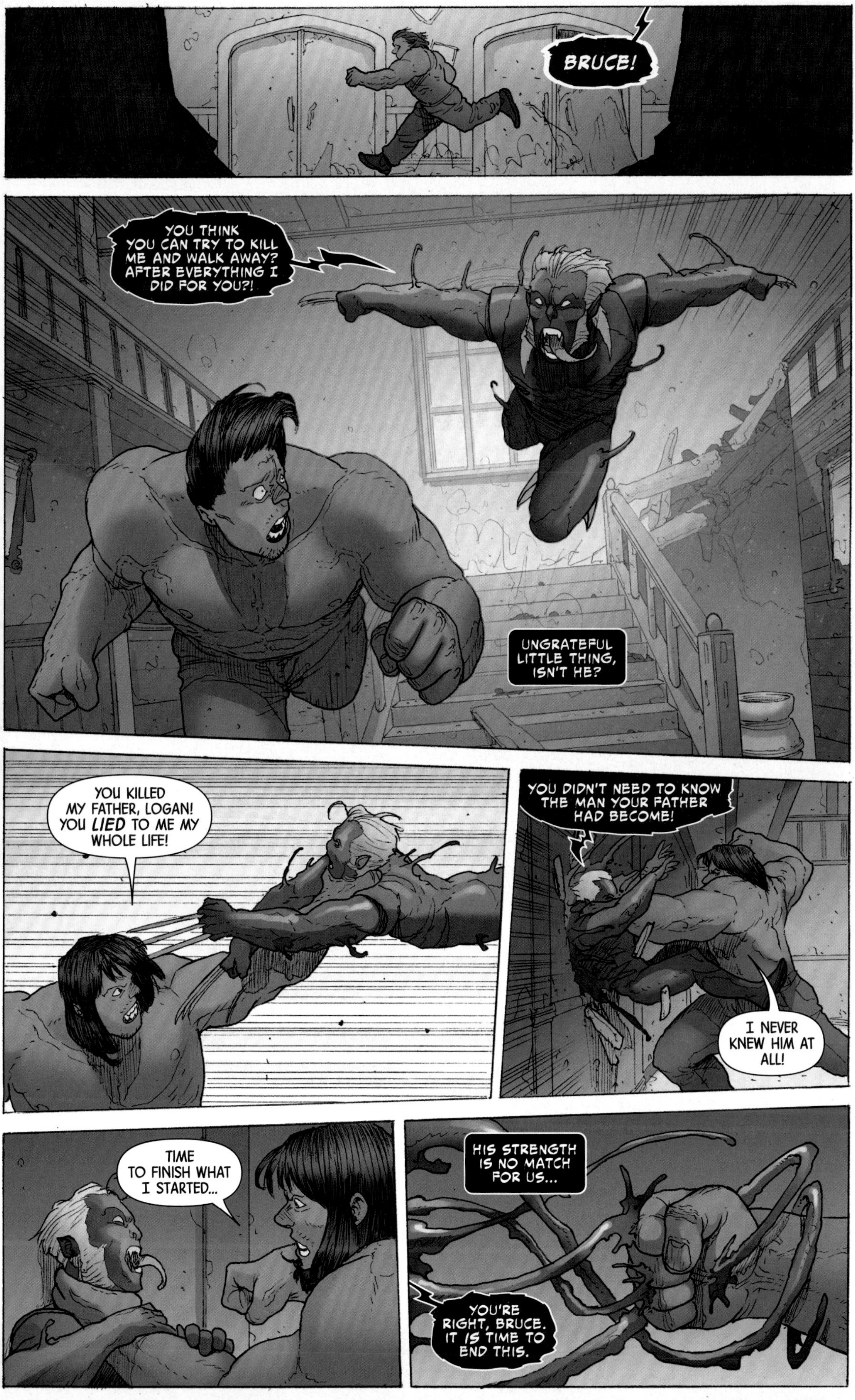
BRUCE!
YOU THINK YOU CAN TRY TO KILL ME AND WALK AWAY? AFTER EVERYTHING I DID FOR YOU?!
UNGRATEFUL LITTLE THING, ISN'T HE?
YOU KILLED MY FATHER, LOGAN! YOU LIED TO ME MY WHOLE LIFE!
YOU DIDN'T NEED TO KNOW THE MAN YOUR FATHER HAD BECOME!
I NEVER KNEW HIM AT ALL!
TIME TO FINISH WHAT I STARTED...
HIS STRENGTH IS NO MATCH FOR US...
YOU'RE RIGHT, BRUCE. IT IS TIME TO END THIS.

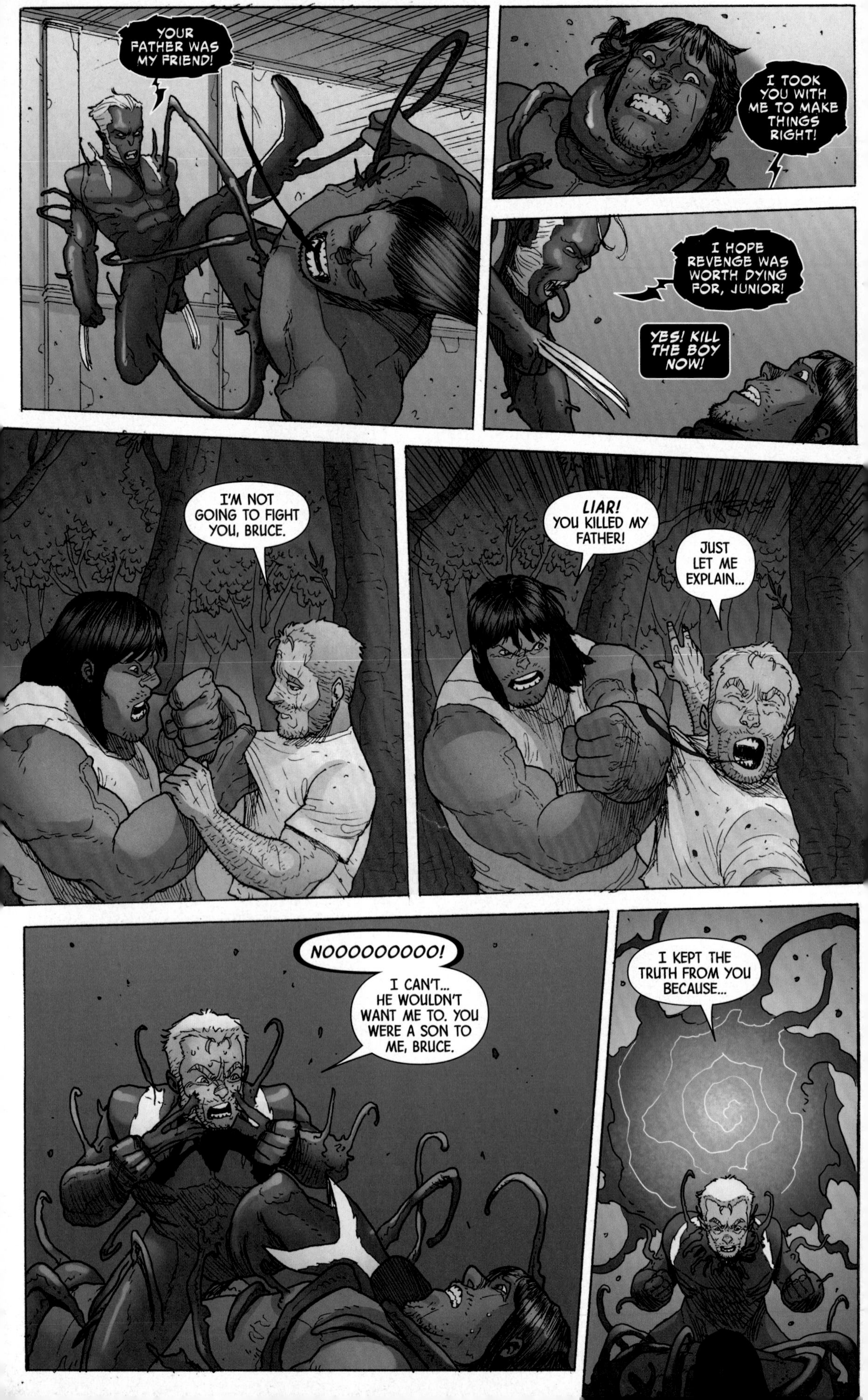
YOUR FATHER WAS MY FRIEND!
I TOOK YOU WITH ME TO MAKE THINGS RIGHT!
I HOPE REVENGE WAS WORTH DYING FOR, JUNIOR!
YES! KILL THE BOY NOW!
I'M NOT GOING TO FIGHT YOU, BRUCE.
LIAR! YOU KILLED MY FATHER!
JUST LET ME EXPLAIN...
NOOOOOOOOO!
I CAN'T... HE WOULDN'T WANT ME TO. YOU WERE A SON TO ME, BRUCE.
I KEPT THE TRUTH FROM YOU BECAUSE...

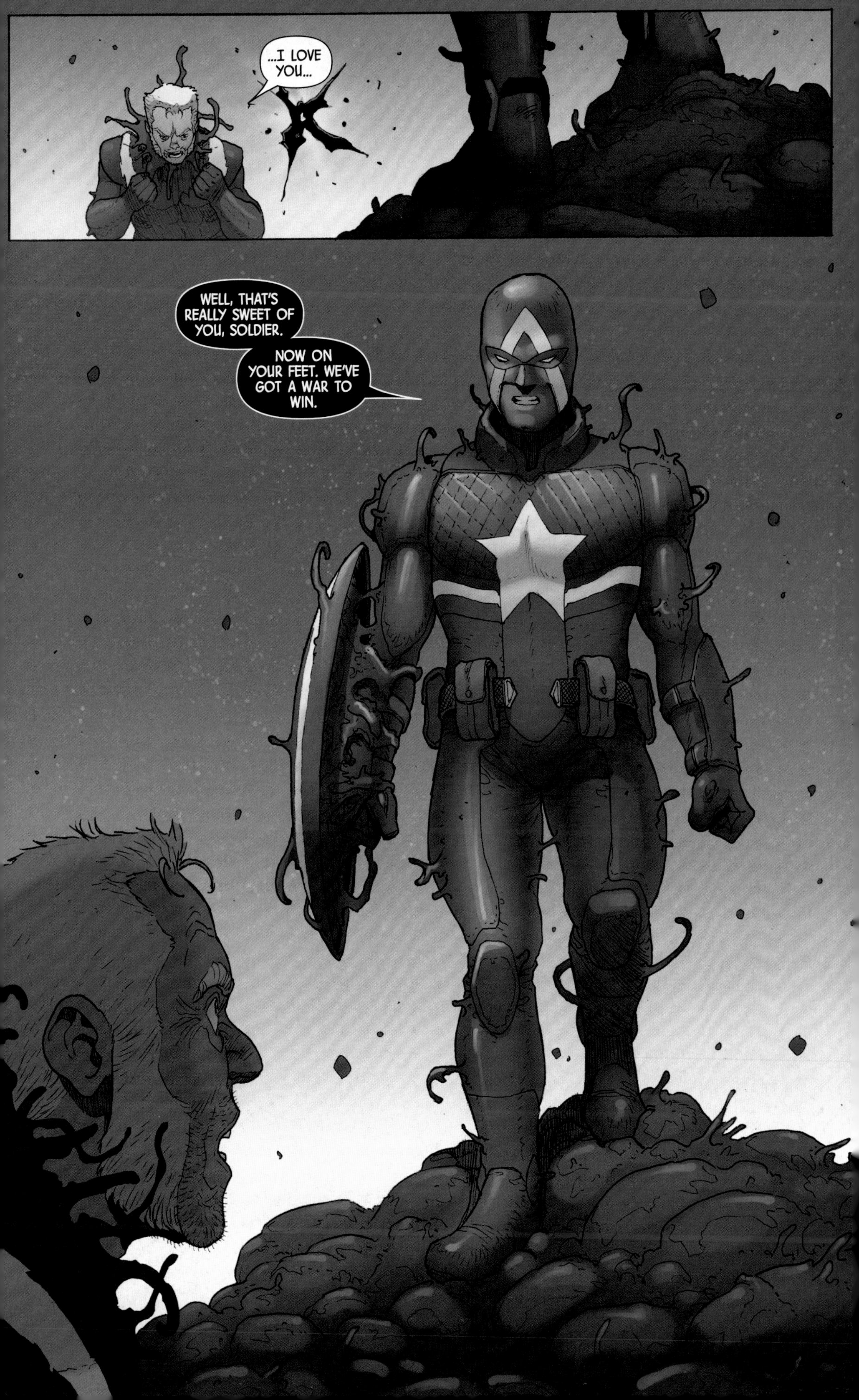
...I LOVE YOU...
WELL, THAT'S REALLY SWEET OF YOU, SOLDIER.
NOW ON YOUR FEET. WE'VE GOT A WAR TO WIN.

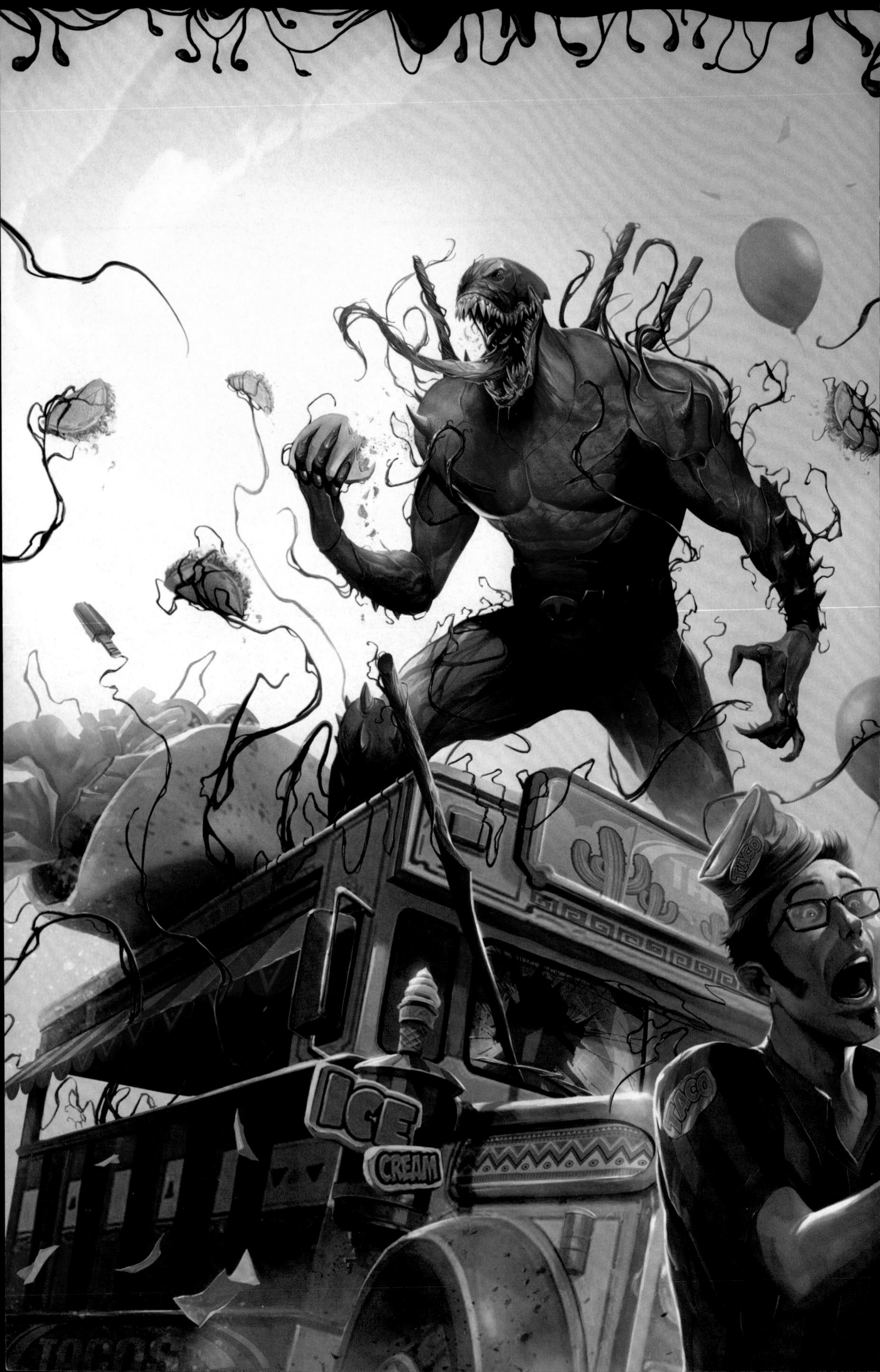
TACO
ICE
CREAM
TACO

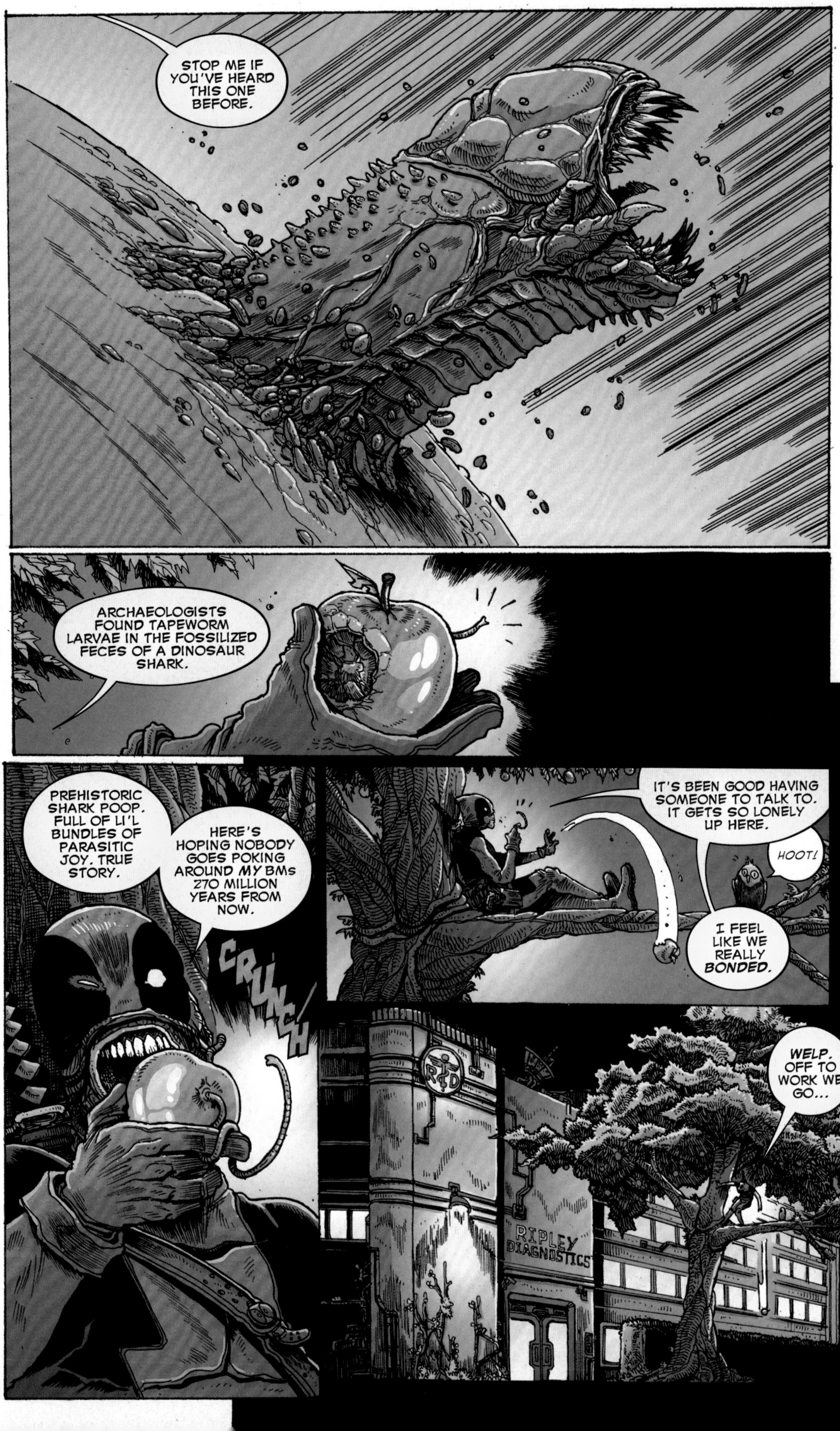
STOP ME IF YOU'VE HEARD THIS ONE BEFORE.
ARCHAEOLOGISTS FOUND TAPEWORM LARVAE IN THE FOSSILIZED FECES OF A DINOSAUR SHARK.
PREHISTORIC SHARK POOP. FULL OF LI'L BUNDLES OF PARASITIC JOY. TRUE STORY.
HERE'S HOPING NOBODY GOES POKING AROUND *MY* BMs 270 MILLION YEARS FROM NOW.
CRUNCH
IT'S BEEN GOOD HAVING SOMEONE TO TALK TO. IT GETS SO LONELY UP HERE.
HOOT!
I FEEL LIKE WE REALLY *BONDED*.
RIPLEY DIAGNOSTICS
WELP. OFF TO WORK WE GO...

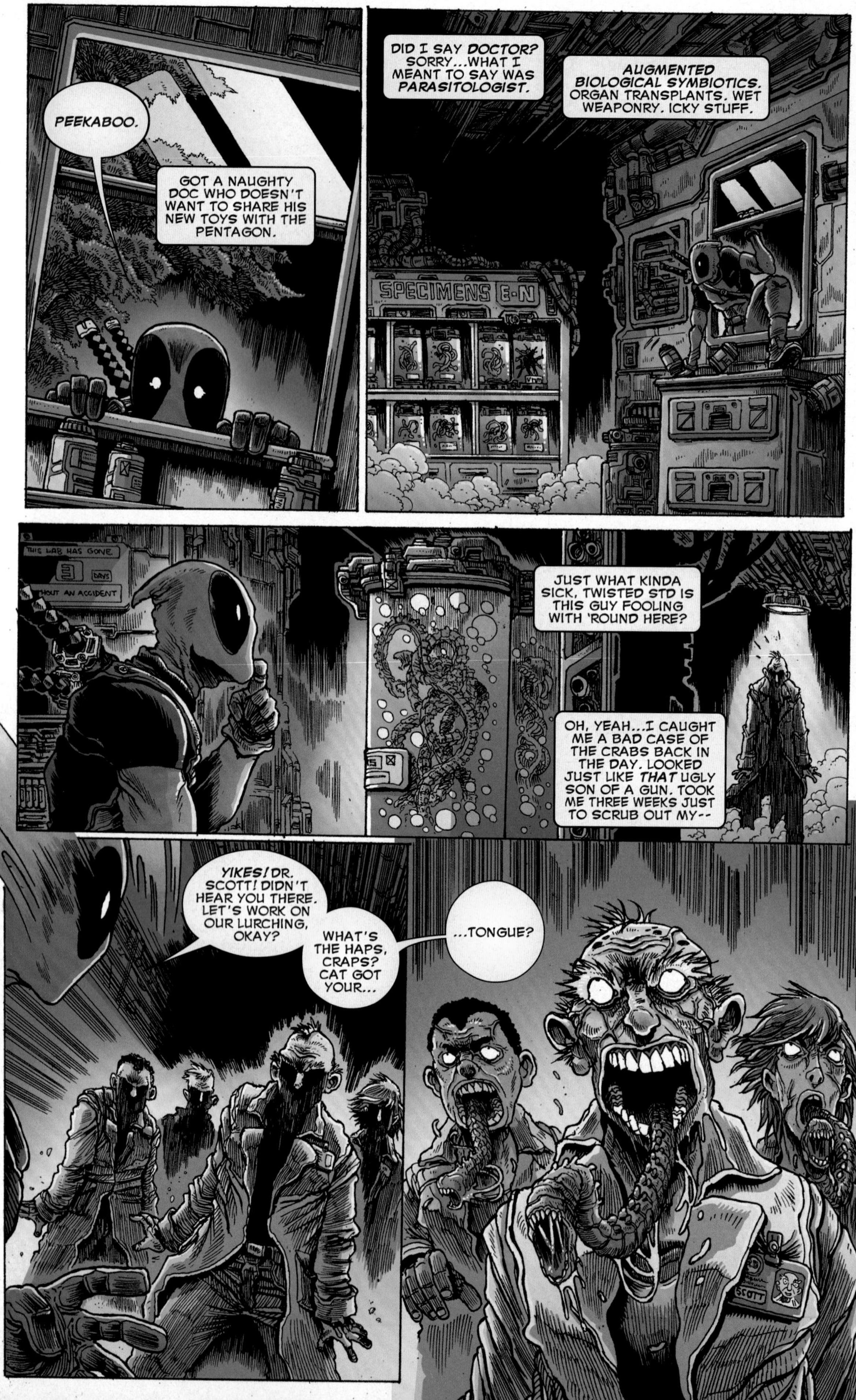
PEEKABOO.
GOT A NAUGHTY DOC WHO DOESN'T WANT TO SHARE HIS NEW TOYS WITH THE PENTAGON.
DID I SAY *DOCTOR?* SORRY...WHAT I MEANT TO SAY WAS *PARASITOLOGIST.*
AUGMENTED BIOLOGICAL SYMBIOTICS. ORGAN TRANSPLANTS. WET WEAPONRY. ICKY STUFF.
SPECIMENS E-N
THIS LAB HAS GONE 3 DAYS ...THOUT AN ACCIDENT
JUST WHAT KINDA SICK, TWISTED STD IS THIS GUY FOOLING WITH 'ROUND HERE?
OH, YEAH...I CAUGHT ME A BAD CASE OF THE CRABS BACK IN THE DAY. LOOKED JUST LIKE *THAT* UGLY SON OF A GUN. TOOK ME THREE WEEKS JUST TO SCRUB OUT MY--
YIKES! DR. SCOTT! DIDN'T HEAR YOU THERE. LET'S WORK ON OUR LURCHING, OKAY?
WHAT'S THE HAPS, CRAPS? CAT GOT YOUR...
...TONGUE?
SCOTT

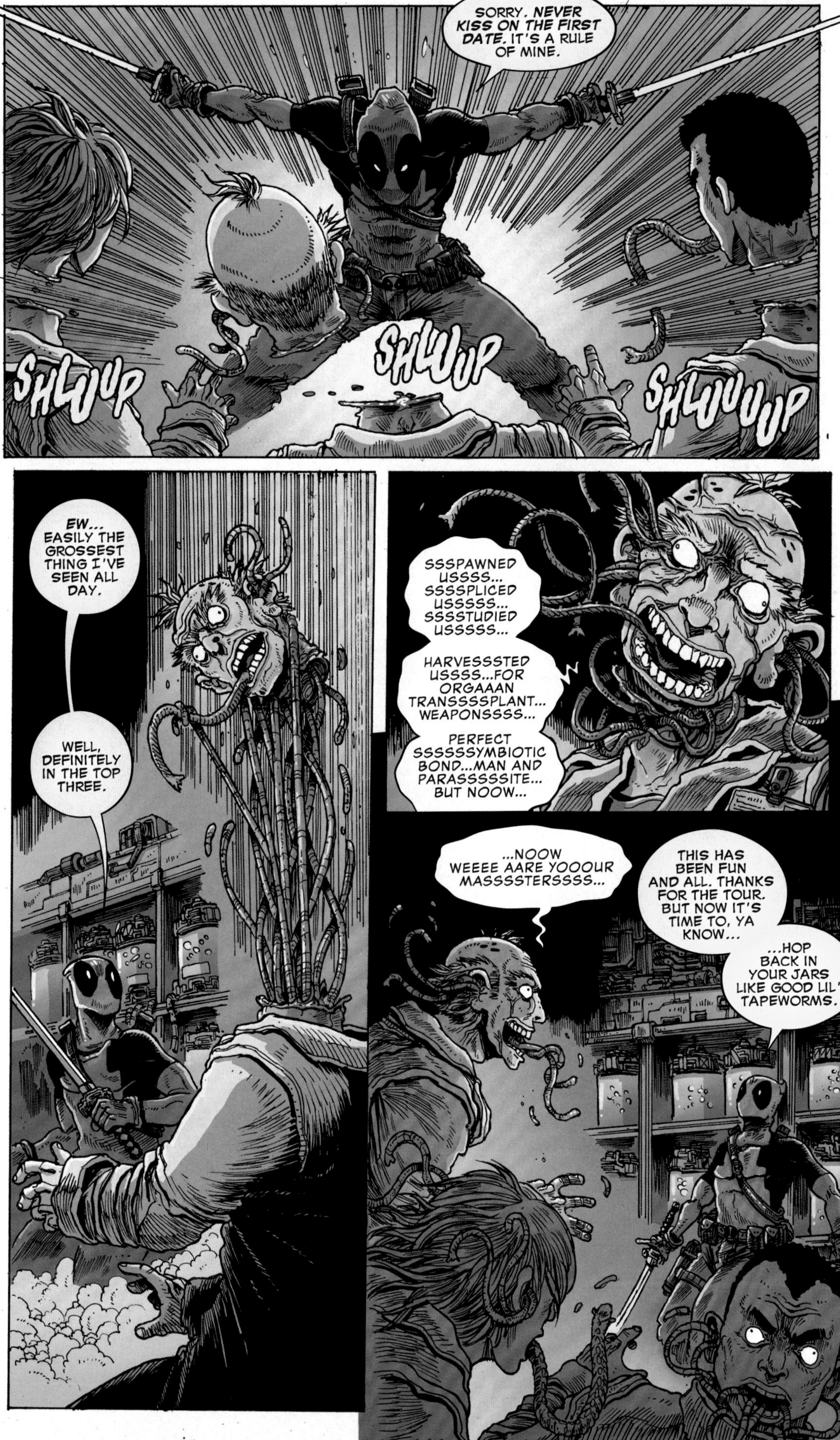
SORRY. NEVER KISS ON THE FIRST DATE. IT'S A RULE OF MINE.
SHLUUP
SHLUUP
SHLUUUUP
EW... EASILY THE GROSSEST THING I'VE SEEN ALL DAY.
WELL, DEFINITELY IN THE TOP THREE.
SSSPAWNED USSSS... SSSSPLICED USSSSS... SSSSTUDIED USSSSS...
HARVESSSTED USSSS...FOR ORGAAAN TRANSSSSPLANT... WEAPONSSSS...
PERFECT SSSSSSYMBIOTIC BOND...MAN AND PARASSSSSITE... BUT NOOW...
...NOOW WEEEE AARE YOOOUR MASSSSTERSSSS...
THIS HAS BEEN FUN AND ALL. THANKS FOR THE TOUR. BUT NOW IT'S TIME TO, YA KNOW...
...HOP BACK IN YOUR JARS LIKE GOOD LIL' TAPEWORMS.

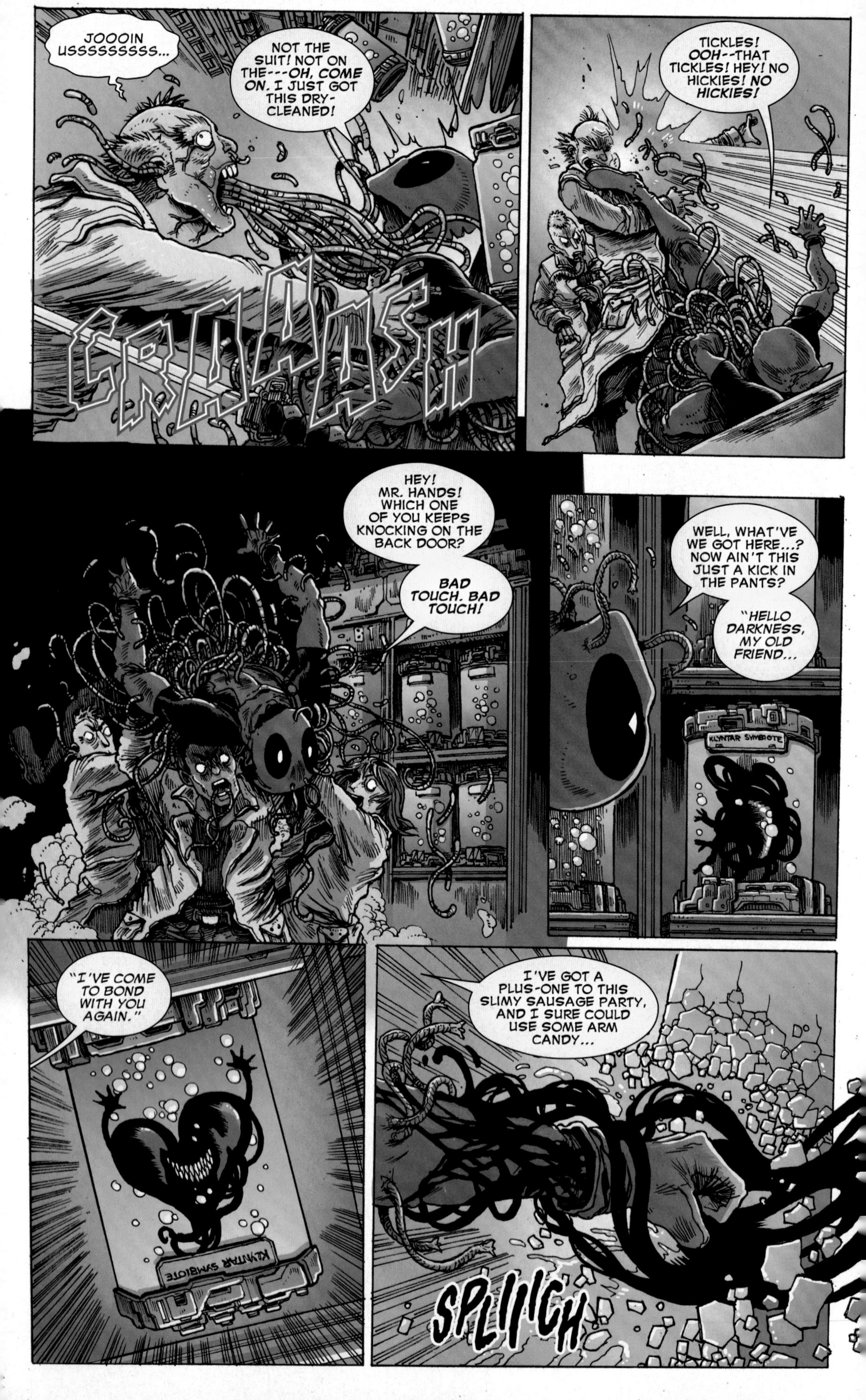
JOOOIN USSSSSSSSS...
NOT THE SUIT! NOT ON THE---OH, COME ON. I JUST GOT THIS DRY-CLEANED!
CRAAASH
TICKLES! OOH--THAT TICKLES! HEY! NO HICKIES! NO HICKIES!
HEY! MR. HANDS! WHICH ONE OF YOU KEEPS KNOCKING ON THE BACK DOOR?
BAD TOUCH. BAD TOUCH!
WELL, WHAT'VE WE GOT HERE...? NOW AIN'T THIS JUST A KICK IN THE PANTS?
"HELLO DARKNESS, MY OLD FRIEND...
KLYNTAR SYMBIOTE
"I'VE COME TO BOND WITH YOU AGAIN."
KLYNTAR SYMBIOTE
I'VE GOT A PLUS-ONE TO THIS SLIMY SAUSAGE PARTY, AND I SURE COULD USE SOME ARM CANDY...
SPLIIICH

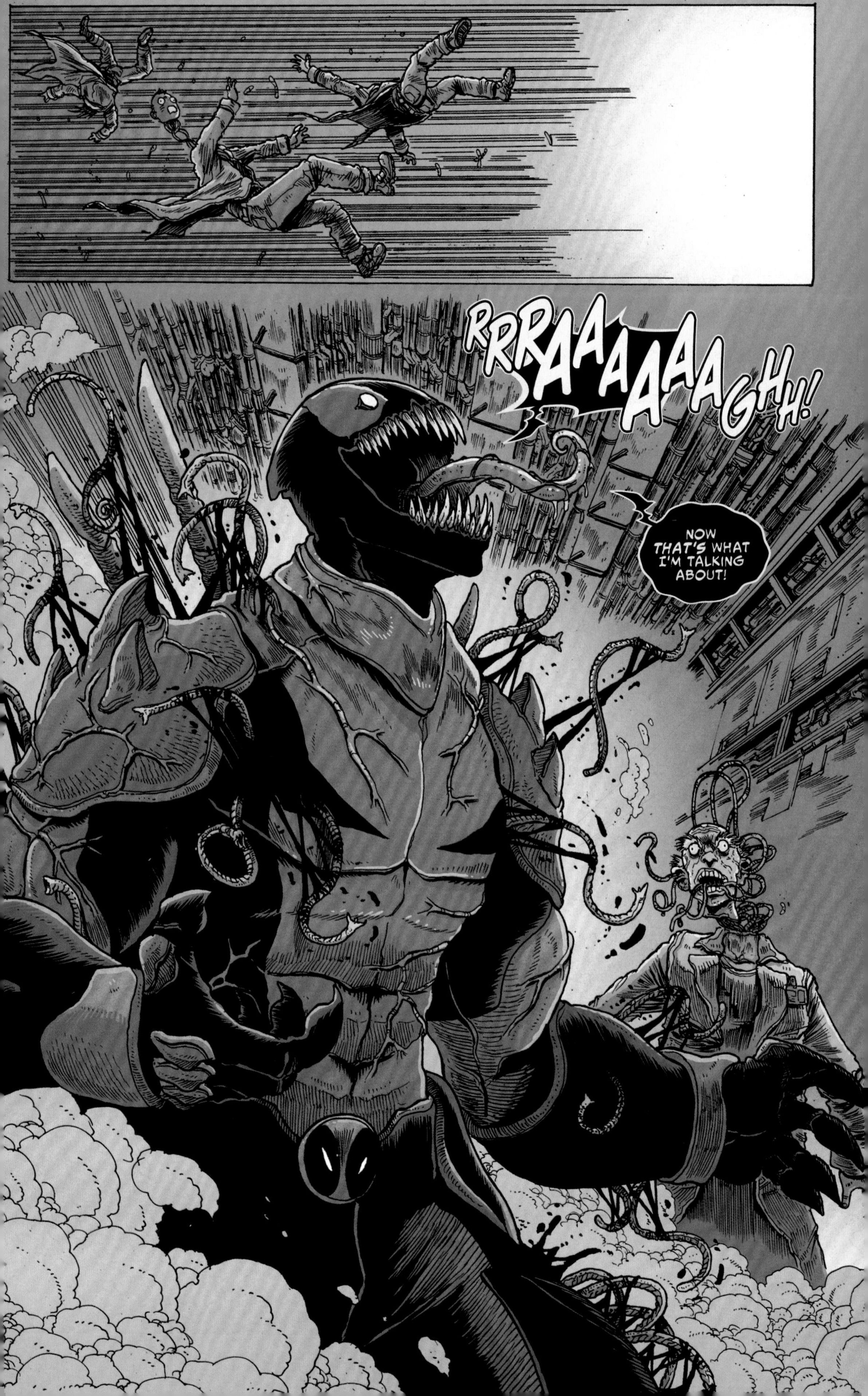
RRRAAAAAAAGHH!
NOW THAT'S WHAT I'M TALKING ABOUT!

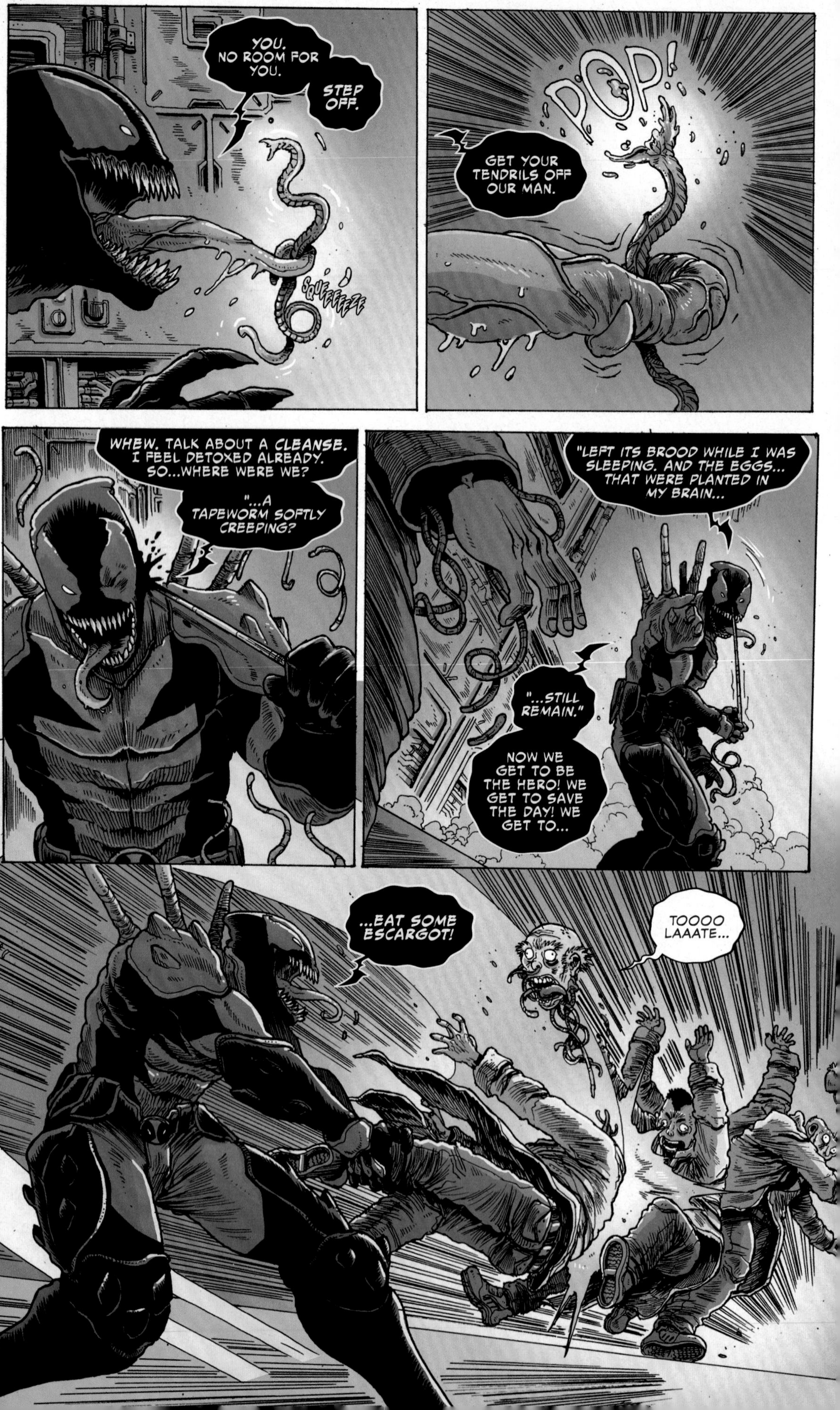
YOU. NO ROOM FOR YOU.
STEP OFF.
SQUEEEEEZE
POP!
GET YOUR TENDRILS OFF OUR MAN.
WHEW. TALK ABOUT A CLEANSE. I FEEL DETOXED ALREADY. SO...WHERE WERE WE?
"...A TAPEWORM SOFTLY CREEPING?
"LEFT ITS BROOD WHILE I WAS SLEEPING. AND THE EGGS... THAT WERE PLANTED IN MY BRAIN...
"...STILL REMAIN."
NOW WE GET TO BE THE HERO! WE GET TO SAVE THE DAY! WE GET TO...
...EAT SOME ESCARGOT!
TOOOO LAAATE...

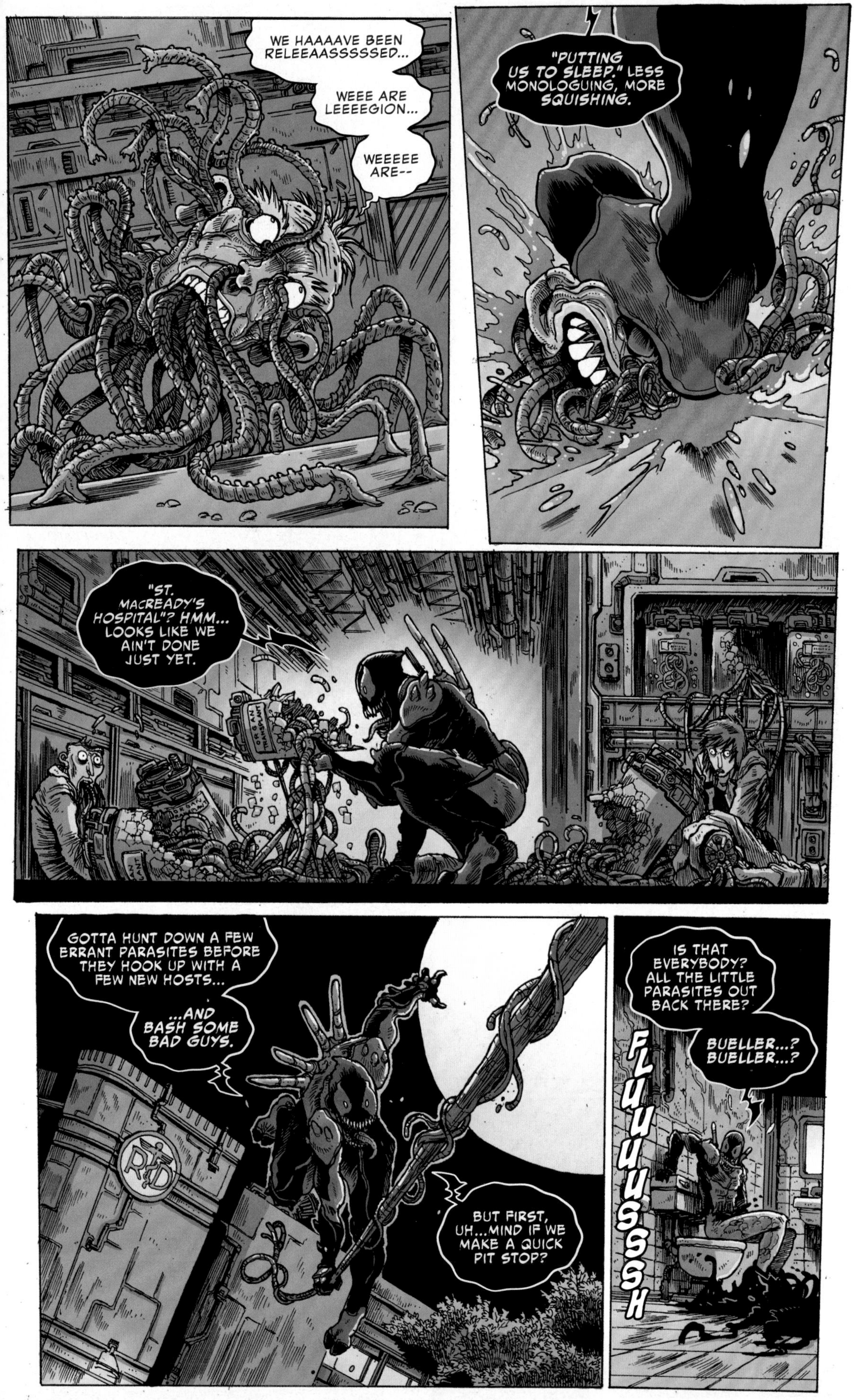

WE HAAAAVE BEEN RELEEAASSSSSED...
WEEE ARE LEEEEGION...
WEEEEE ARE--
"PUTTING US TO SLEEP." LESS MONOLOGUING, MORE SQUISHING.
"ST. MACREADY'S HOSPITAL"? HMM... LOOKS LIKE WE AIN'T DONE JUST YET.
ORGAN TRANSPLANT
GOTTA HUNT DOWN A FEW ERRANT PARASITES BEFORE THEY HOOK UP WITH A FEW NEW HOSTS...
...AND BASH SOME BAD GUYS.
BUT FIRST, UH...MIND IF WE MAKE A QUICK PIT STOP?
IS THAT EVERYBODY? ALL THE LITTLE PARASITES OUT BACK THERE?
BUELLER...? BUELLER...?
FLUUUUSSSH

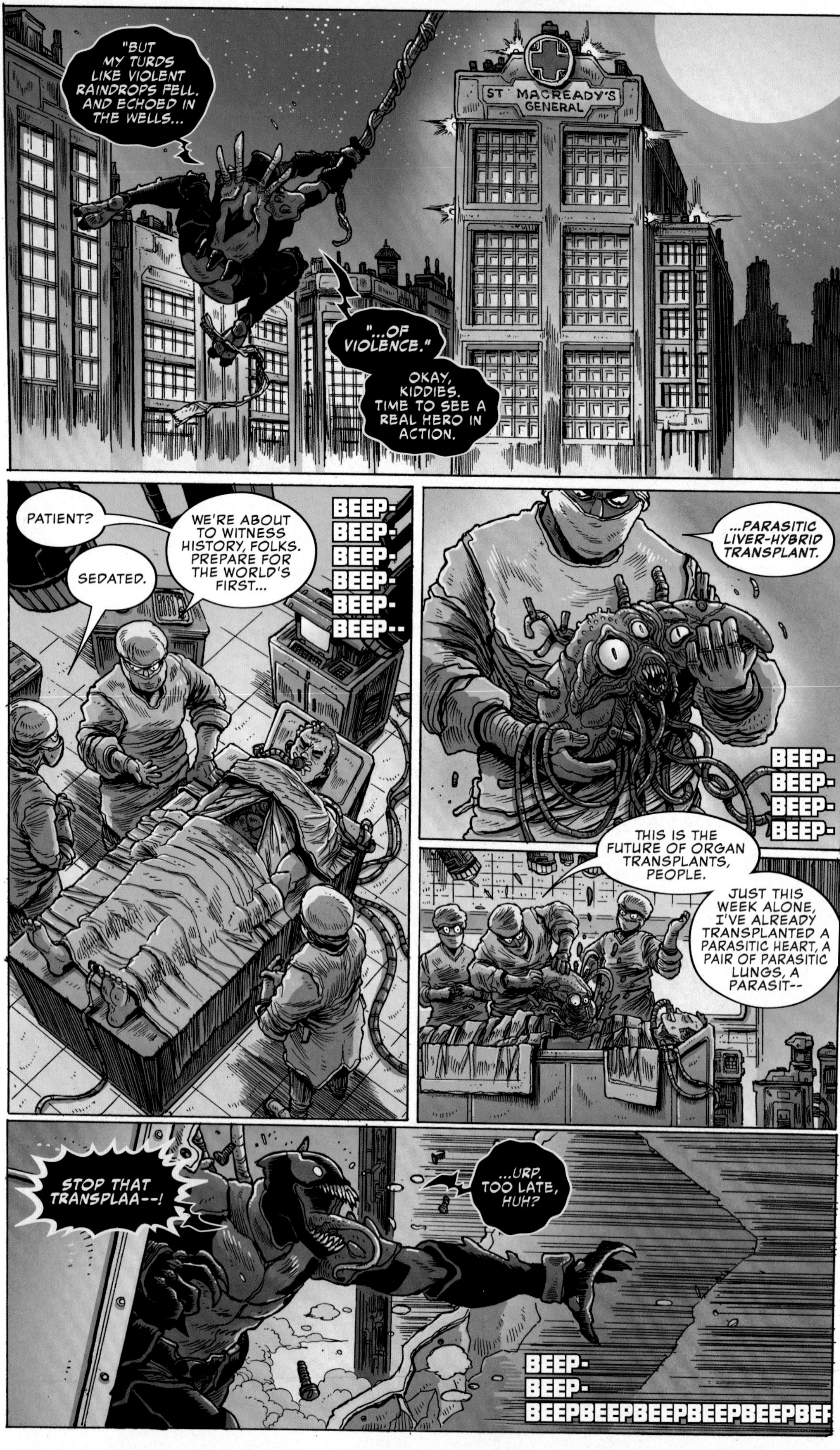
"BUT MY TURDS LIKE VIOLENT RAINDROPS FELL. AND ECHOED IN THE WELLS...
ST MACREADY'S GENERAL
"...OF VIOLENCE."
OKAY, KIDDIES. TIME TO SEE A REAL HERO IN ACTION.
PATIENT?
SEDATED.
WE'RE ABOUT TO WITNESS HISTORY, FOLKS. PREPARE FOR THE WORLD'S FIRST...
BEEP- BEEP- BEEP- BEEP- BEEP- BEEP--
...PARASITIC LIVER-HYBRID TRANSPLANT.
BEEP- BEEP- BEEP- BEEP-
THIS IS THE FUTURE OF ORGAN TRANSPLANTS, PEOPLE.
JUST THIS WEEK ALONE, I'VE ALREADY TRANSPLANTED A PARASITIC HEART, A PAIR OF PARASITIC LUNGS, A PARASIT--
STOP THAT TRANSPLAA--!
...URP. TOO LATE, HUH?
BEEP- BEEP- BEEPBEEPBEEPBEEPBEEPBEEPBEEPBEE

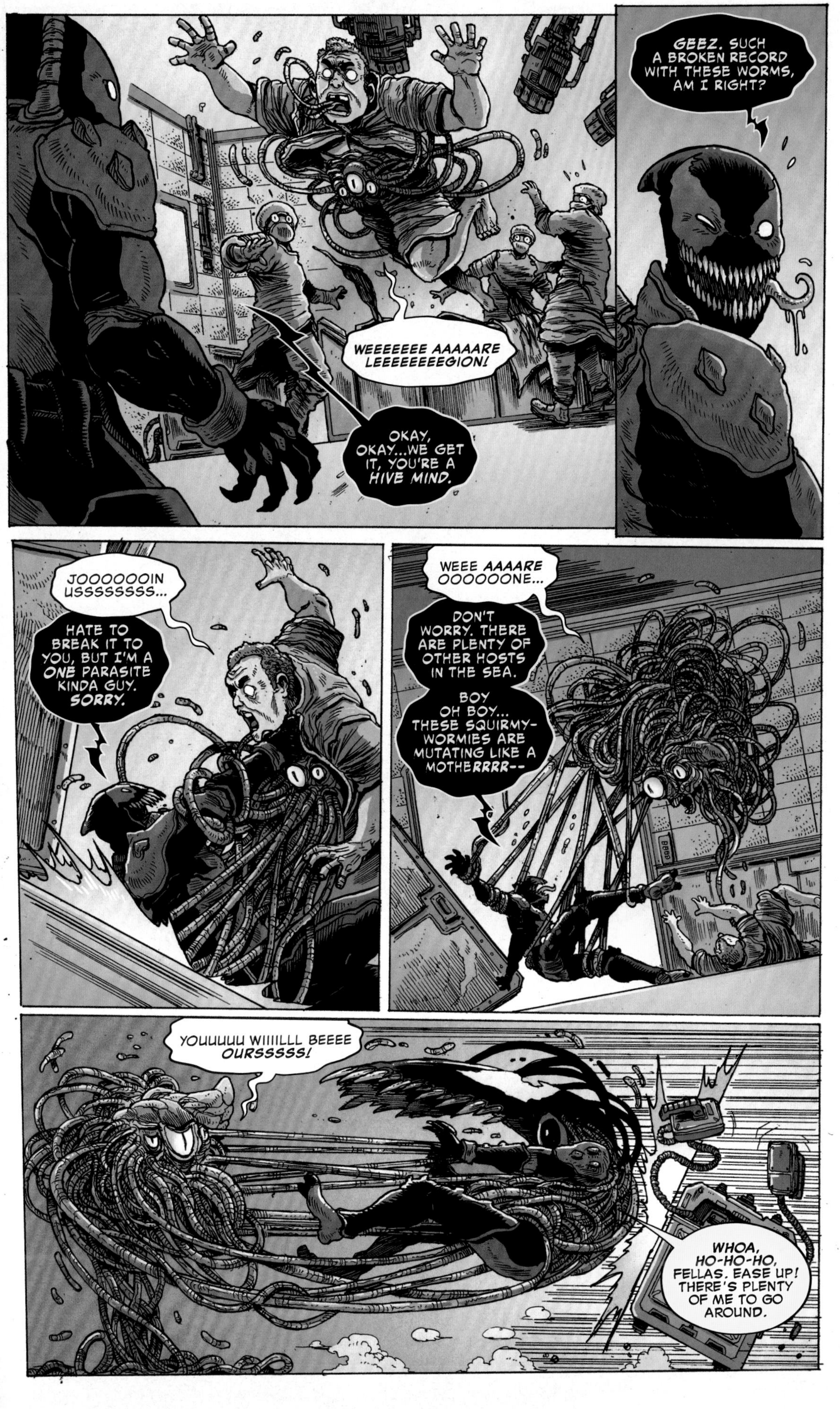
WEEEEEEE AAAAARE LEEEEEEEEGION!
OKAY, OKAY...WE GET IT, YOU'RE A *HIVE MIND.*
GEEZ. SUCH A BROKEN RECORD WITH THESE WORMS, AM I RIGHT?
JOOOOOOIN USSSSSSSS...
HATE TO BREAK IT TO YOU, BUT I'M A *ONE* PARASITE KINDA GUY. ***SORRY.***
WEEE *AAAARE* OOOOOONE...
DON'T WORRY. THERE ARE PLENTY OF OTHER HOSTS IN THE SEA.
BOY OH BOY... THESE SQUIRMY-WORMIES ARE MUTATING LIKE A MOTHER*RRR*--
YOUUUUU WIIIILLL BEEEE *OURSSSSS!*
WHOA, HO-HO-HO, FELLAS. EASE UP! THERE'S PLENTY OF ME TO GO AROUND.

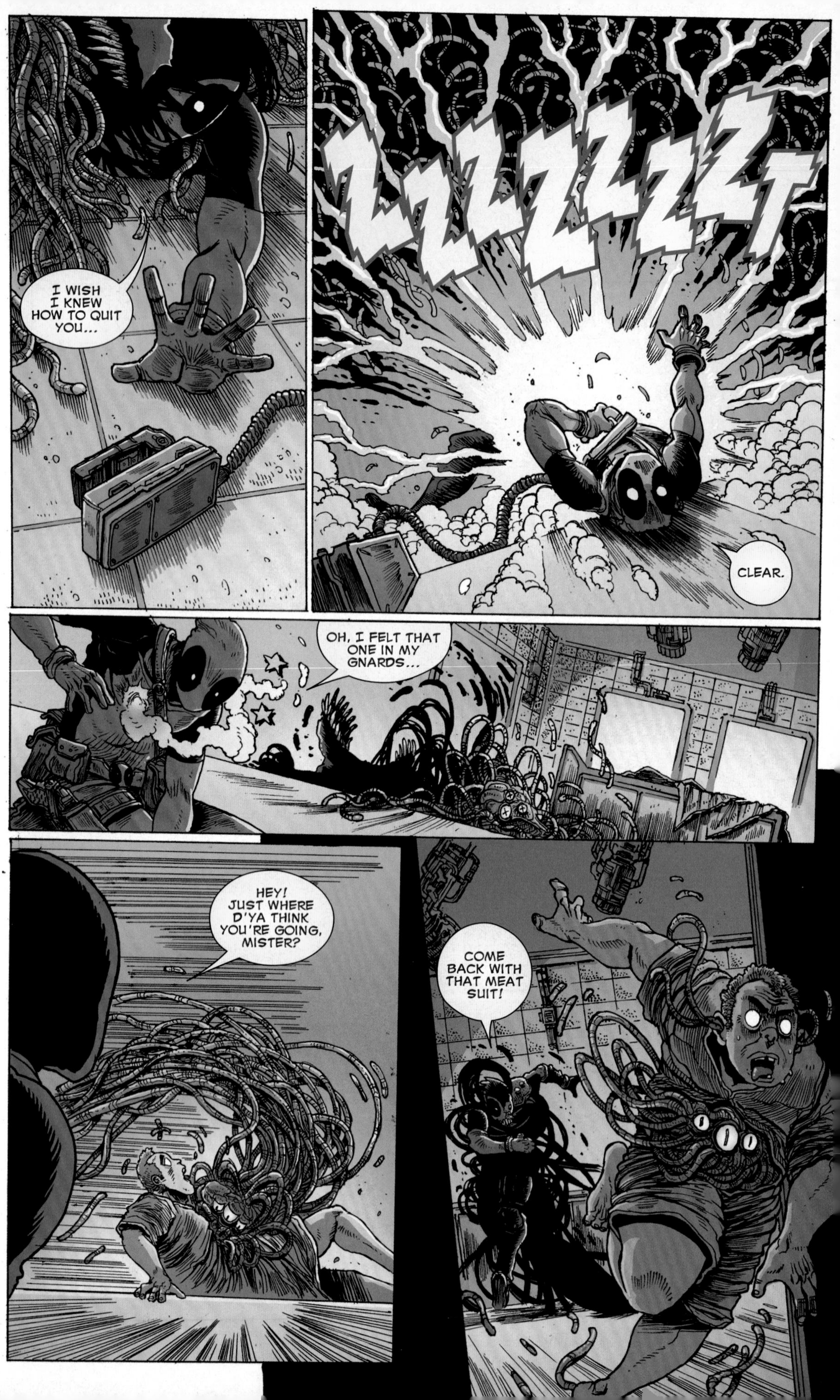
I WISH I KNEW HOW TO QUIT YOU...
ZZZZZZZT
CLEAR.
OH, I FELT THAT ONE IN MY GNARDS...
HEY! JUST WHERE D'YA THINK YOU'RE GOING, MISTER?
COME BACK WITH THAT MEAT SUIT!

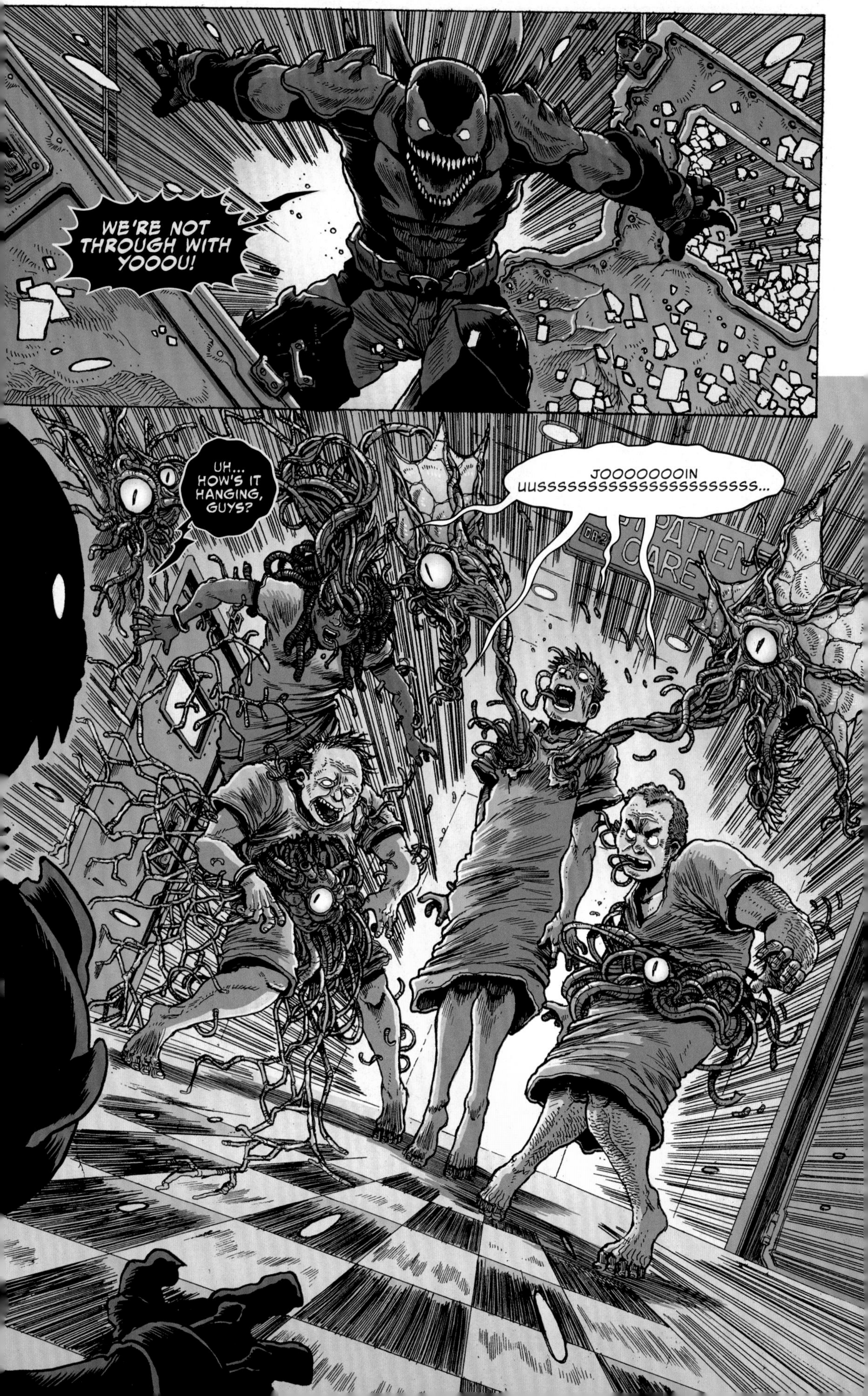
WE'RE NOT THROUGH WITH YOOOU!
UH... HOW'S IT HANGING, GUYS?
JOOOOOOOIN UUSSSSSSSSSSSSSSSSSSSSS...

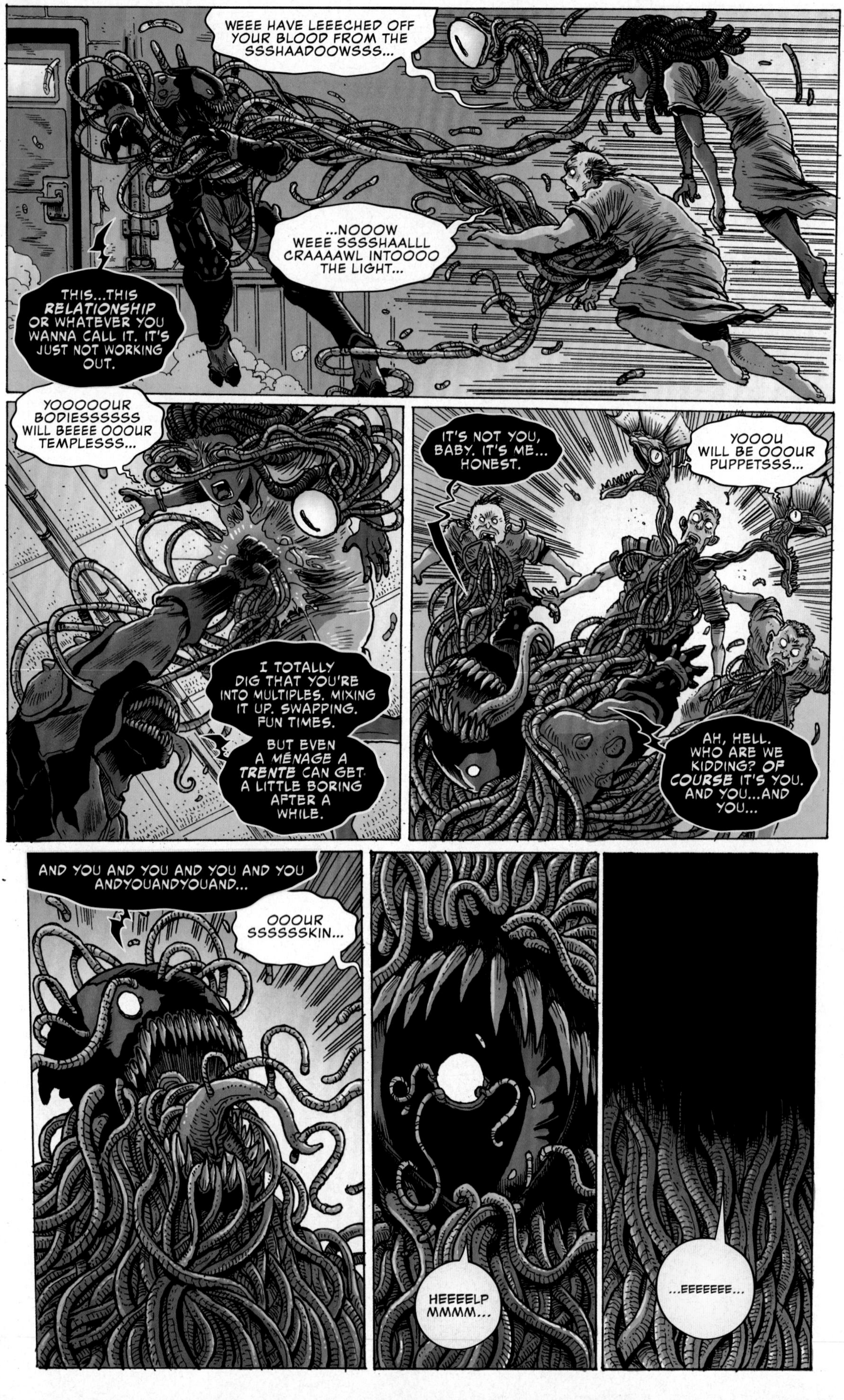
WEEE HAVE LEEECHED OFF YOUR BLOOD FROM THE SSSHAADOOWSSS...
...NOOOW WEEE SSSSHAALLL CRAAAAWL INTOOOO THE LIGHT...
THIS...THIS RELATIONSHIP OR WHATEVER YOU WANNA CALL IT. IT'S JUST NOT WORKING OUT.
YOOOOOUR BODIESSSSSS WILL BEEEE OOOUR TEMPLESSS...
I TOTALLY DIG THAT YOU'RE INTO MULTIPLES. MIXING IT UP. SWAPPING. FUN TIMES.
BUT EVEN A MÉNAGE A TRENTE CAN GET A LITTLE BORING AFTER A WHILE.
IT'S NOT YOU, BABY. IT'S ME... HONEST.
YOOOU WILL BE OOOUR PUPPETSSS...
AH, HELL. WHO ARE WE KIDDING? OF COURSE IT'S YOU. AND YOU...AND YOU...
AND YOU AND YOU AND YOU AND YOU ANDYOUANDYOUAND...
OOOUR SSSSSSKIN...
HEEEELP MMMM...
...EEEEEEE...

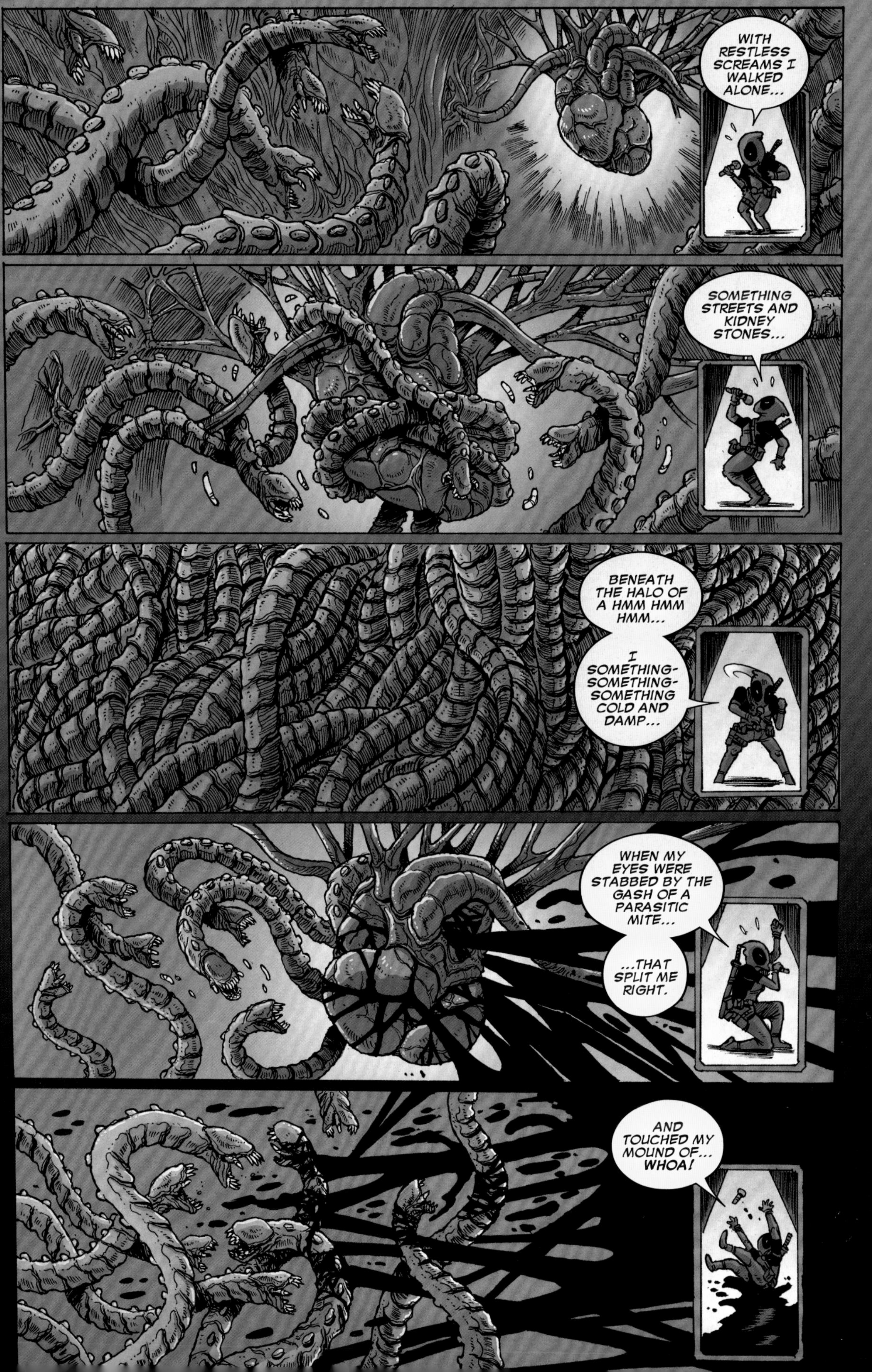

WITH RESTLESS SCREAMS I WALKED ALONE...
SOMETHING STREETS AND KIDNEY STONES...
BENEATH THE HALO OF A HMM HMM HMM...
I SOMETHING-SOMETHING-SOMETHING COLD AND DAMP...
WHEN MY EYES WERE STABBED BY THE GASH OF A PARASITIC MITE...
...THAT SPLIT ME RIGHT.
AND TOUCHED MY MOUND OF... WHOA!

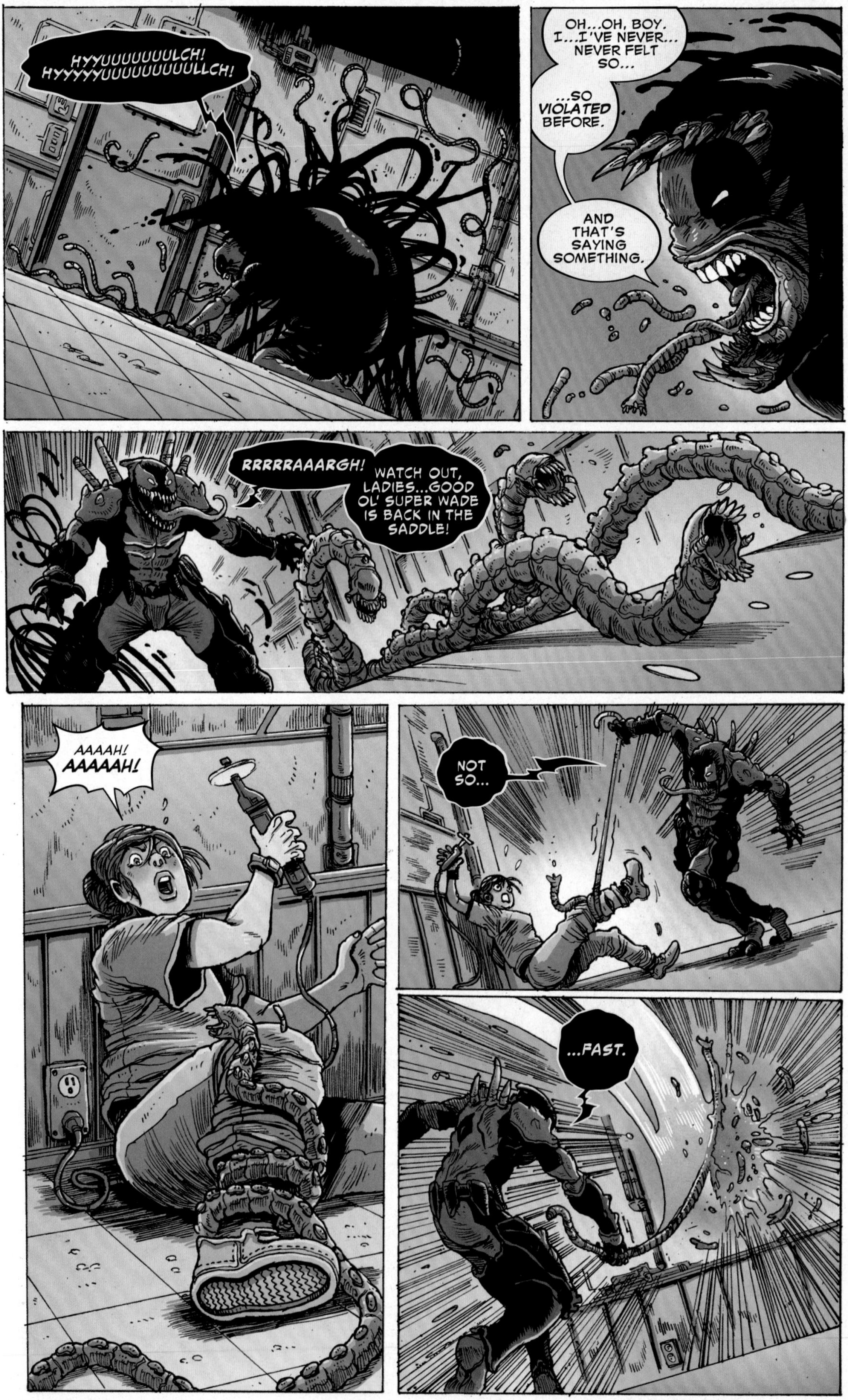
HYYUUUUUUULCH! HYYYYYUUUUUUUUULLCH!
OH...OH, BOY. I...I'VE NEVER... NEVER FELT SO...
...SO VIOLATED BEFORE.
AND THAT'S SAYING SOMETHING.
RRRRRAAARGH!
WATCH OUT, LADIES...GOOD OL' SUPER WADE IS BACK IN THE SADDLE!
AAAAH! AAAAAH!
NOT SO...
...FAST.

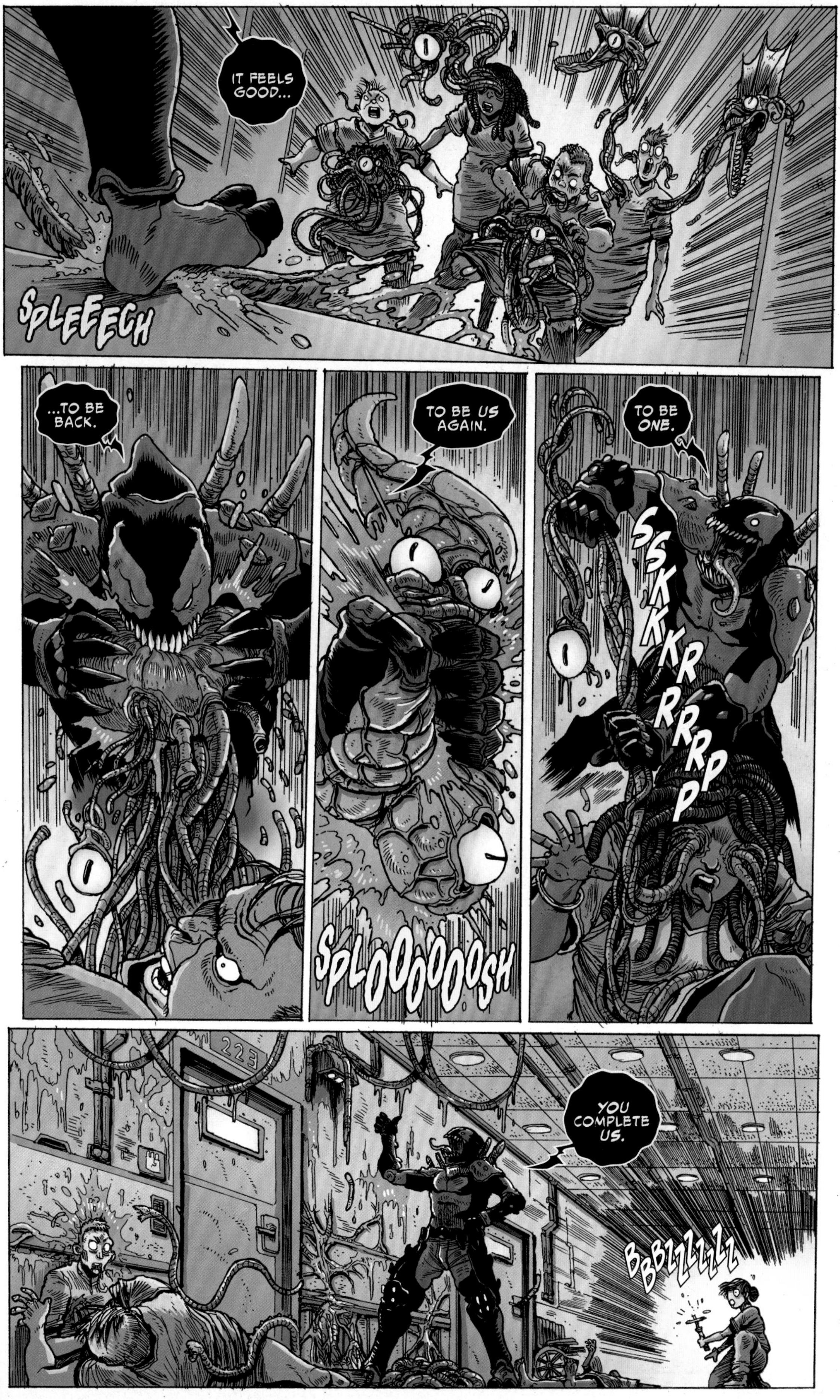
IT FEELS GOOD...
SPLEEEECH
...TO BE BACK.
TO BE US AGAIN.
SPLOOOOOOOSH
TO BE ONE.
SSKKRRRRP
YOU COMPLETE US.
223
BBBZZZZZZ

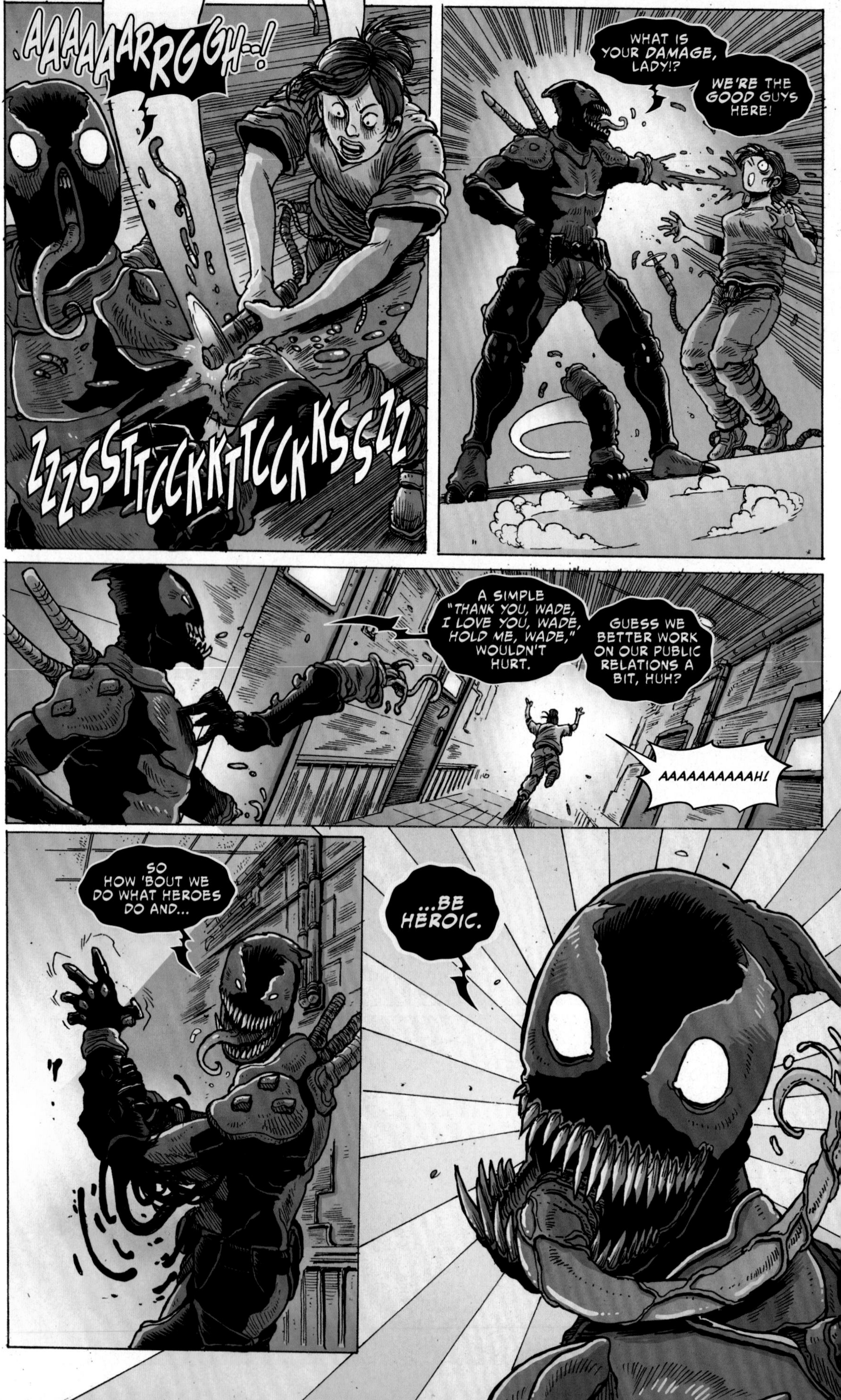
AAAAARRGGH--!
ZZZSSTTCCKKTTCCKKSSZZ
WHAT IS YOUR DAMAGE, LADY!?
WE'RE THE GOOD GUYS HERE!
A SIMPLE "THANK YOU, WADE, I LOVE YOU, WADE, HOLD ME, WADE," WOULDN'T HURT.
GUESS WE BETTER WORK ON OUR PUBLIC RELATIONS A BIT, HUH?
AAAAAAAAAAH!
SO HOW 'BOUT WE DO WHAT HEROES DO AND...
...BE HEROIC.

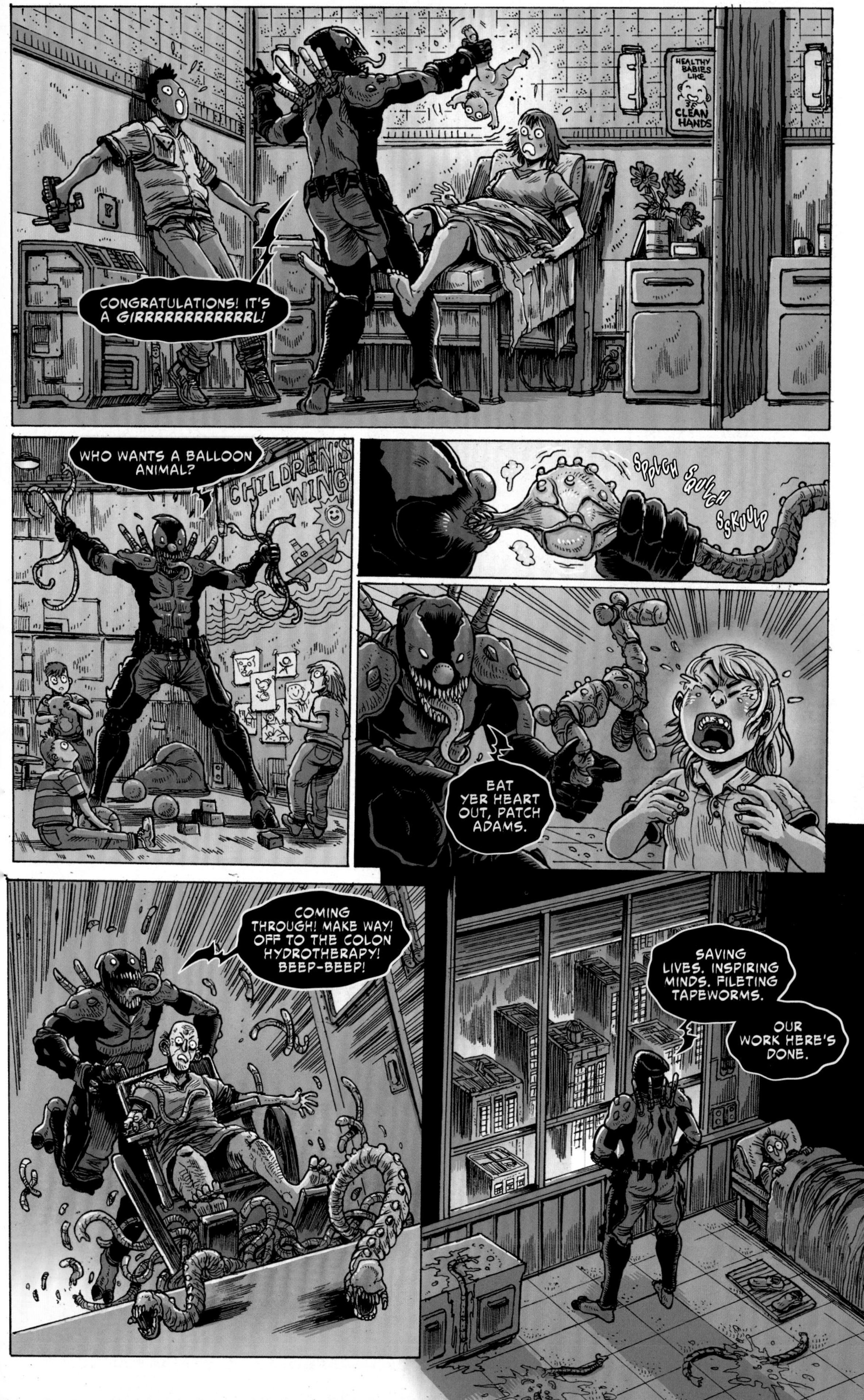
HEALTHY BABIES LIKE CLEAN HANDS
CONGRATULATIONS! IT'S A GIRRRRRRRRRRRL!
WHO WANTS A BALLOON ANIMAL?
CHILDREN'S WING
SPPLCH SQULCH SSKUULP
EAT YER HEART OUT, PATCH ADAMS.
COMING THROUGH! MAKE WAY! OFF TO THE COLON HYDROTHERAPY! BEEP-BEEP!
SAVING LIVES. INSPIRING MINDS. FILETING TAPEWORMS.
OUR WORK HERE'S DONE.

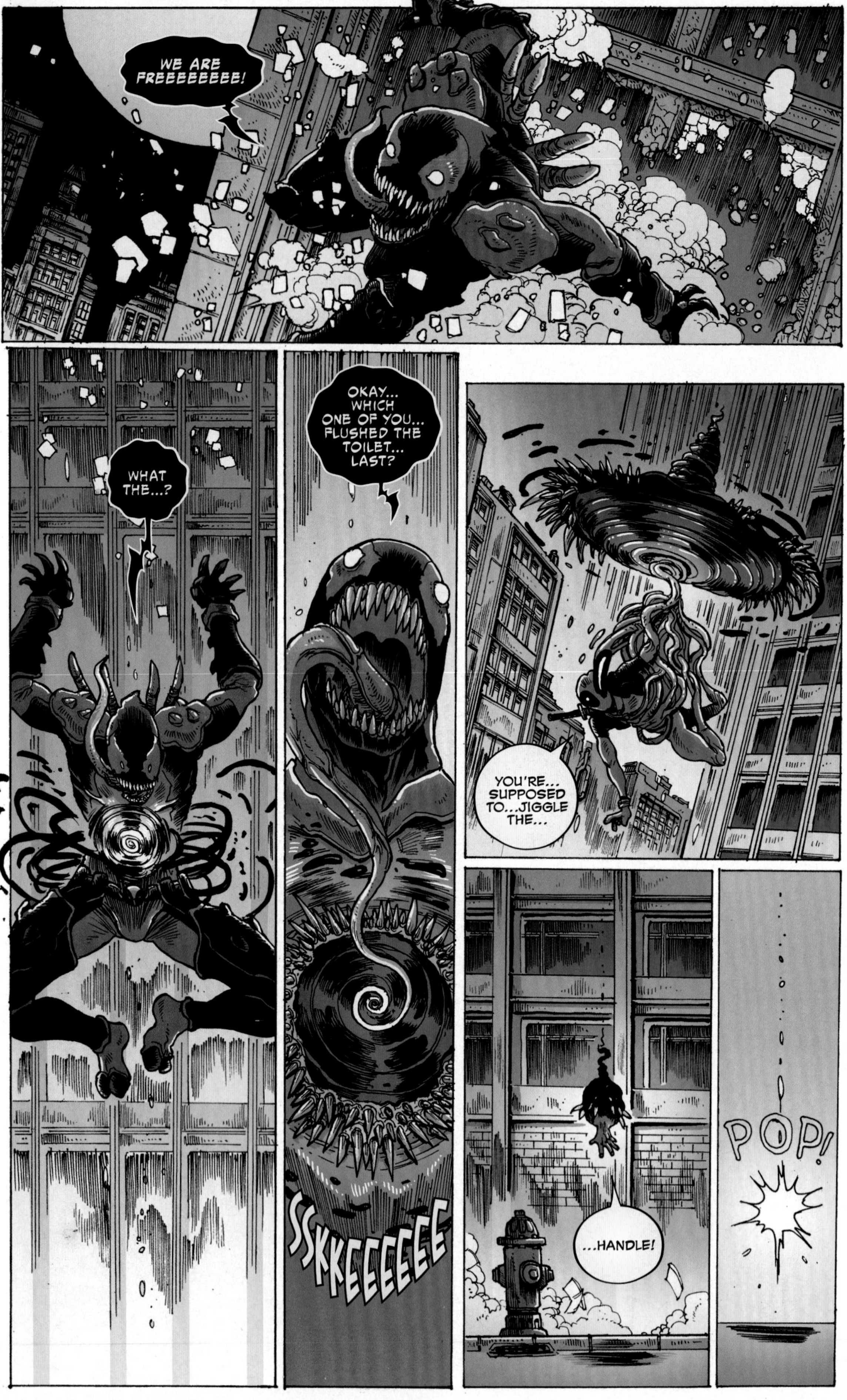
WE ARE FREEEEEEEE!
WHAT THE...?
OKAY... WHICH ONE OF YOU... FLUSHED THE TOILET... LAST?
SSKKEEEEEE
YOU'RE... SUPPOSED TO...JIGGLE THE...
...HANDLE!
POP!

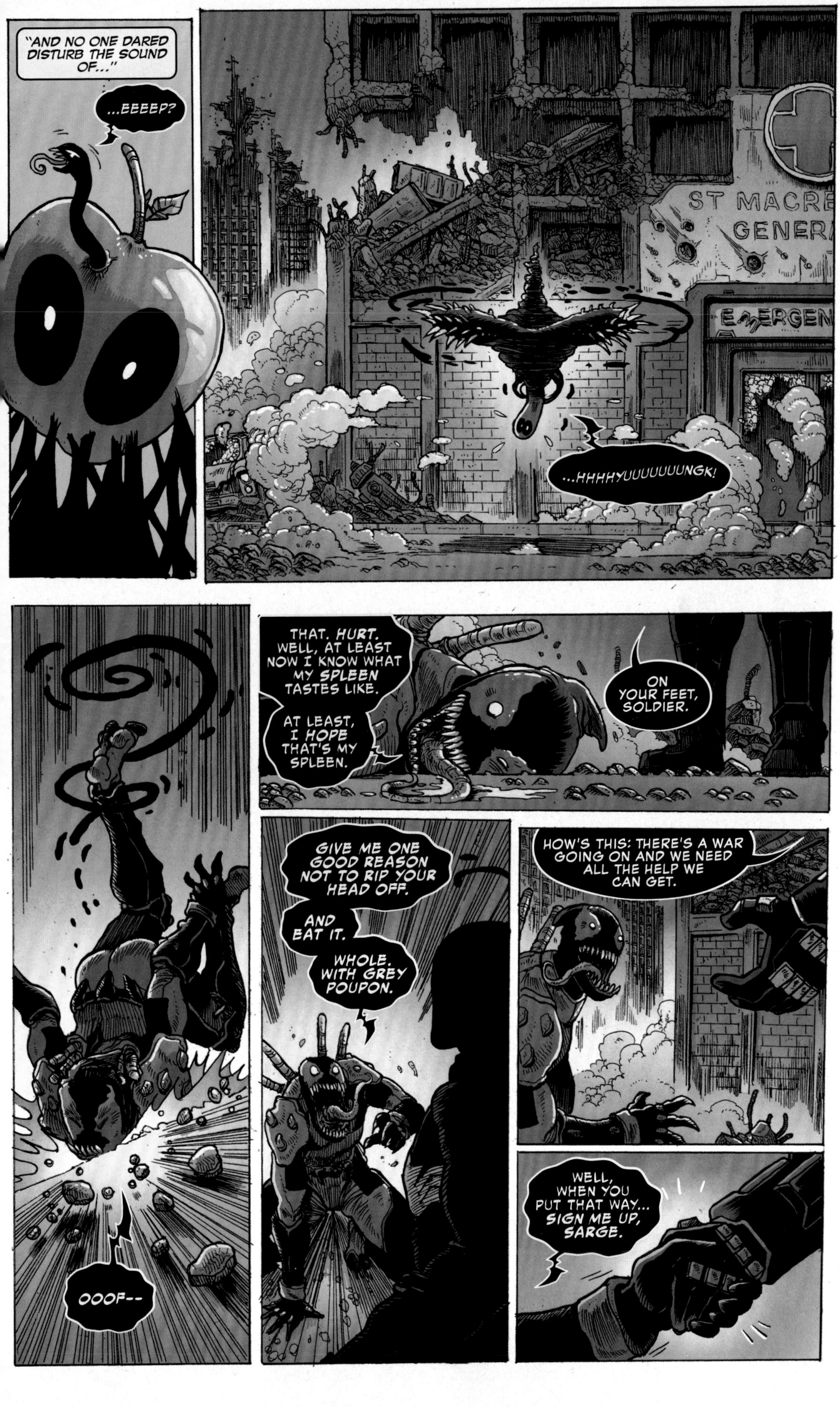
"AND NO ONE DARED DISTURB THE SOUND OF..."
...EEEEP?
ST MACRE
GENER
EMERGEN
...HHHHYUUUUUUUNGK!
OOOF--
THAT. HURT. WELL, AT LEAST NOW I KNOW WHAT MY SPLEEN TASTES LIKE.
AT LEAST, I HOPE THAT'S MY SPLEEN.
ON YOUR FEET, SOLDIER.
GIVE ME ONE GOOD REASON NOT TO RIP YOUR HEAD OFF.
AND EAT IT.
WHOLE. WITH GREY POUPON.
HOW'S THIS: THERE'S A WAR GOING ON AND WE NEED ALL THE HELP WE CAN GET.
WELL, WHEN YOU PUT THAT WAY... SIGN ME UP, SARGE.

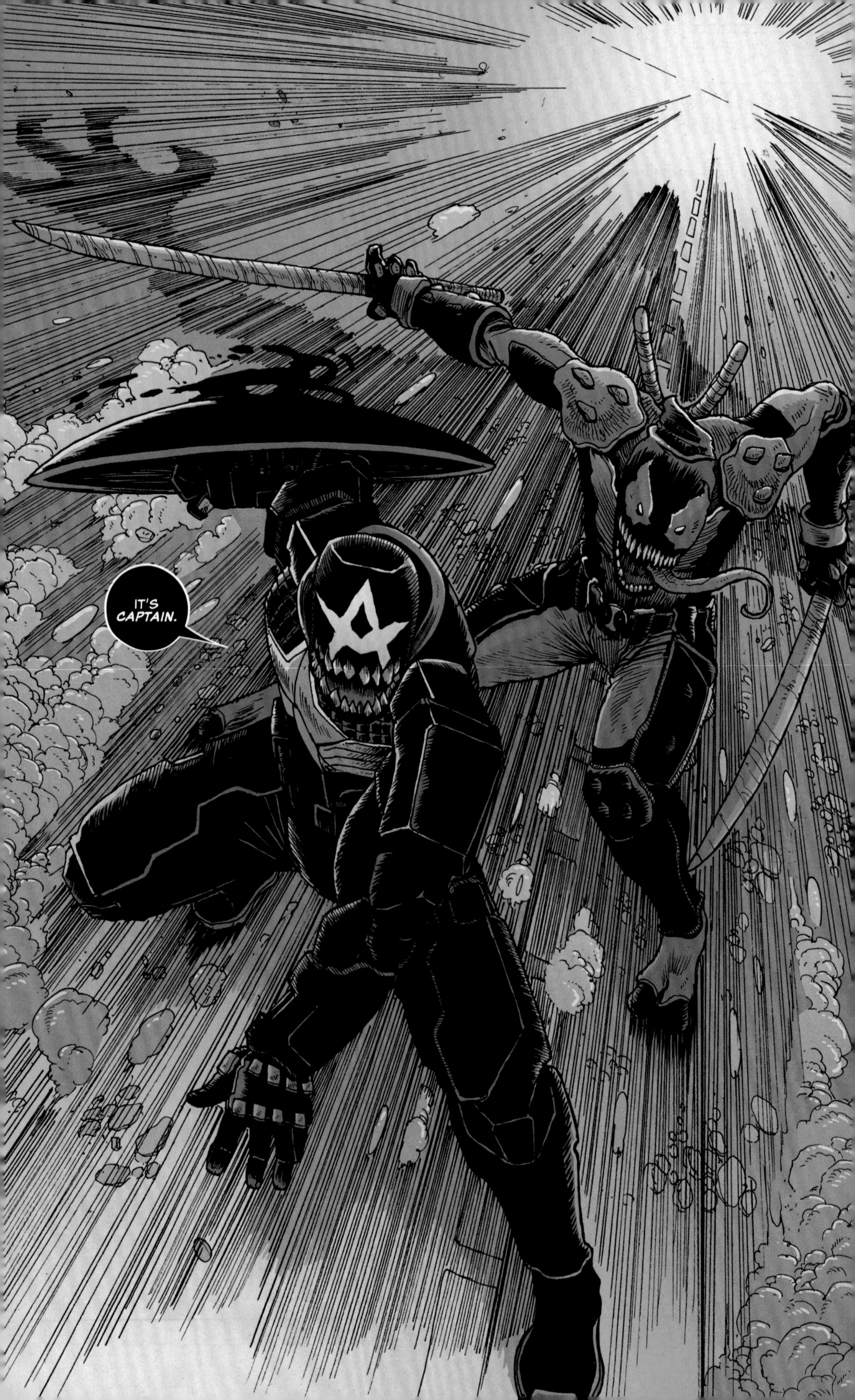
IT'S CAPTAIN.

VENOMVERSE: WAR STORIES 1

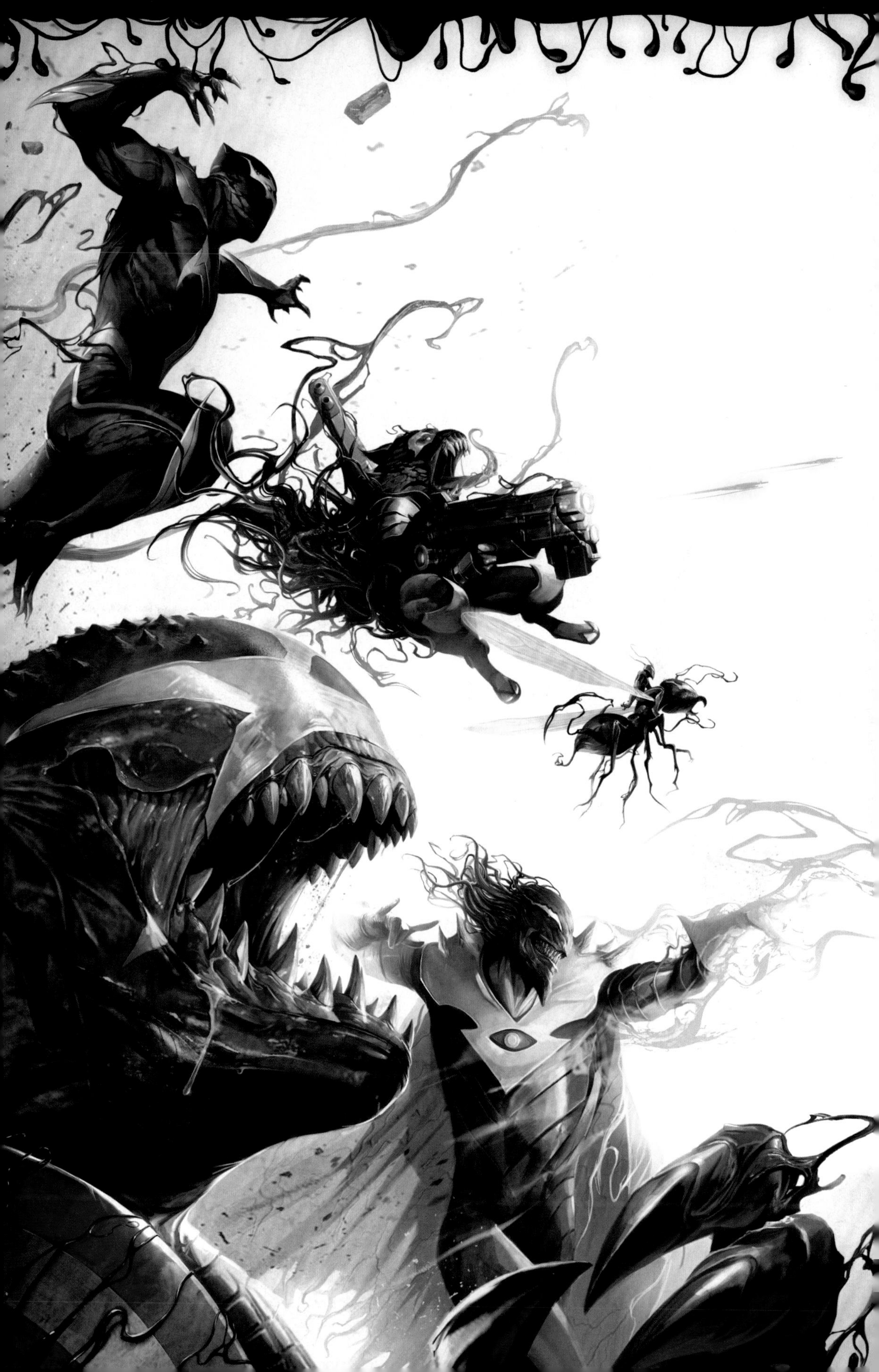

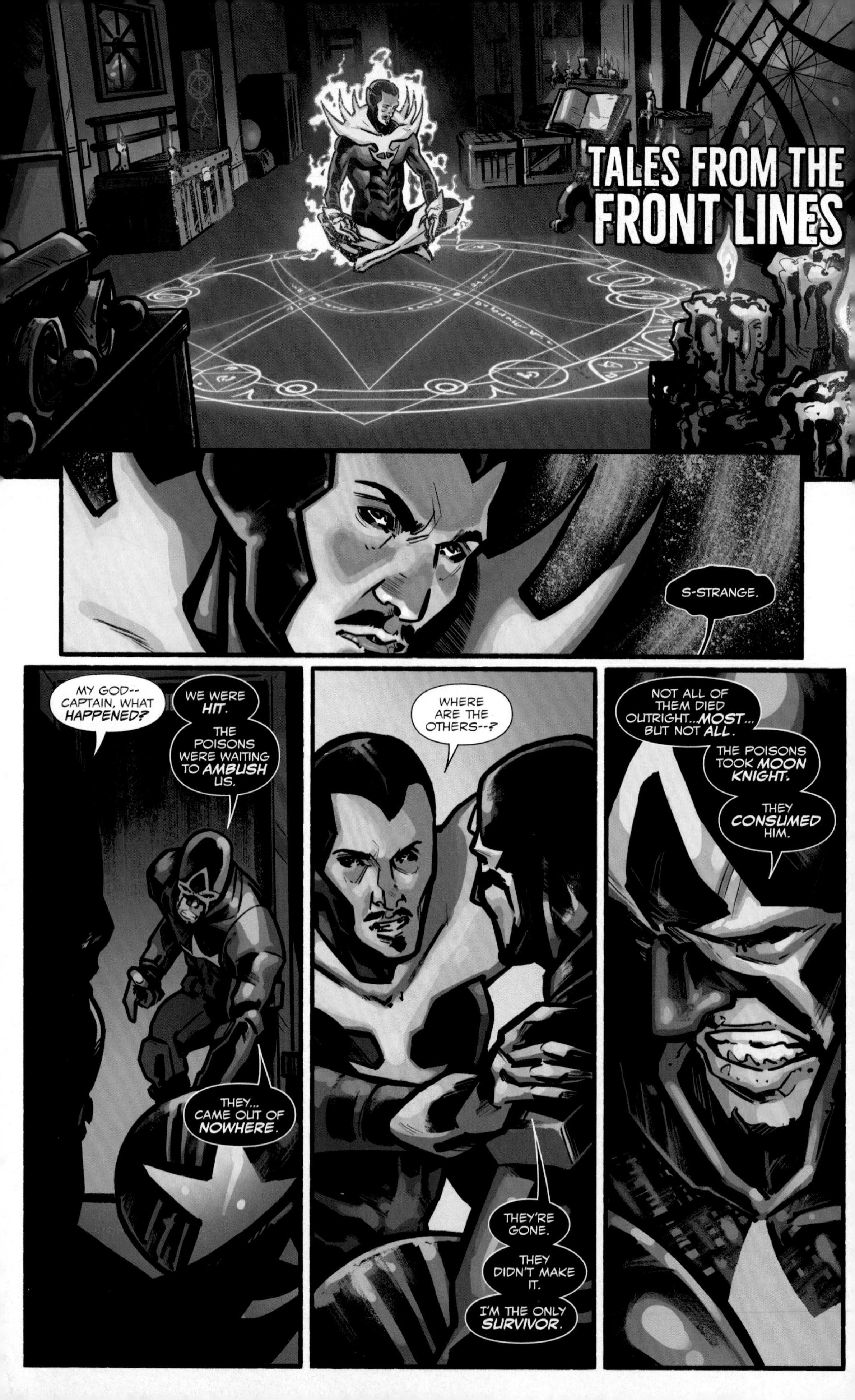
TALES FROM THE FRONT LINES
S-STRANGE.
MY GOD-- CAPTAIN, WHAT HAPPENED?
WE WERE HIT.
THE POISONS WERE WAITING TO AMBUSH US.
THEY... CAME OUT OF NOWHERE.
WHERE ARE THE OTHERS--?
THEY'RE GONE.
THEY DIDN'T MAKE IT.
I'M THE ONLY SURVIVOR.
NOT ALL OF THEM DIED OUTRIGHT...MOST... BUT NOT ALL.
THE POISONS TOOK MOON KNIGHT.
THEY CONSUMED HIM.

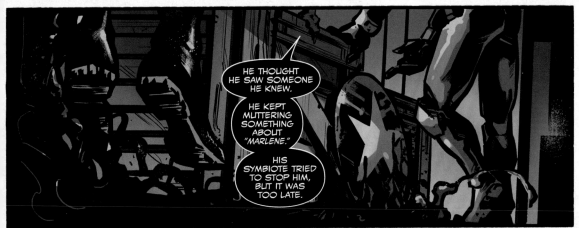

HE THOUGHT HE SAW SOMEONE HE KNEW.

HE KEPT MUTTERING SOMETHING ABOUT "MARLENE."

HIS SYMBIOTE TRIED TO STOP HIM, BUT IT WAS TOO LATE.

WE CANNOT STAY HERE.

IF THEY HAVE MOON KNIGHT, THEY KNOW WHERE WE ARE.

ARE WE *ALONE* NOW?

HAVE YOU EXHAUSTED OUR RESOURCES?

I'M NOT THROWING IN THE TOWEL--FAR FROM IT--BUT I JUST WANT TO KNOW IF WE'RE THE LAST MEN STANDING.

WE ARE NOT ALONE.

NOT YET.

THERE ARE COUNTLESS *WORLDS*... COUNTLESS *VENOM* SYMBIOTES.

"COUNTLESS."

AND WE'RE STILL RUNNING OUT FASTER THAN YOU CAN BRING THEM OVER.

I HAVE REGAINED SOME OF MY STRENGTH SINCE THE LAST SUMMONING.

BUT BOLSTERING OUR FORCES SO QUICKLY WILL *TAX* ME.

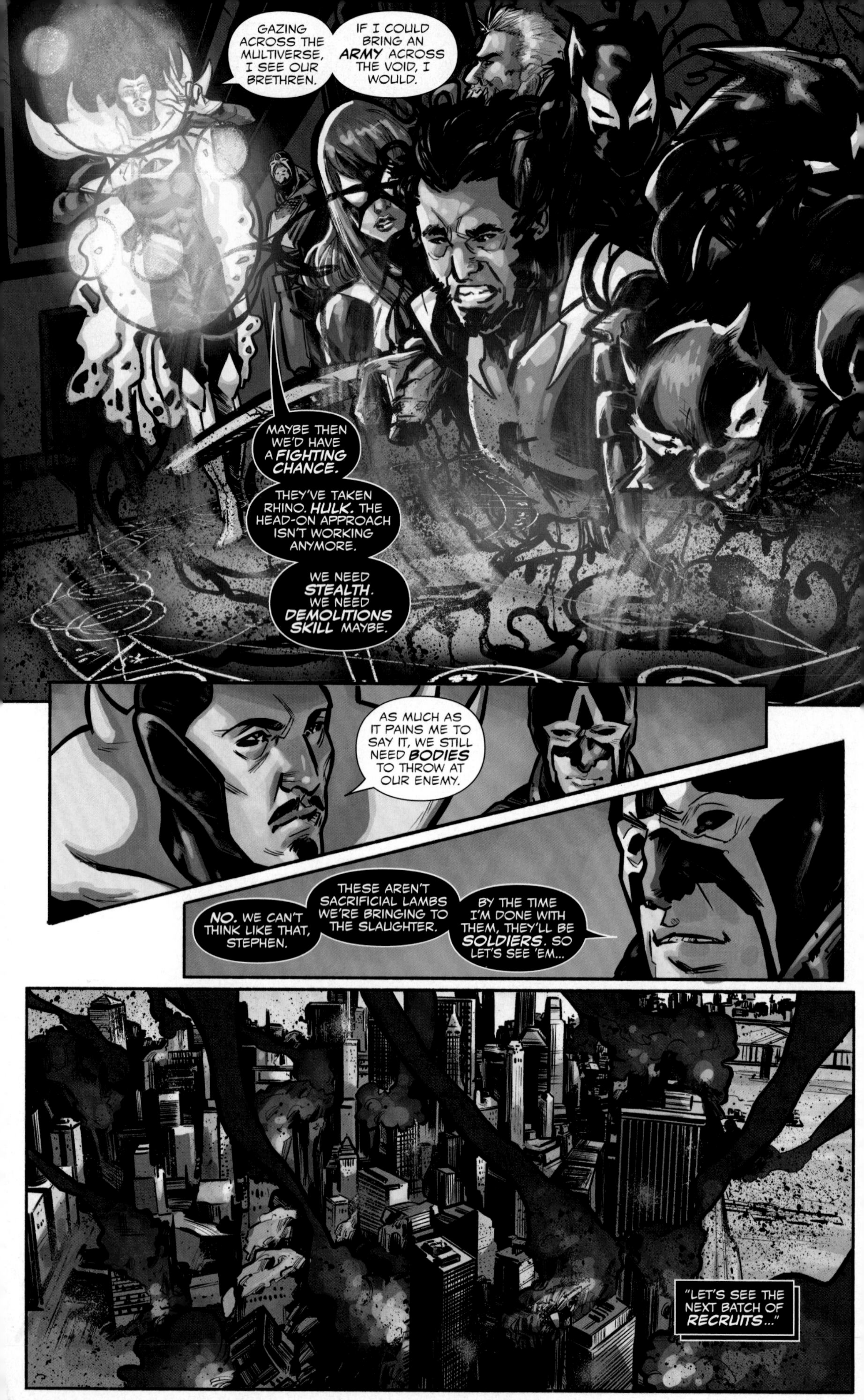
GAZING ACROSS THE MULTIVERSE, I SEE OUR BRETHREN.
IF I COULD BRING AN ARMY ACROSS THE VOID, I WOULD.
MAYBE THEN WE'D HAVE A FIGHTING CHANCE.
THEY'VE TAKEN RHINO. HULK. THE HEAD-ON APPROACH ISN'T WORKING ANYMORE.
WE NEED STEALTH. WE NEED DEMOLITIONS SKILL MAYBE.
AS MUCH AS IT PAINS ME TO SAY IT, WE STILL NEED BODIES TO THROW AT OUR ENEMY.
NO. WE CAN'T THINK LIKE THAT, STEPHEN.
THESE AREN'T SACRIFICIAL LAMBS WE'RE BRINGING TO THE SLAUGHTER.
BY THE TIME I'M DONE WITH THEM, THEY'LL BE SOLDIERS. SO LET'S SEE 'EM...
"LET'S SEE THE NEXT BATCH OF RECRUITS..."

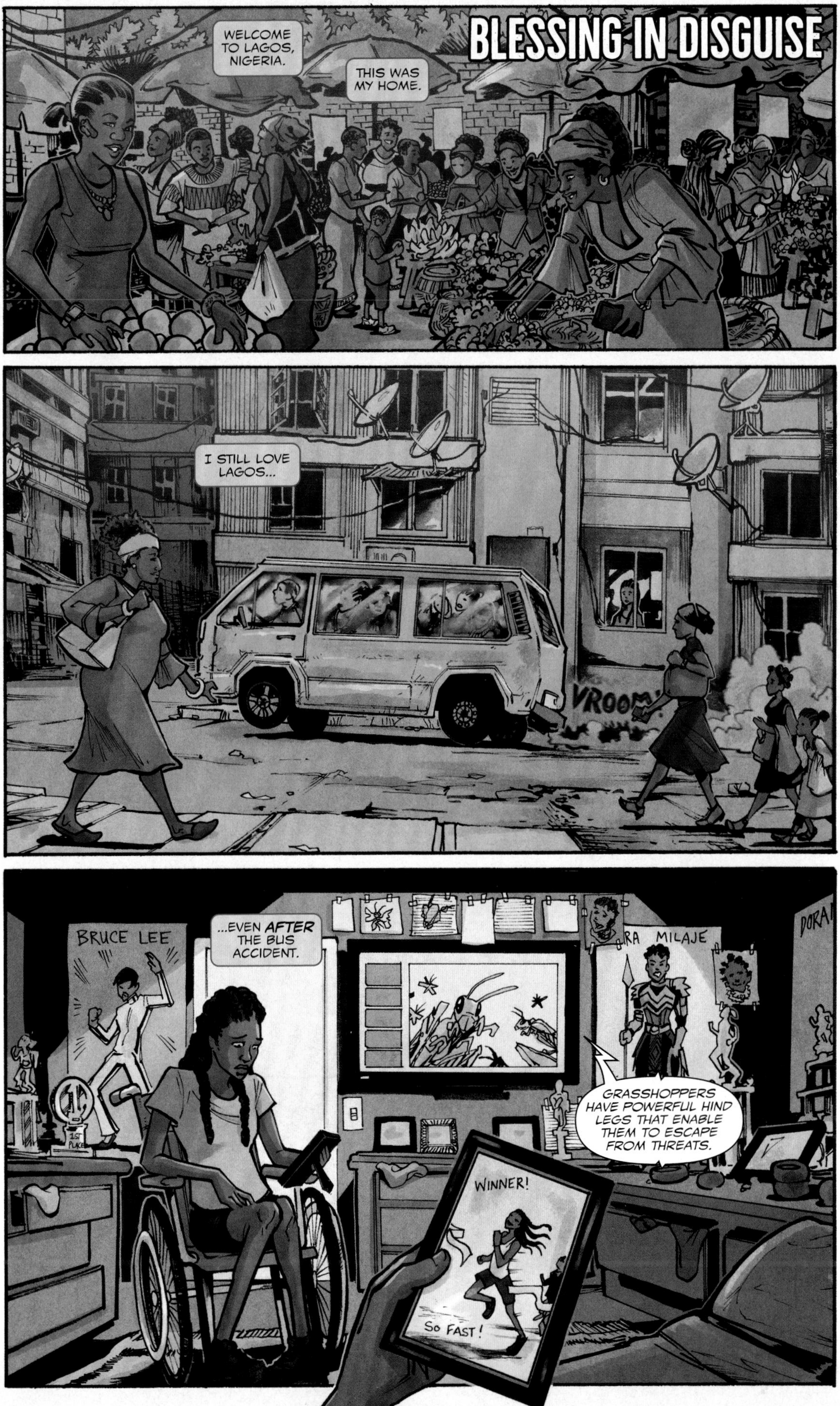
BLESSING IN DISGUISE
WELCOME TO LAGOS, NIGERIA.
THIS WAS MY HOME.
I STILL LOVE LAGOS...
VROOM!
...EVEN AFTER THE BUS ACCIDENT.
BRUCE LEE
1ST PLACE
GRASSHOPPERS HAVE POWERFUL HIND LEGS THAT ENABLE THEM TO ESCAPE FROM THREATS.
WINNER!
So FAST!

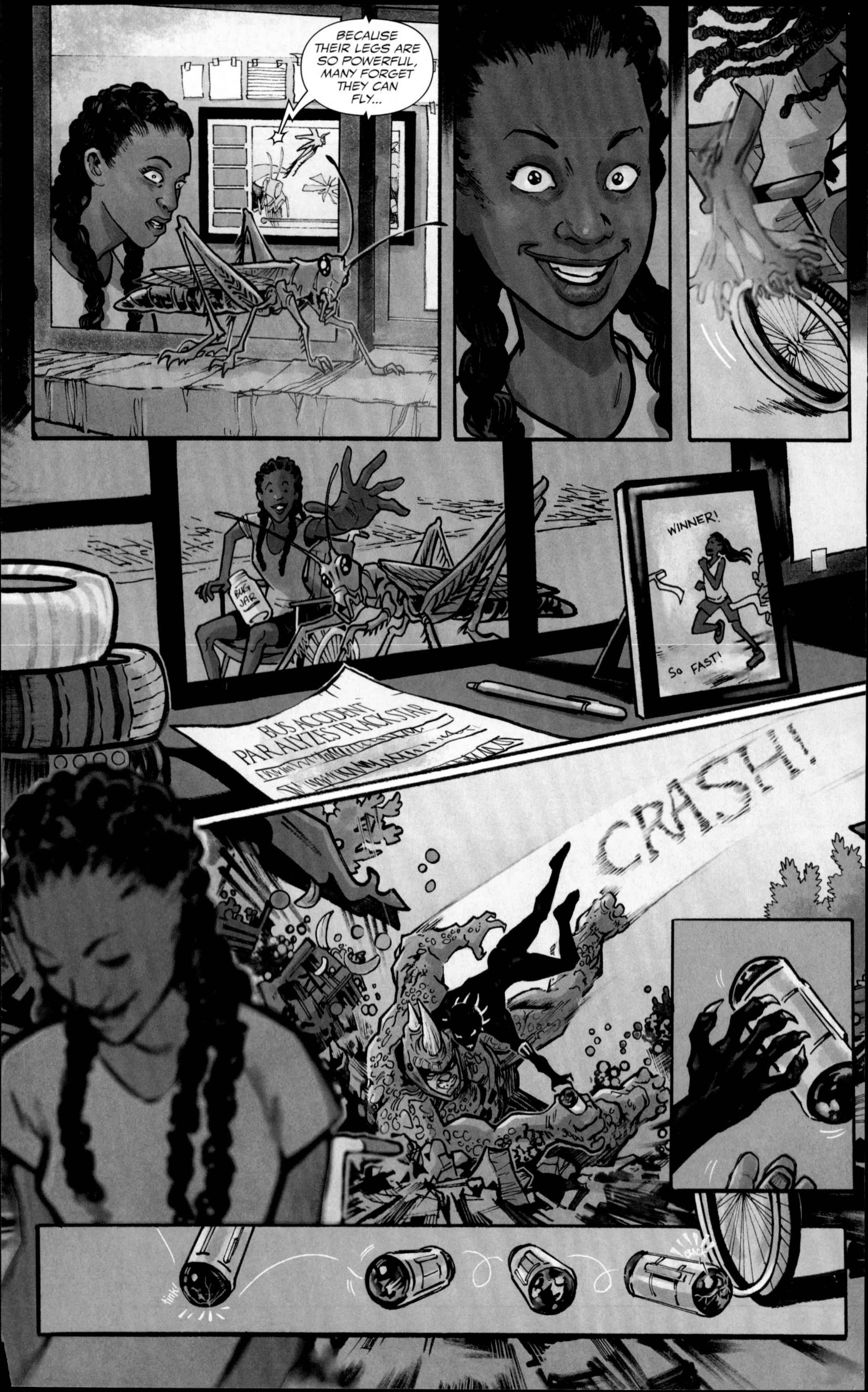
BECAUSE THEIR LEGS ARE SO POWERFUL, MANY FORGET THEY CAN FLY...
BUG JAR
WINNER!
SO FAST!
BUS ACCIDENT PARALYZES TRACK STAR
CRASH!
tink!

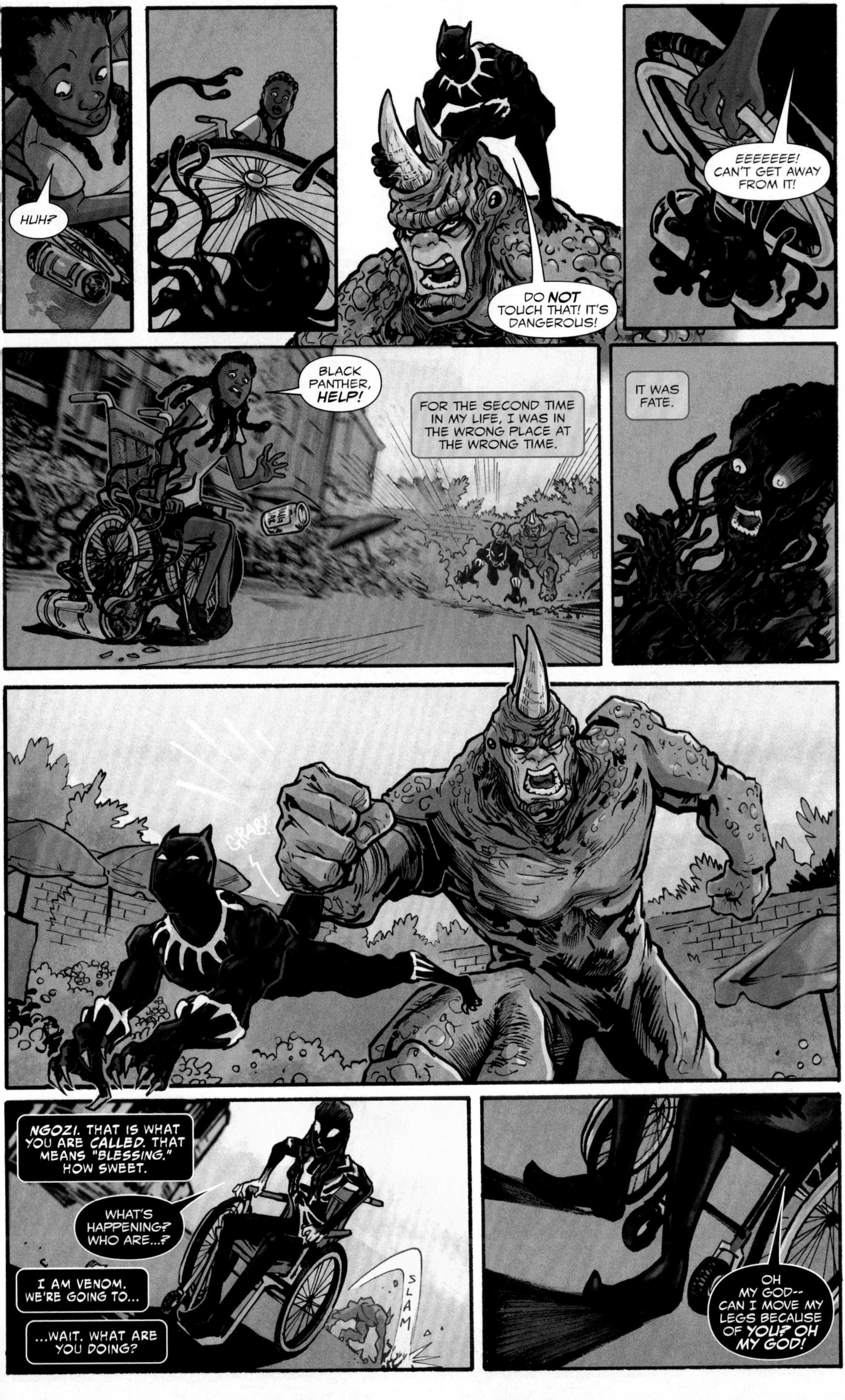
HUH?
DO NOT TOUCH THAT! IT'S DANGEROUS!
EEEEEEE! CAN'T GET AWAY FROM IT!
BLACK PANTHER, HELP!
FOR THE SECOND TIME IN MY LIFE, I WAS IN THE WRONG PLACE AT THE WRONG TIME.
IT WAS FATE.
GRAB!
NGOZI. THAT IS WHAT YOU ARE CALLED. THAT MEANS "BLESSING." HOW SWEET.
WHAT'S HAPPENING? WHO ARE...?
I AM VENOM. WE'RE GOING TO...
...WAIT. WHAT ARE YOU DOING?
SLAM
OH MY GOD-- CAN I MOVE MY LEGS BECAUSE OF YOU? OH MY GOD!

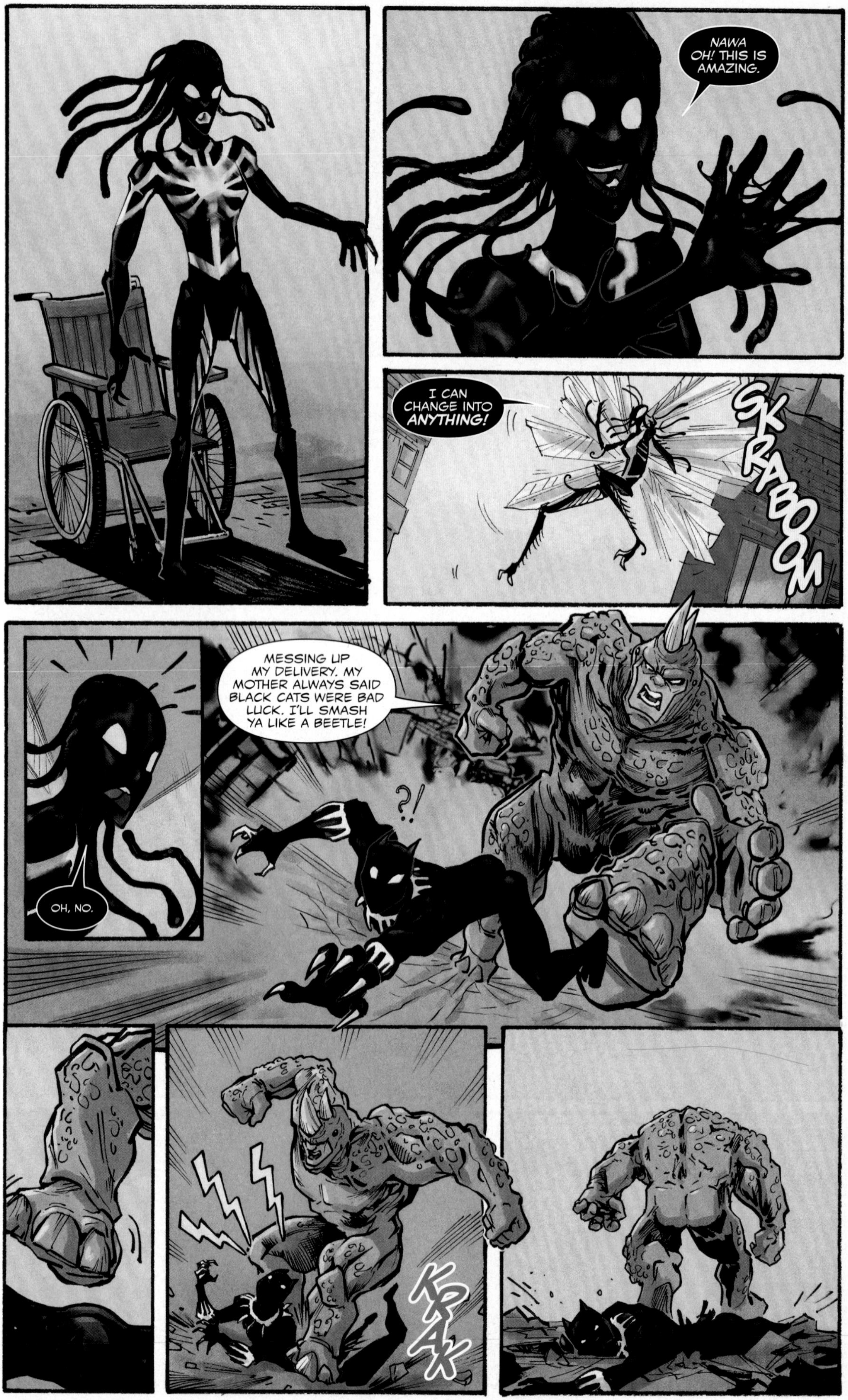
NAWA OH! THIS IS AMAZING.
I CAN CHANGE INTO ANYTHING!
SKRABOOM
OH, NO.
MESSING UP MY DELIVERY. MY MOTHER ALWAYS SAID BLACK CATS WERE BAD LUCK. I'LL SMASH YA LIKE A BEETLE!
?!
KRAK

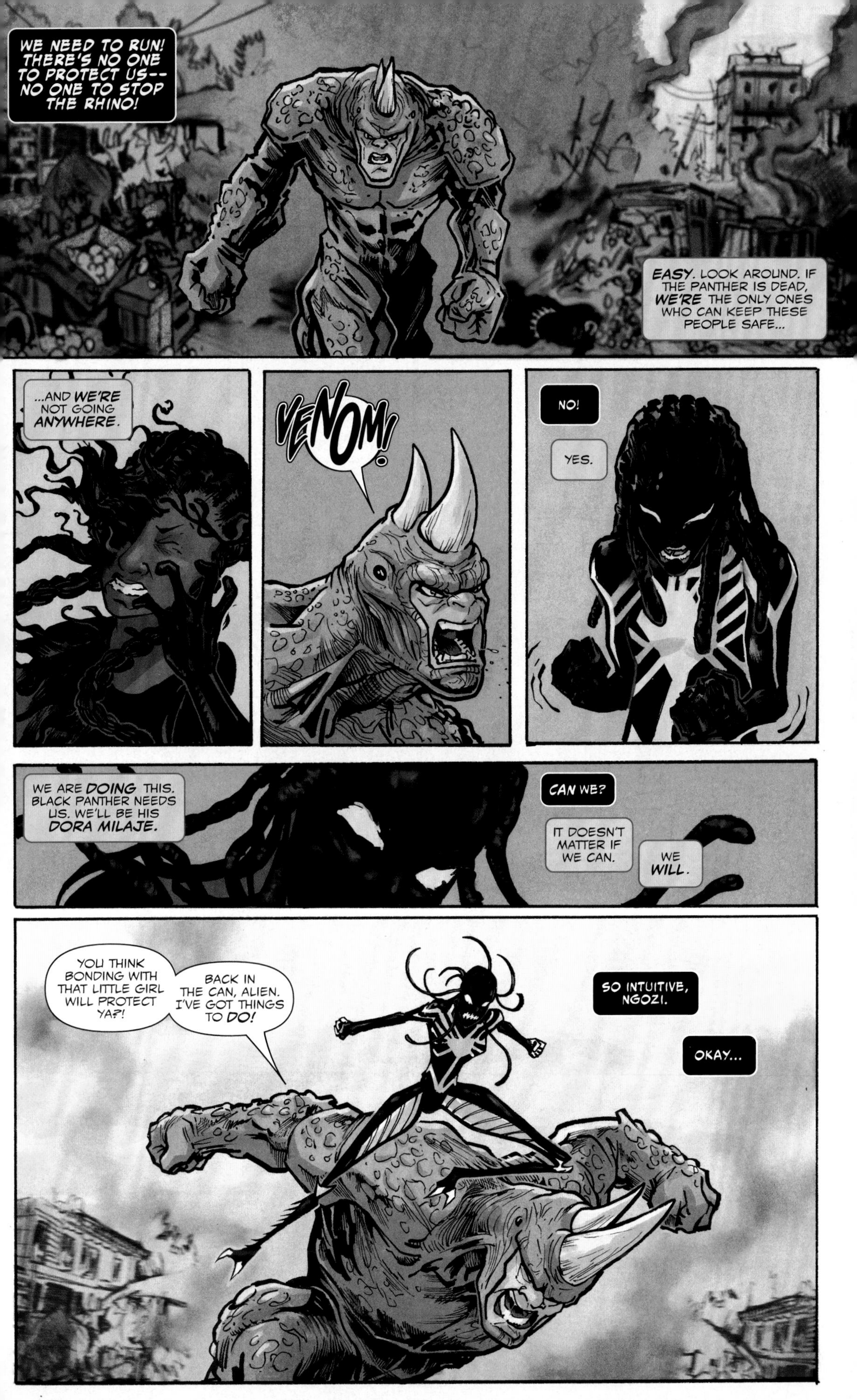
WE NEED TO RUN! THERE'S NO ONE TO PROTECT US-- NO ONE TO STOP THE RHINO!
EASY. LOOK AROUND. IF THE PANTHER IS DEAD, WE'RE THE ONLY ONES WHO CAN KEEP THESE PEOPLE SAFE...
...AND WE'RE NOT GOING ANYWHERE.
VENOM!
NO!
YES.
WE ARE DOING THIS. BLACK PANTHER NEEDS US. WE'LL BE HIS DORA MILAJE.
CAN WE?
IT DOESN'T MATTER IF WE CAN.
WE WILL.
YOU THINK BONDING WITH THAT LITTLE GIRL WILL PROTECT YA?!
BACK IN THE CAN, ALIEN. I'VE GOT THINGS TO DO!
SO INTUITIVE, NGOZI.
OKAY...

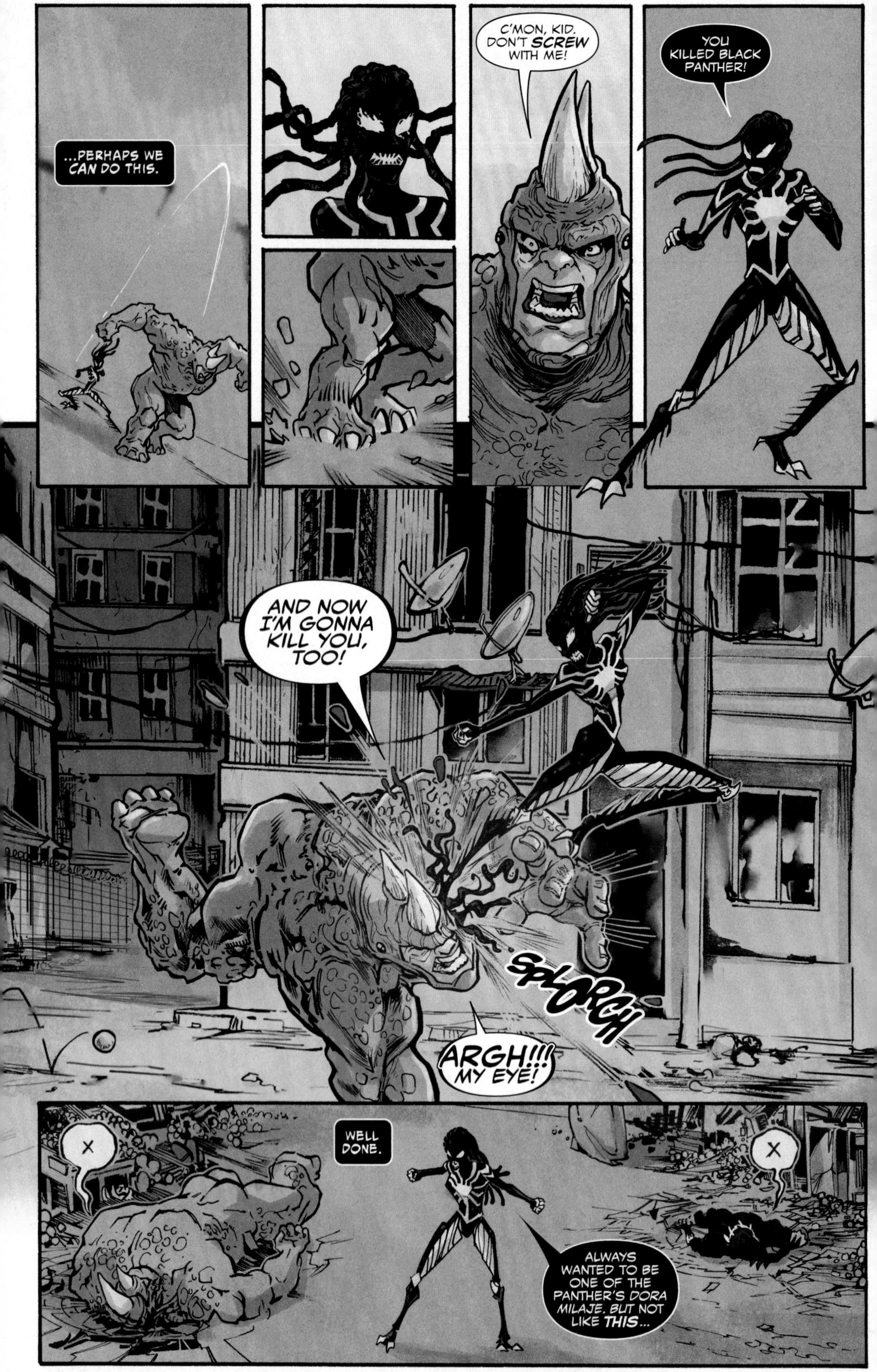

...PERHAPS WE CAN DO THIS.
C'MON, KID. DON'T SCREW WITH ME!
YOU KILLED BLACK PANTHER!
AND NOW I'M GONNA KILL YOU, TOO!
SPLORCH
ARGH!!! MY EYE!
X
WELL DONE.
X
ALWAYS WANTED TO BE ONE OF THE PANTHER'S DORA MILAJE. BUT NOT LIKE THIS...

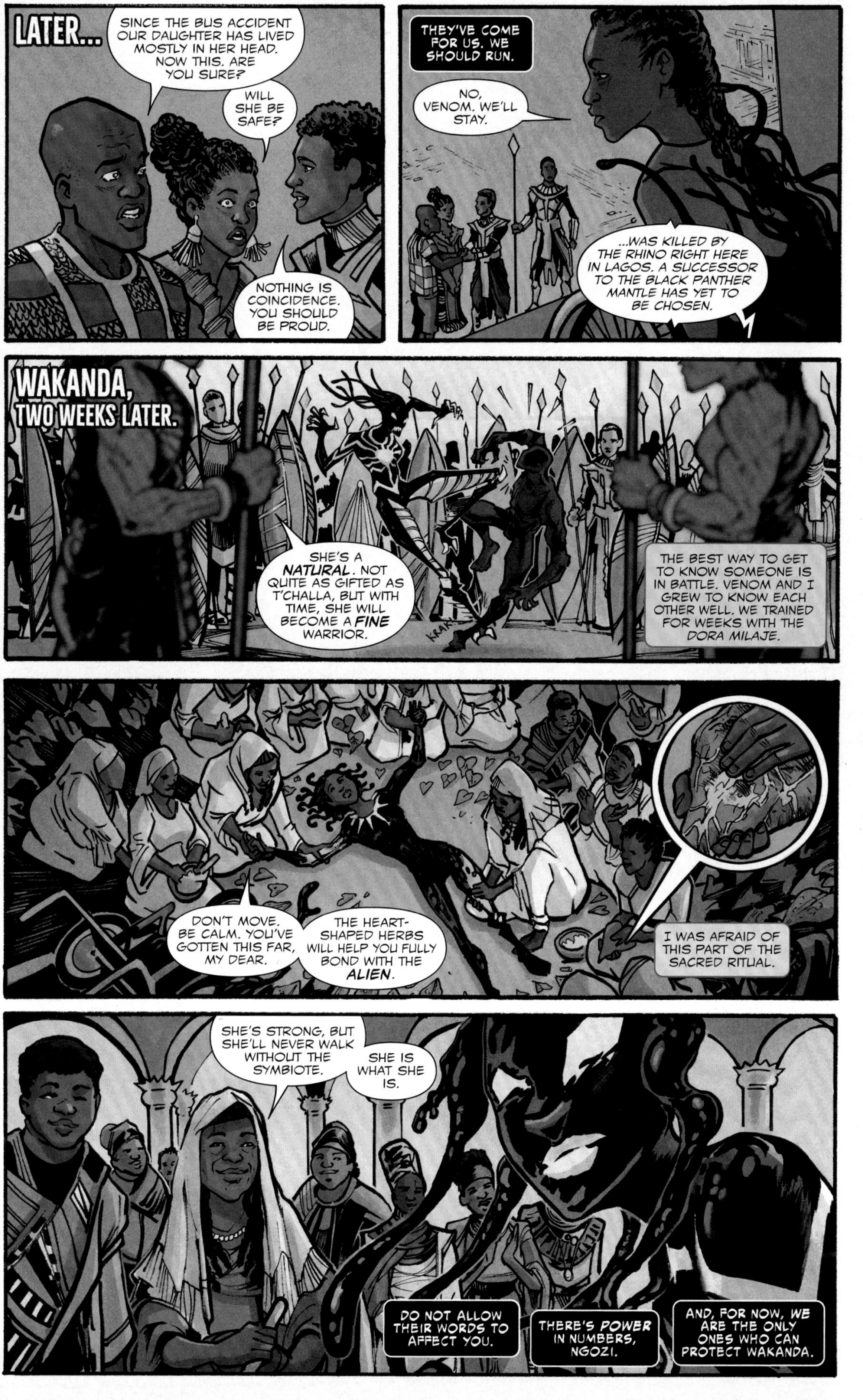
LATER...
SINCE THE BUS ACCIDENT OUR DAUGHTER HAS LIVED MOSTLY IN HER HEAD. NOW THIS. ARE YOU SURE?
WILL SHE BE SAFE?
NOTHING IS COINCIDENCE. YOU SHOULD BE PROUD.
THEY'VE COME FOR US. WE SHOULD RUN.
NO, VENOM. WE'LL STAY.
...WAS KILLED BY THE RHINO RIGHT HERE IN LAGOS. A SUCCESSOR TO THE BLACK PANTHER MANTLE HAS YET TO BE CHOSEN.
WAKANDA, TWO WEEKS LATER.
SHE'S A NATURAL. NOT QUITE AS GIFTED AS T'CHALLA, BUT WITH TIME, SHE WILL BECOME A FINE WARRIOR.
KRAK!
THE BEST WAY TO GET TO KNOW SOMEONE IS IN BATTLE. VENOM AND I GREW TO KNOW EACH OTHER WELL. WE TRAINED FOR WEEKS WITH THE DORA MILAJE.
DON'T MOVE. BE CALM. YOU'VE GOTTEN THIS FAR, MY DEAR.
THE HEART-SHAPED HERBS WILL HELP YOU FULLY BOND WITH THE ALIEN.
I WAS AFRAID OF THIS PART OF THE SACRED RITUAL.
SHE'S STRONG, BUT SHE'LL NEVER WALK WITHOUT THE SYMBIOTE.
SHE IS WHAT SHE IS.
DO NOT ALLOW THEIR WORDS TO AFFECT YOU.
THERE'S POWER IN NUMBERS, NGOZI.
AND, FOR NOW, WE ARE THE ONLY ONES WHO CAN PROTECT WAKANDA.

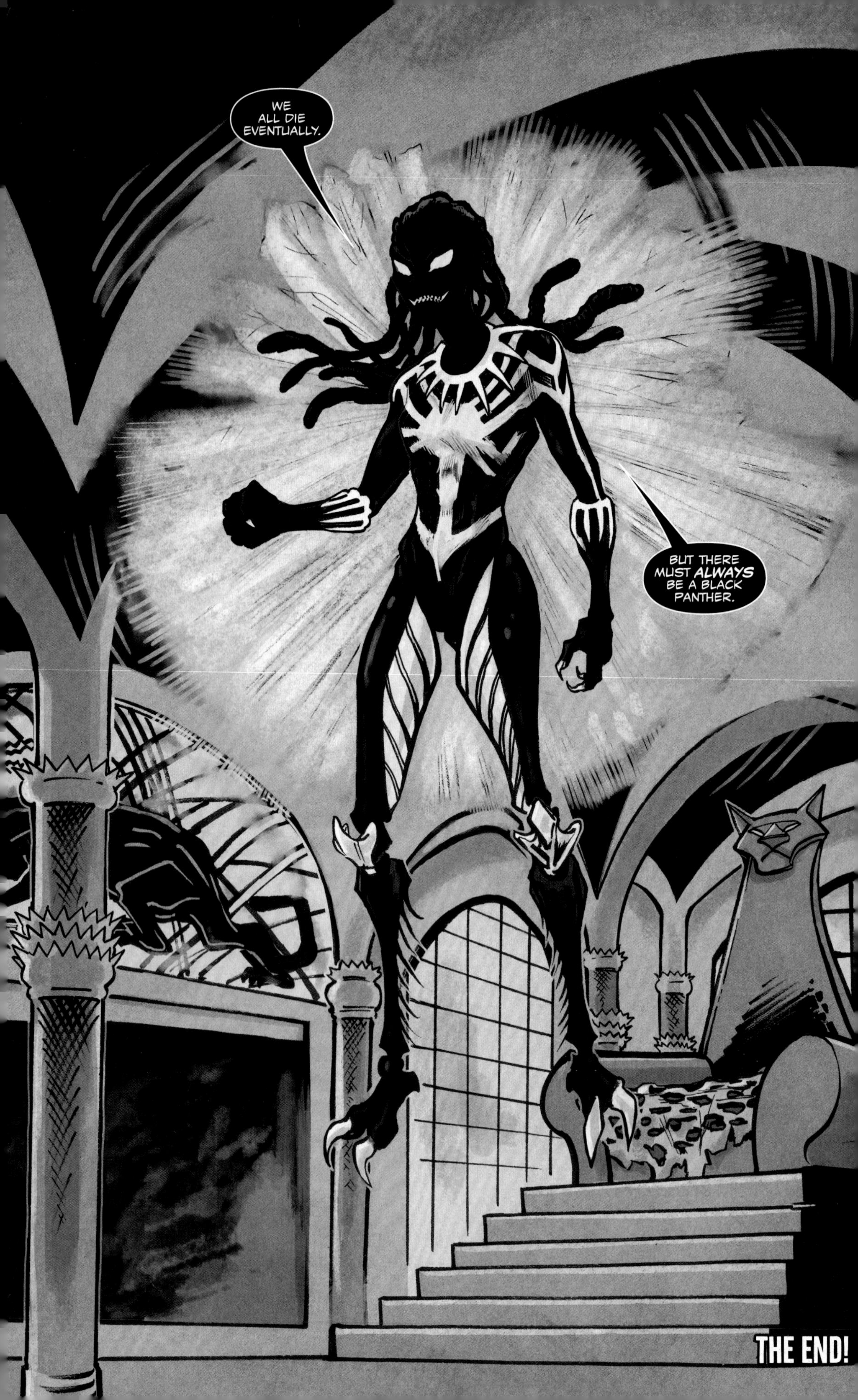

WE ALL DIE EVENTUALLY.
BUT THERE MUST ALWAYS BE A BLACK PANTHER.
THE END!

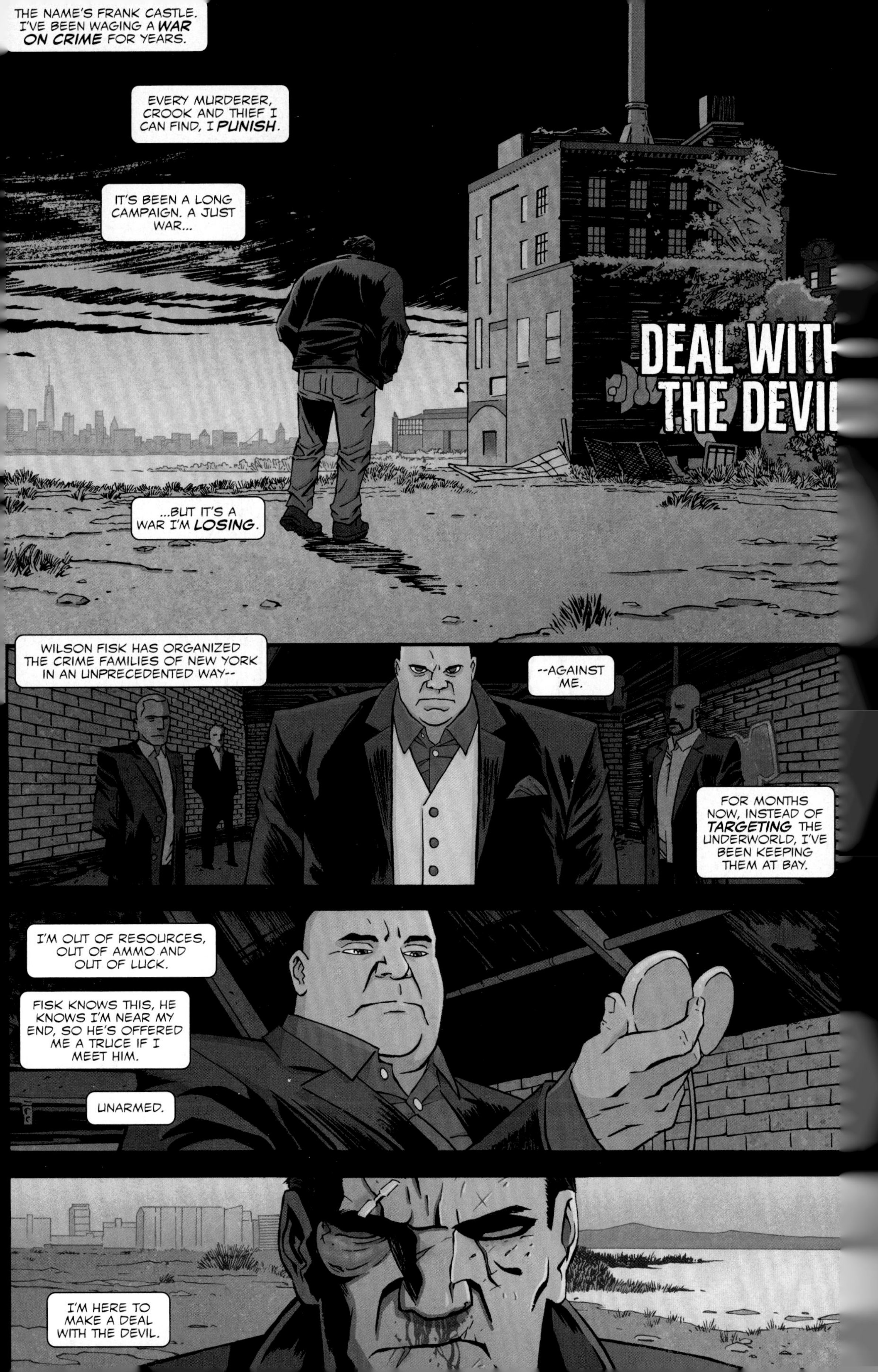
THE NAME'S FRANK CASTLE. I'VE BEEN WAGING A WAR ON CRIME FOR YEARS.
EVERY MURDERER, CROOK AND THIEF I CAN FIND, I PUNISH.
IT'S BEEN A LONG CAMPAIGN. A JUST WAR...
DEAL WITH THE DEVIL
...BUT IT'S A WAR I'M LOSING.
WILSON FISK HAS ORGANIZED THE CRIME FAMILIES OF NEW YORK IN AN UNPRECEDENTED WAY--
--AGAINST ME.
FOR MONTHS NOW, INSTEAD OF TARGETING THE UNDERWORLD, I'VE BEEN KEEPING THEM AT BAY.
I'M OUT OF RESOURCES, OUT OF AMMO AND OUT OF LUCK.
FISK KNOWS THIS, HE KNOWS I'M NEAR MY END, SO HE'S OFFERED ME A TRUCE IF I MEET HIM.
UNARMED.
I'M HERE TO MAKE A DEAL WITH THE DEVIL.

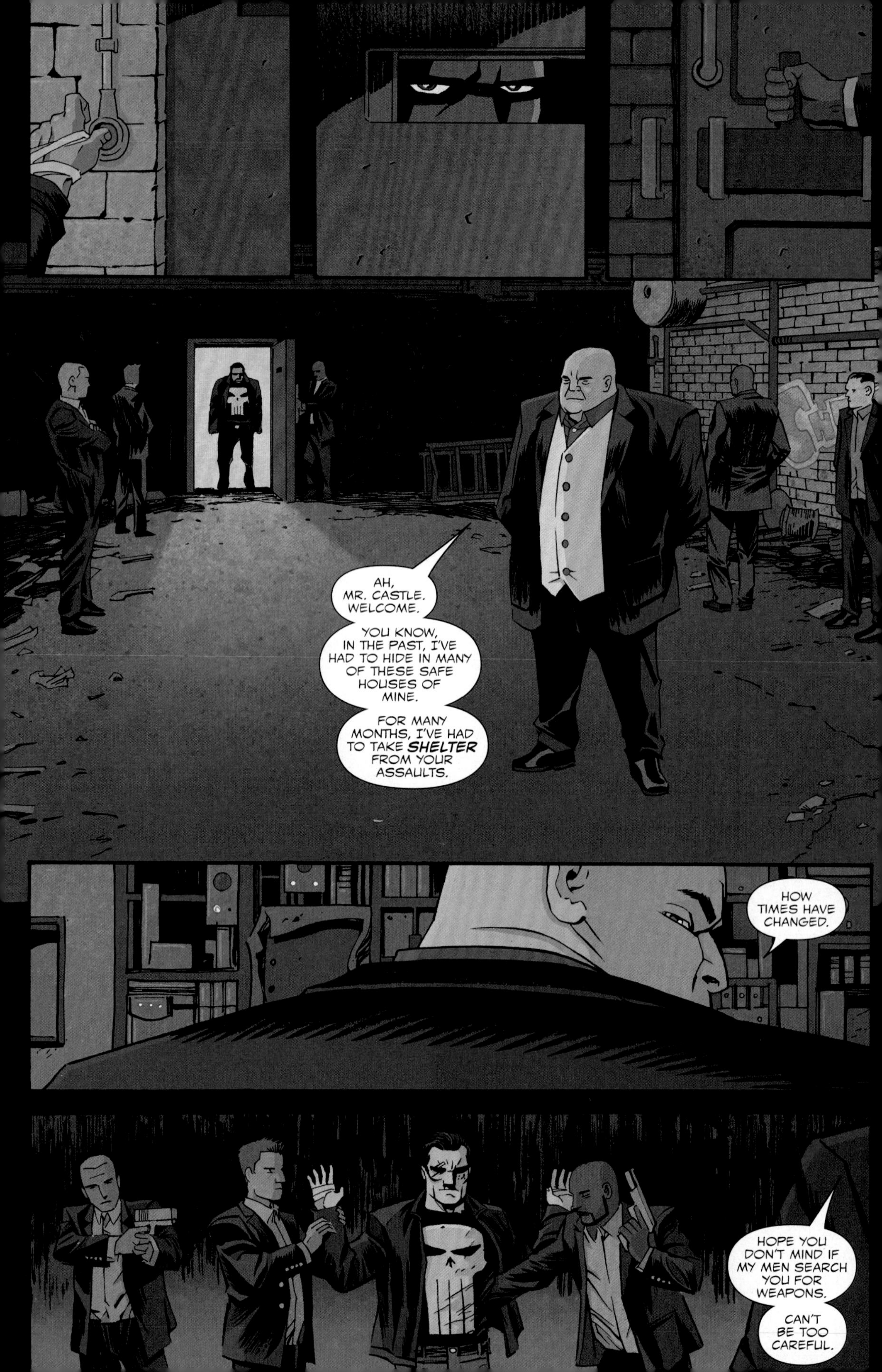
AH, MR. CASTLE. WELCOME.
YOU KNOW, IN THE PAST, I'VE HAD TO HIDE IN MANY OF THESE SAFE HOUSES OF MINE.
FOR MANY MONTHS, I'VE HAD TO TAKE SHELTER FROM YOUR ASSAULTS.
HOW TIMES HAVE CHANGED.
HOPE YOU DON'T MIND IF MY MEN SEARCH YOU FOR WEAPONS.
CAN'T BE TOO CAREFUL.

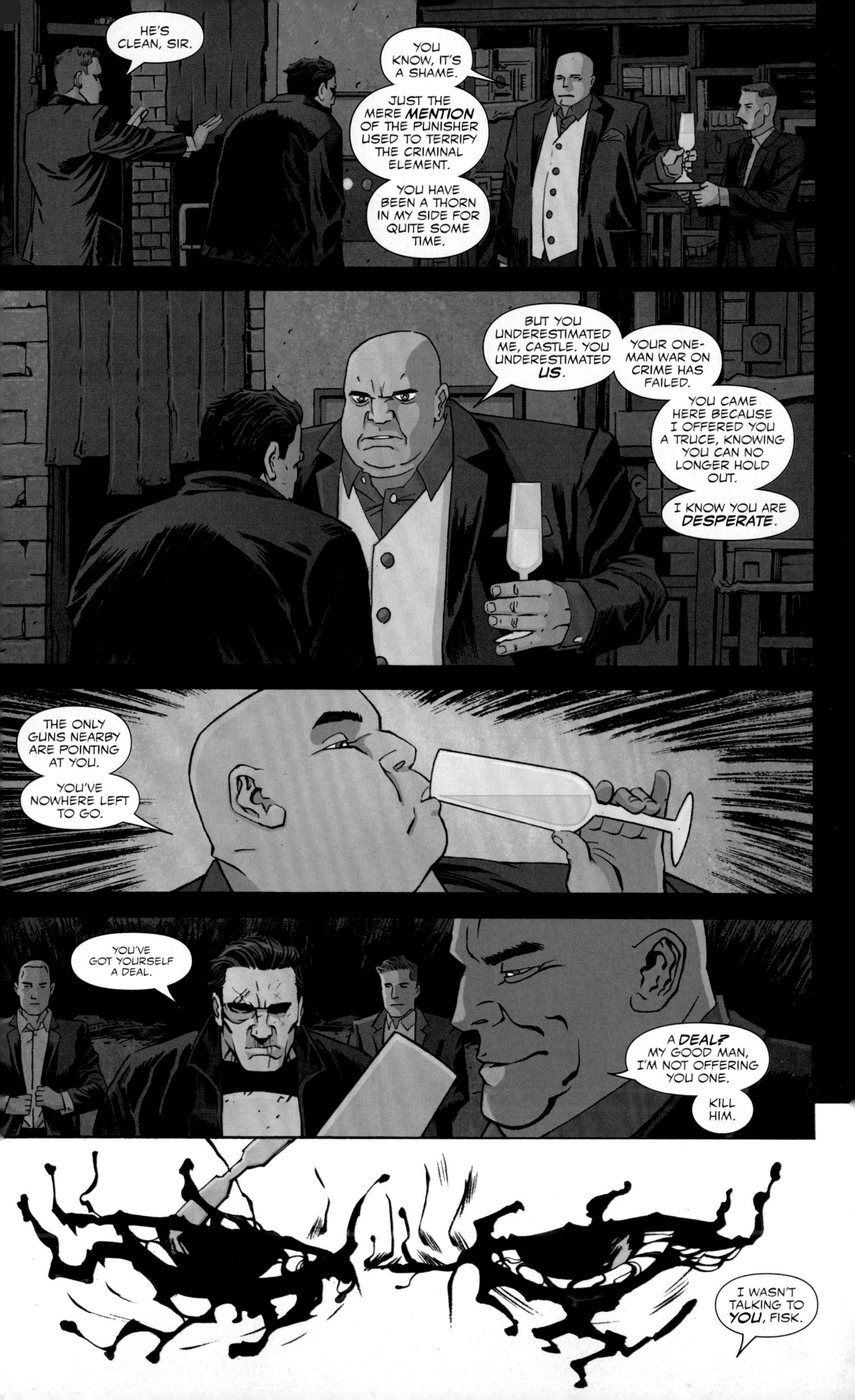
HE'S CLEAN, SIR.
YOU KNOW, IT'S A SHAME.
JUST THE MERE MENTION OF THE PUNISHER USED TO TERRIFY THE CRIMINAL ELEMENT.
YOU HAVE BEEN A THORN IN MY SIDE FOR QUITE SOME TIME.
BUT YOU UNDERESTIMATED ME, CASTLE. YOU UNDERESTIMATED US.
YOUR ONE-MAN WAR ON CRIME HAS FAILED.
YOU CAME HERE BECAUSE I OFFERED YOU A TRUCE, KNOWING YOU CAN NO LONGER HOLD OUT.
I KNOW YOU ARE DESPERATE.
THE ONLY GUNS NEARBY ARE POINTING AT YOU.
YOU'VE NOWHERE LEFT TO GO.
YOU'VE GOT YOURSELF A DEAL.
A DEAL? MY GOOD MAN, I'M NOT OFFERING YOU ONE.
KILL HIM.
I WASN'T TALKING TO YOU, FISK.

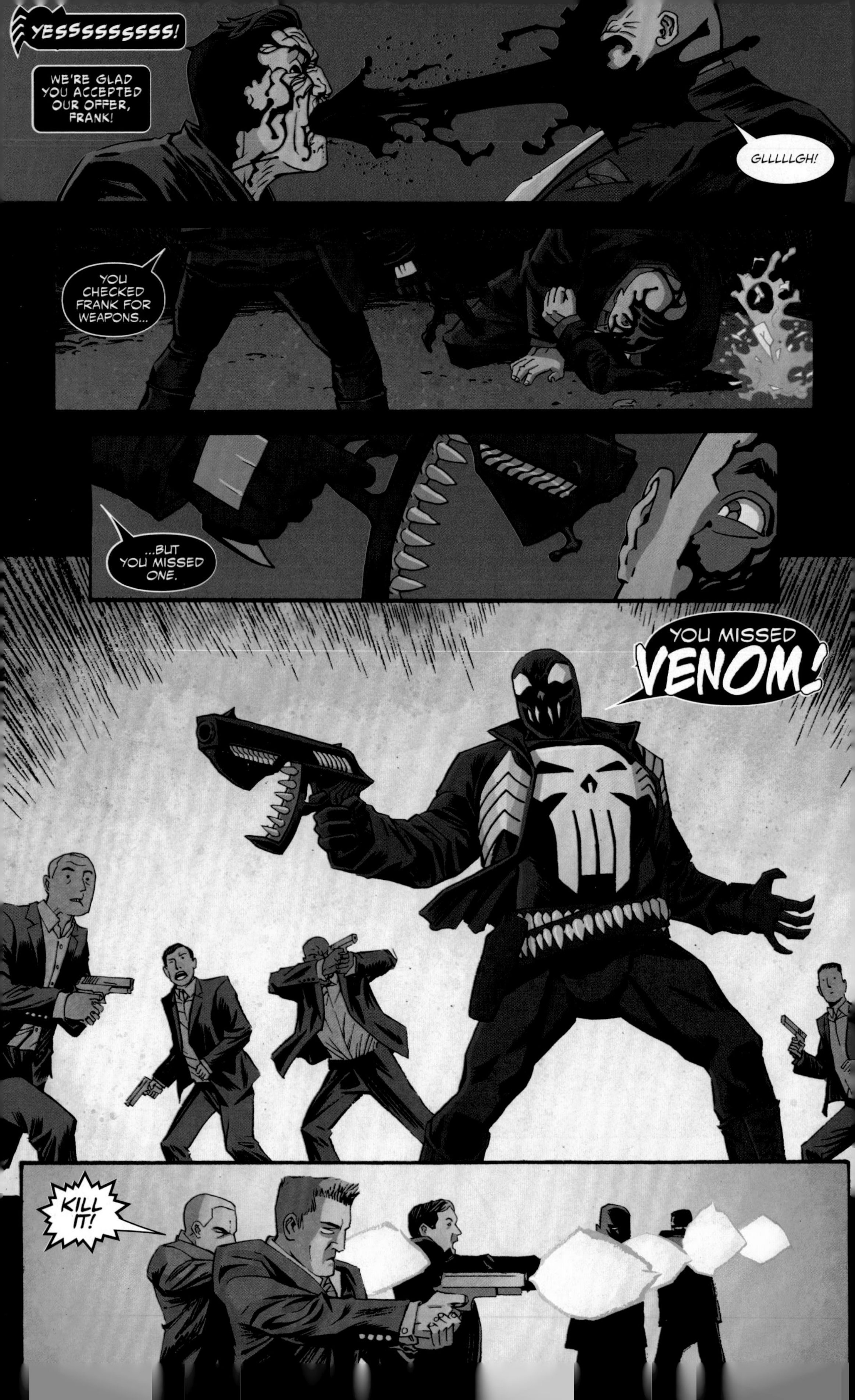
YESSSSSSSSS!
WE'RE GLAD YOU ACCEPTED OUR OFFER, FRANK!
GLLLLLGH!
YOU CHECKED FRANK FOR WEAPONS...
...BUT YOU MISSED ONE.
YOU MISSED VENOM!
KILL IT!

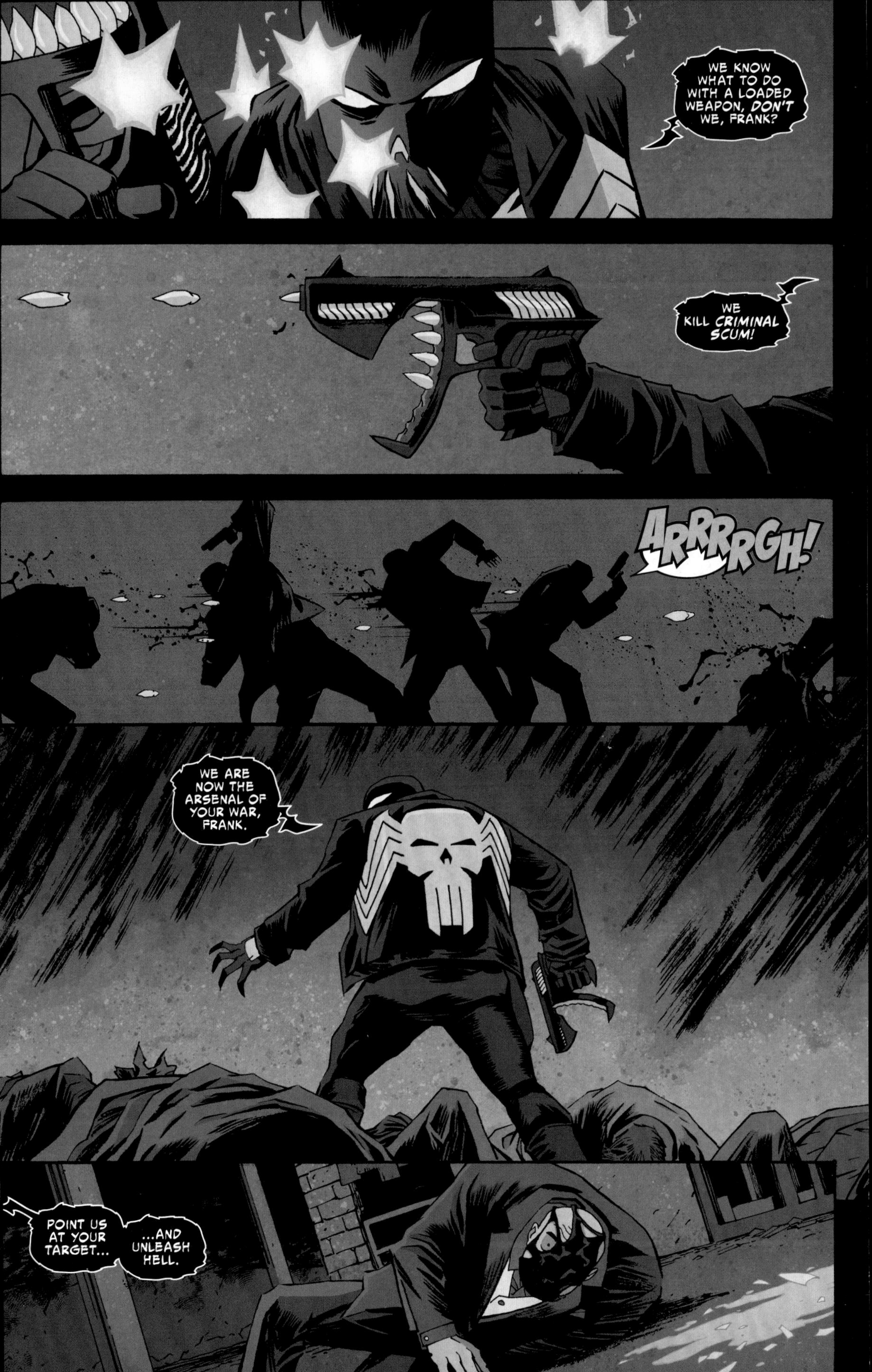
WE KNOW WHAT TO DO WITH A LOADED WEAPON, DON'T WE, FRANK?
WE KILL CRIMINAL SCUM!
ARRRRGH!
WE ARE NOW THE ARSENAL OF YOUR WAR, FRANK.
POINT US AT YOUR TARGET...
...AND UNLEASH HELL.

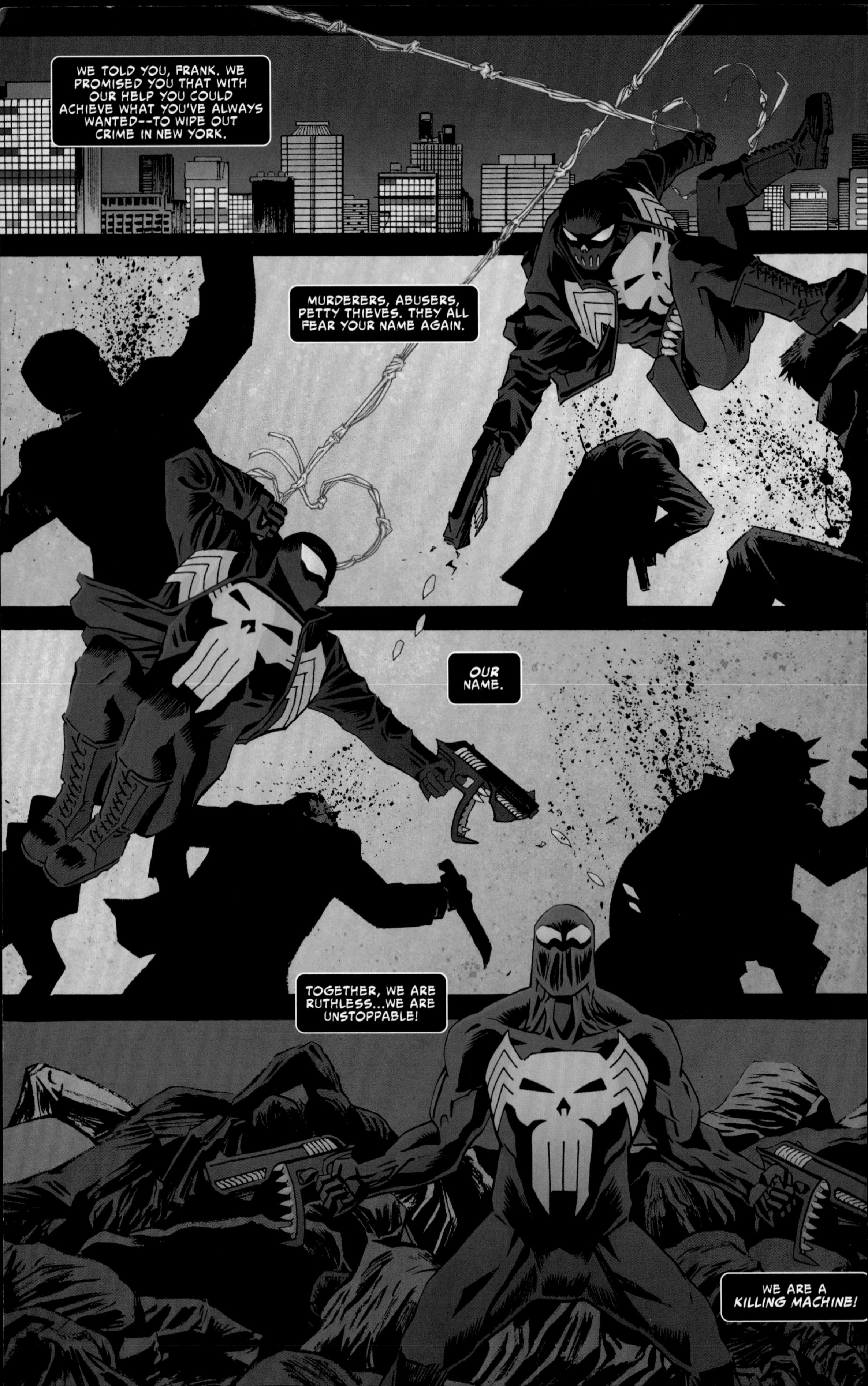
WE TOLD YOU, FRANK. WE PROMISED YOU THAT WITH OUR HELP YOU COULD ACHIEVE WHAT YOU'VE ALWAYS WANTED--TO WIPE OUT CRIME IN NEW YORK.
MURDERERS, ABUSERS, PETTY THIEVES. THEY ALL FEAR YOUR NAME AGAIN.
OUR NAME.
TOGETHER, WE ARE RUTHLESS...WE ARE UNSTOPPABLE!
WE ARE A KILLING MACHINE!

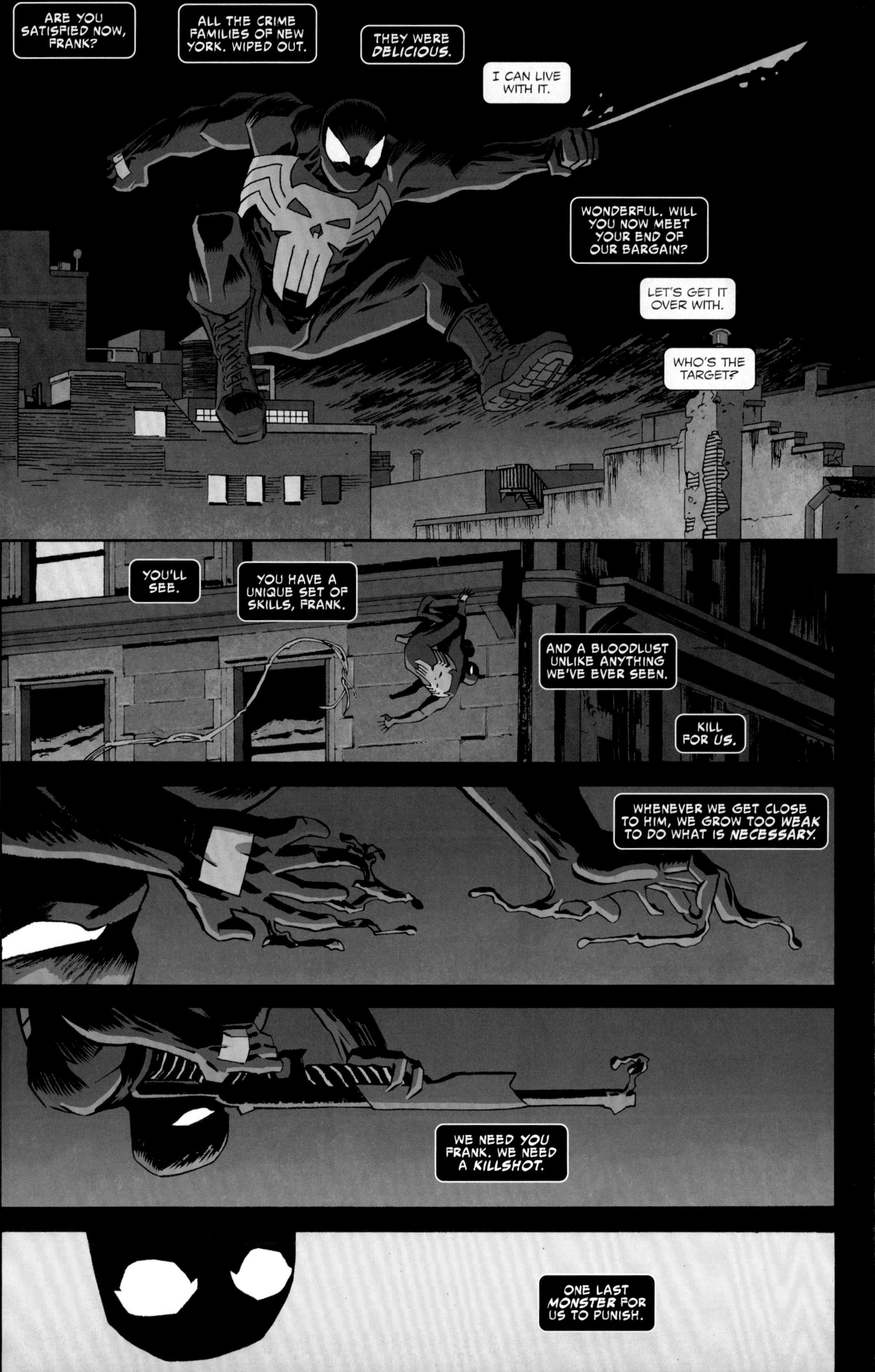
ARE YOU SATISFIED NOW, FRANK?
ALL THE CRIME FAMILIES OF NEW YORK. WIPED OUT.
THEY WERE *DELICIOUS.*
I CAN LIVE WITH IT.
WONDERFUL. WILL YOU NOW MEET YOUR END OF OUR BARGAIN?
LET'S GET IT OVER WITH.
WHO'S THE TARGET?
YOU'LL SEE.
YOU HAVE A UNIQUE SET OF SKILLS, FRANK.
AND A BLOODLUST UNLIKE ANYTHING WE'VE EVER SEEN.
KILL FOR *US.*
WHENEVER WE GET CLOSE TO HIM, WE GROW TOO *WEAK* TO DO WHAT IS *NECESSARY.*
WE NEED *YOU* FRANK. WE NEED A *KILLSHOT.*
ONE LAST *MONSTER* FOR US TO PUNISH.

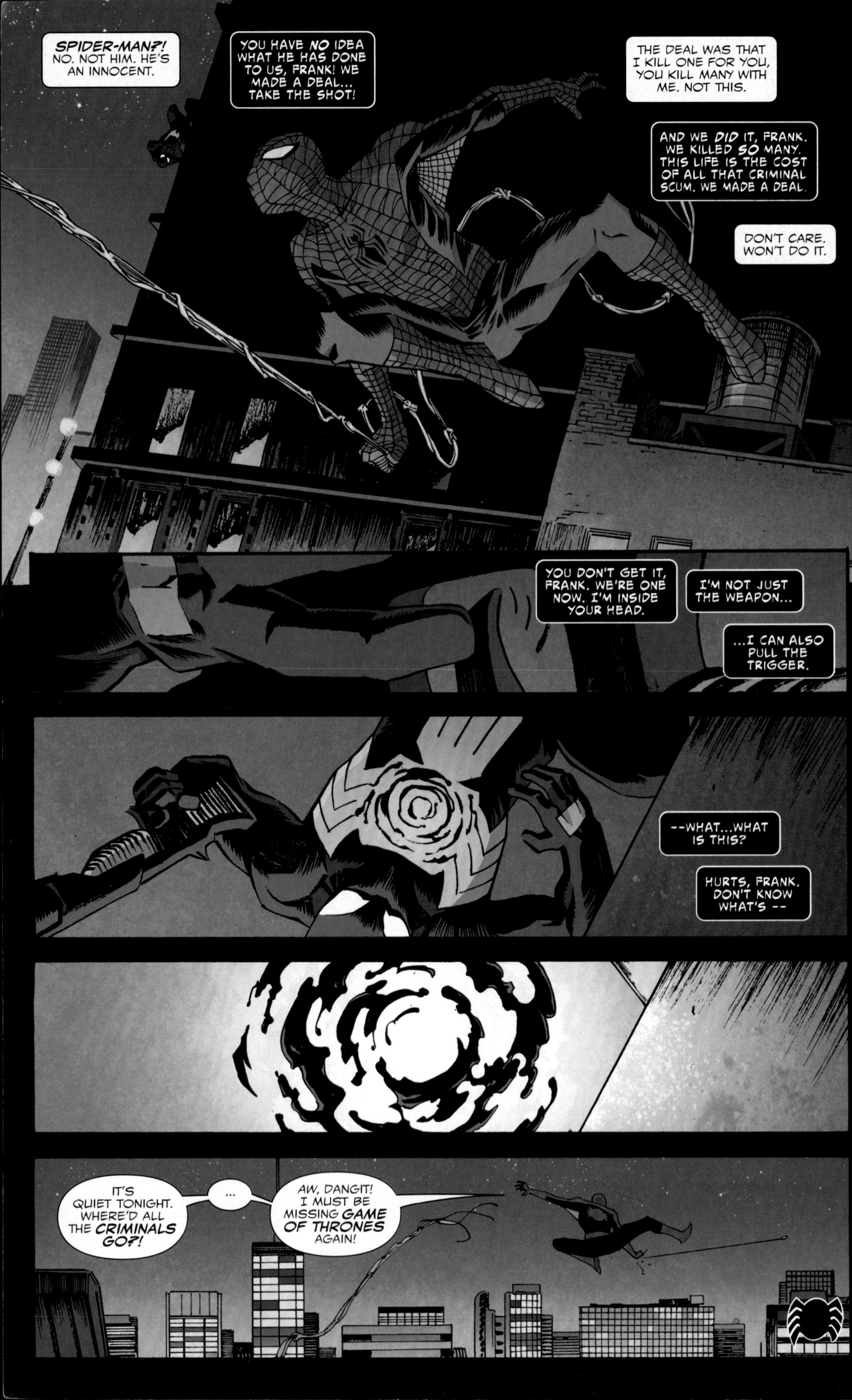
SPIDER-MAN?! NO. NOT HIM. HE'S AN INNOCENT.
YOU HAVE NO IDEA WHAT HE HAS DONE TO US, FRANK! WE MADE A DEAL... TAKE THE SHOT!
THE DEAL WAS THAT I KILL ONE FOR YOU, YOU KILL MANY WITH ME. NOT THIS.
AND WE DID IT, FRANK. WE KILLED SO MANY. THIS LIFE IS THE COST OF ALL THAT CRIMINAL SCUM. WE MADE A DEAL.
DON'T CARE. WON'T DO IT.
YOU DON'T GET IT, FRANK. WE'RE ONE NOW. I'M INSIDE YOUR HEAD.
I'M NOT JUST THE WEAPON...
...I CAN ALSO PULL THE TRIGGER.
--WHAT...WHAT IS THIS?
HURTS, FRANK. DON'T KNOW WHAT'S --
IT'S QUIET TONIGHT. WHERE'D ALL THE CRIMINALS GO?!
...
AW, DANGIT! I MUST BE MISSING GAME OF THRONES AGAIN!

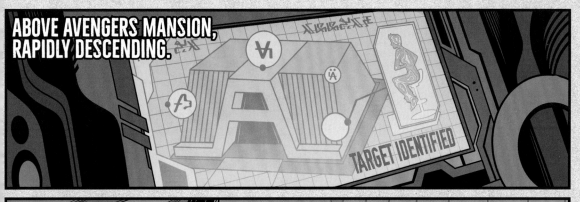

ABOVE AVENGERS MANSION, RAPIDLY DESCENDING.

TARGET IDENTIFIED

"TARGET IDENTIFIED," HUH? YOU *SURE* ABOUT THAT?

AFFIRMATIVE.

LAST TIME YOU WERE *"AFFIRMATIVE,"* IT ENDED UP BEING *A-BOMB* INSTEAD OF THE *THING.*

IT'S LIKE YOU'RE TRYING TO GET ME *KILLED.* YOU WAITING FOR THE ROBOT UPRISING? GONNA FINALLY TAKE ME OUT?

AFFIRMATIVE.

I *KNEW* I LIKED YOU.

3 2 1

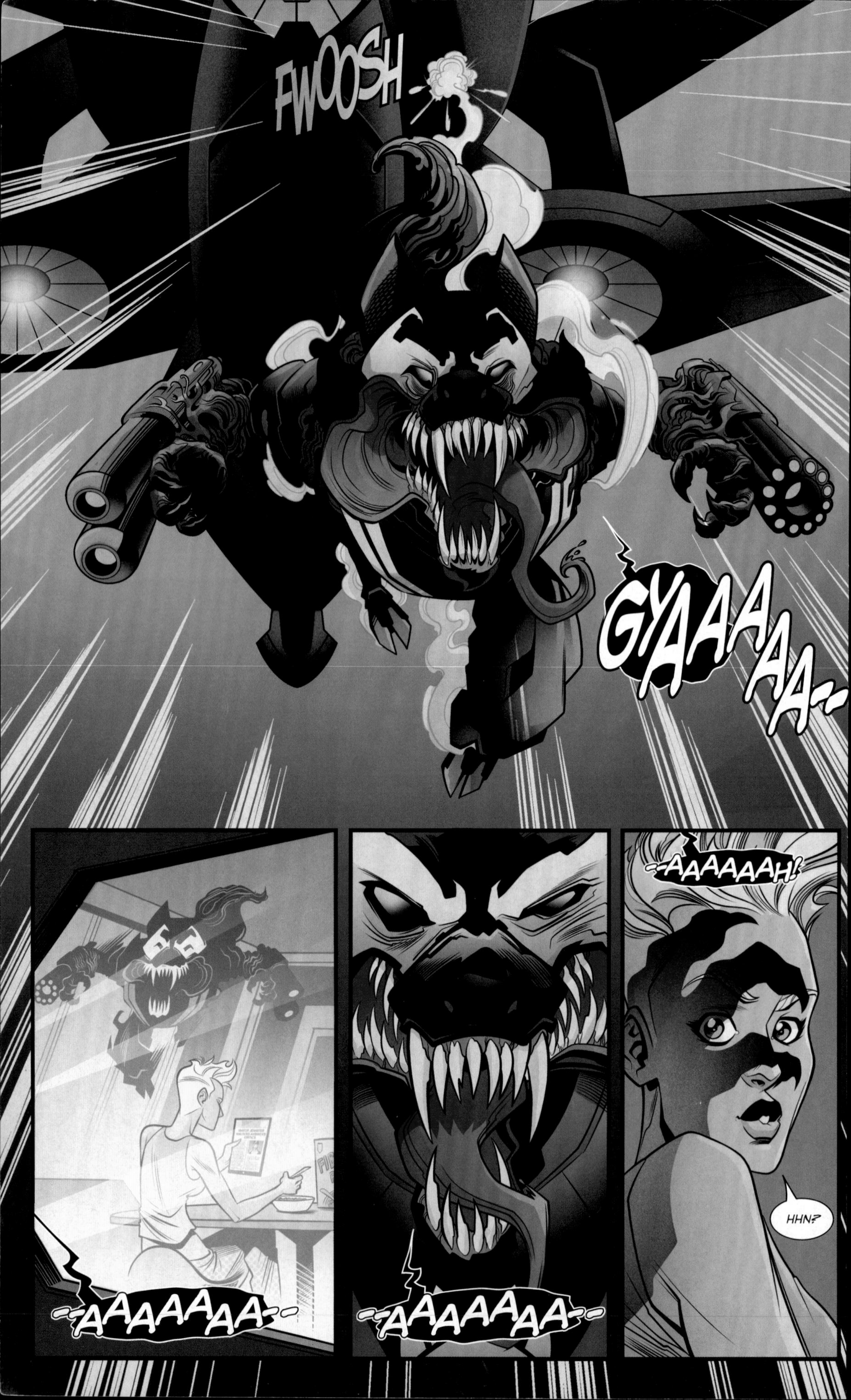
FWOOSH
GYAAAAAA--
--AAAAAAA--
--AAAAAAA--
--AAAAAAH!
HHN?

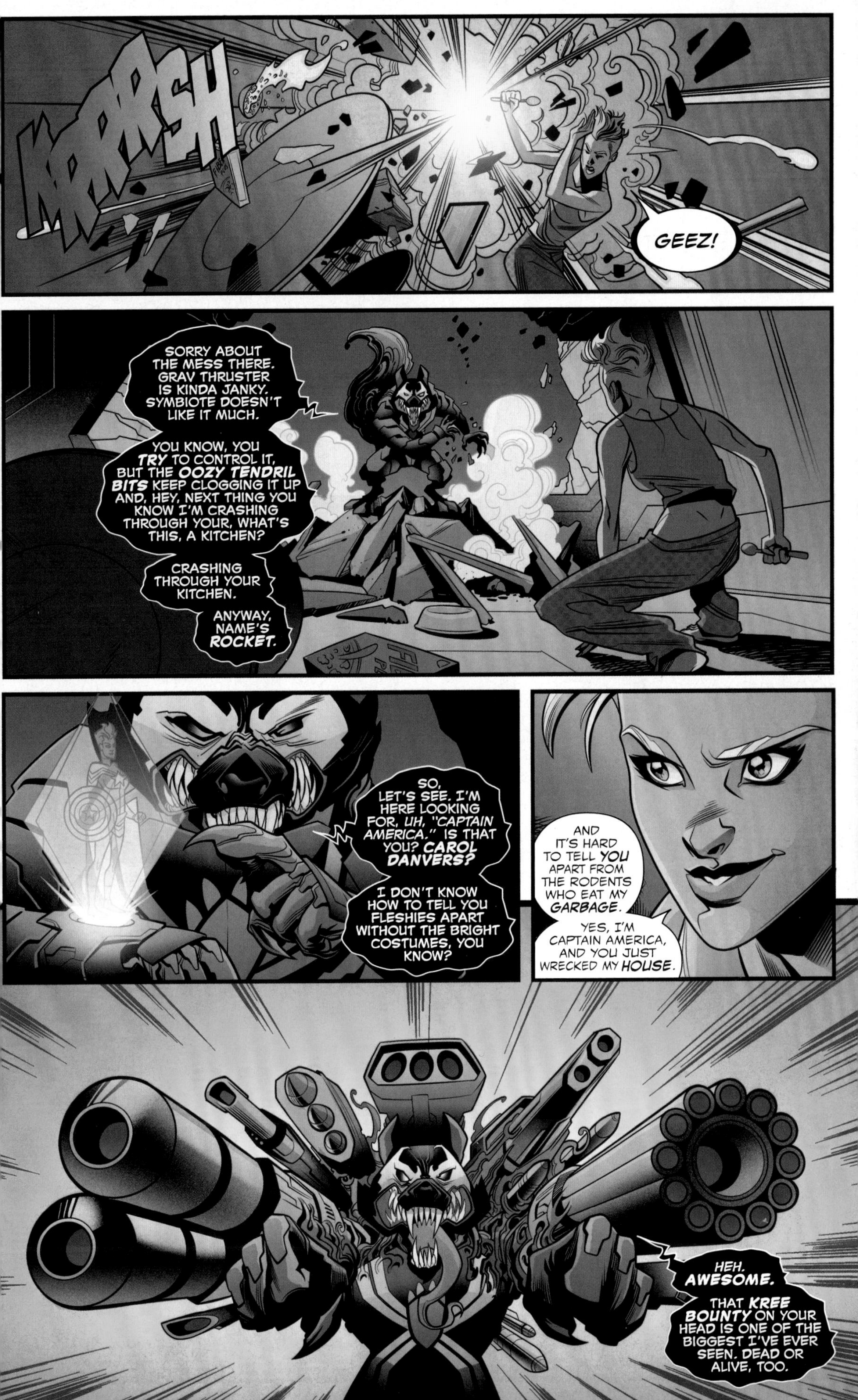
KRRRSH
GEEZ!
SORRY ABOUT THE MESS THERE. GRAV THRUSTER IS KINDA JANKY. SYMBIOTE DOESN'T LIKE IT MUCH.
YOU KNOW, YOU TRY TO CONTROL IT, BUT THE OOZY TENDRIL BITS KEEP CLOGGING IT UP AND, HEY, NEXT THING YOU KNOW I'M CRASHING THROUGH YOUR, WHAT'S THIS, A KITCHEN?
CRASHING THROUGH YOUR KITCHEN.
ANYWAY, NAME'S ROCKET.
SO, LET'S SEE. I'M HERE LOOKING FOR, UH, "CAPTAIN AMERICA." IS THAT YOU? CAROL DANVERS?
I DON'T KNOW HOW TO TELL YOU FLESHIES APART WITHOUT THE BRIGHT COSTUMES, YOU KNOW?
AND IT'S HARD TO TELL YOU APART FROM THE RODENTS WHO EAT MY GARBAGE.
YES, I'M CAPTAIN AMERICA, AND YOU JUST WRECKED MY HOUSE.
HEH. AWESOME.
THAT KREE BOUNTY ON YOUR HEAD IS ONE OF THE BIGGEST I'VE EVER SEEN. DEAD OR ALIVE, TOO.

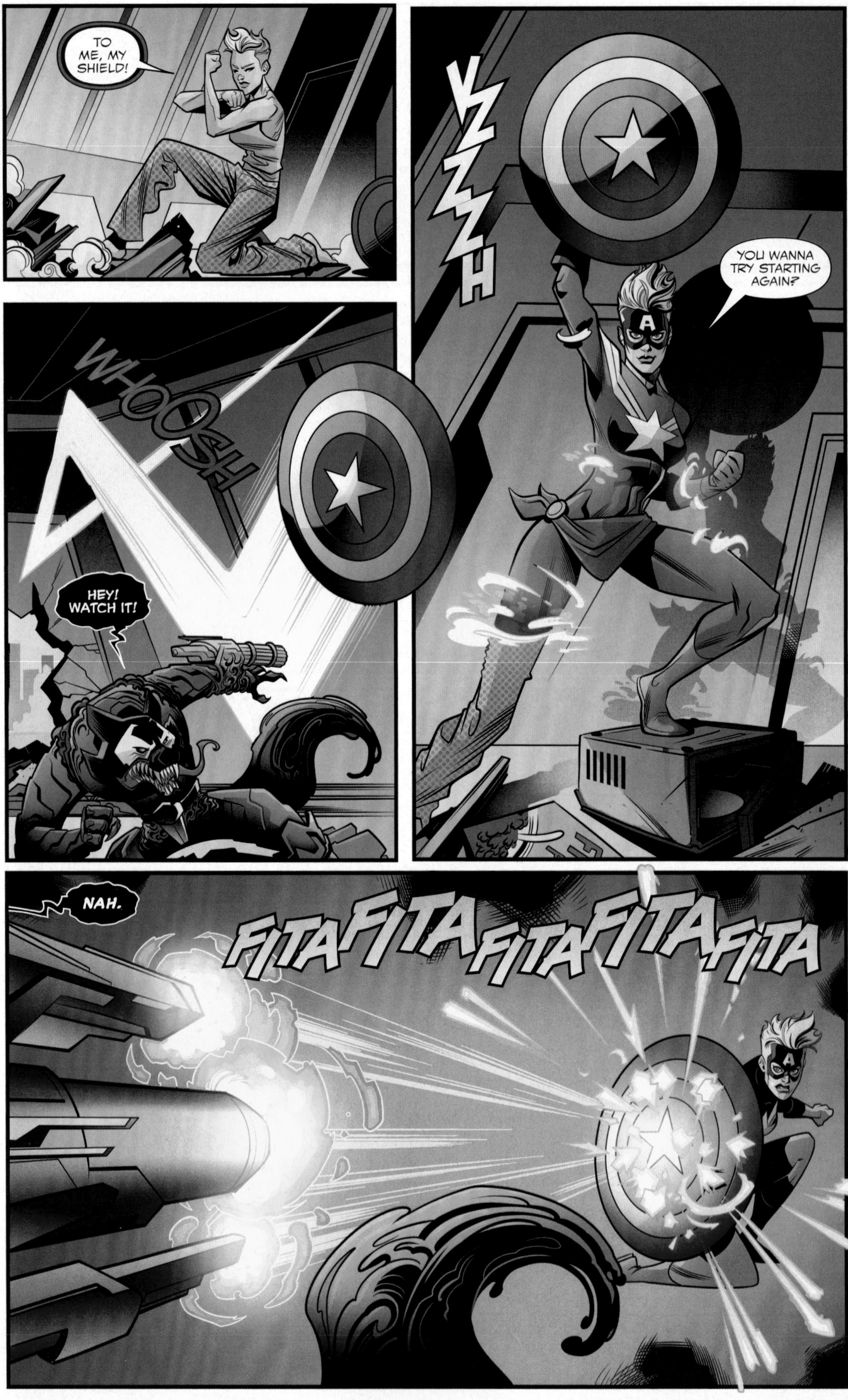
TO ME, MY SHIELD!
VZZZZH
YOU WANNA TRY STARTING AGAIN?
WHOOOSH
HEY! WATCH IT!
NAH.
FITAFITAFITAFITAFITAFITA

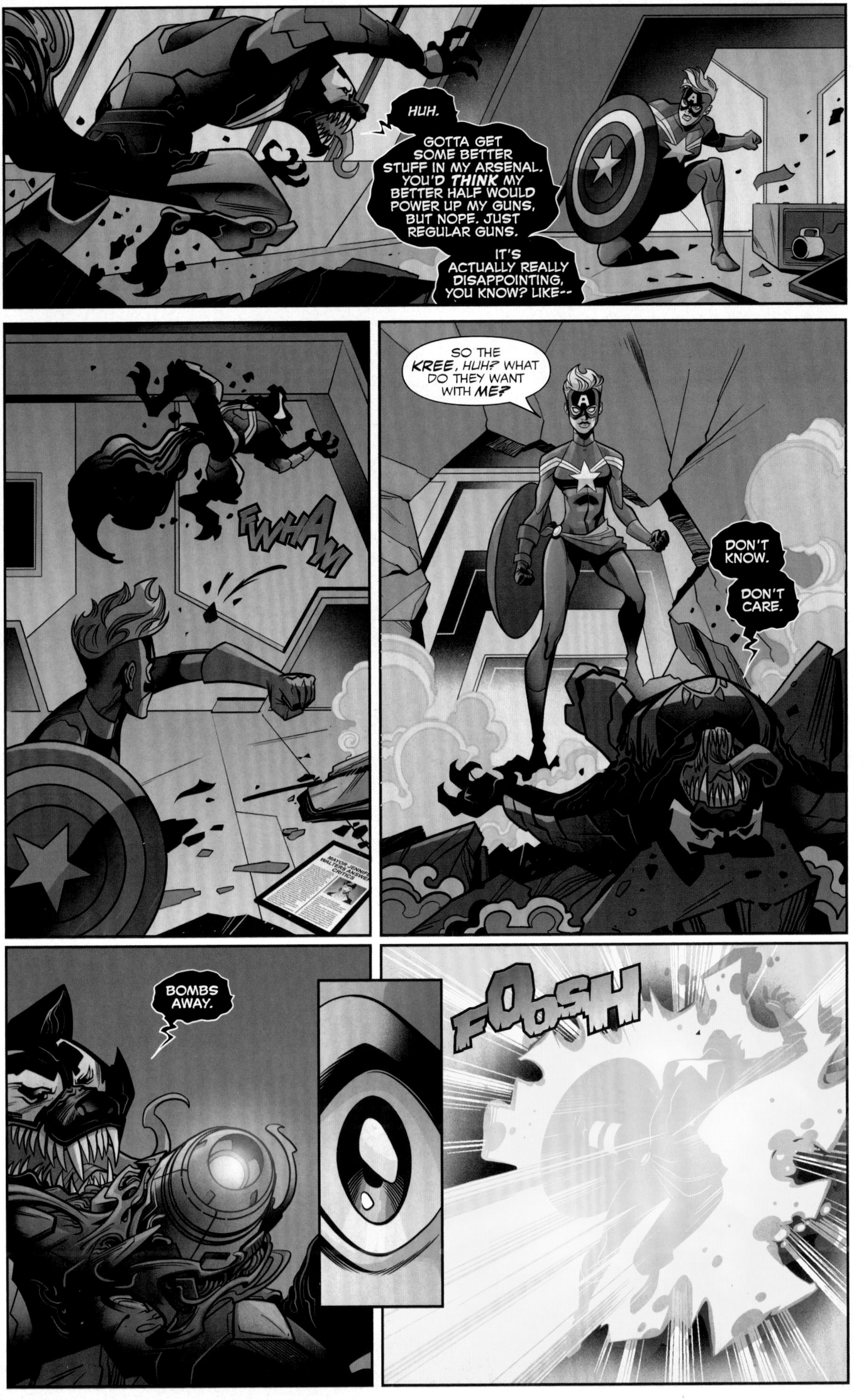

HUH.
GOTTA GET SOME BETTER STUFF IN MY ARSENAL. YOU'D THINK MY BETTER HALF WOULD POWER UP MY GUNS, BUT NOPE. JUST REGULAR GUNS.
IT'S ACTUALLY REALLY DISAPPOINTING, YOU KNOW? LIKE--
FWHAM
SO THE KREE, HUH? WHAT DO THEY WANT WITH ME?
DON'T KNOW.
DON'T CARE.
BOMBS AWAY.
FOOSH

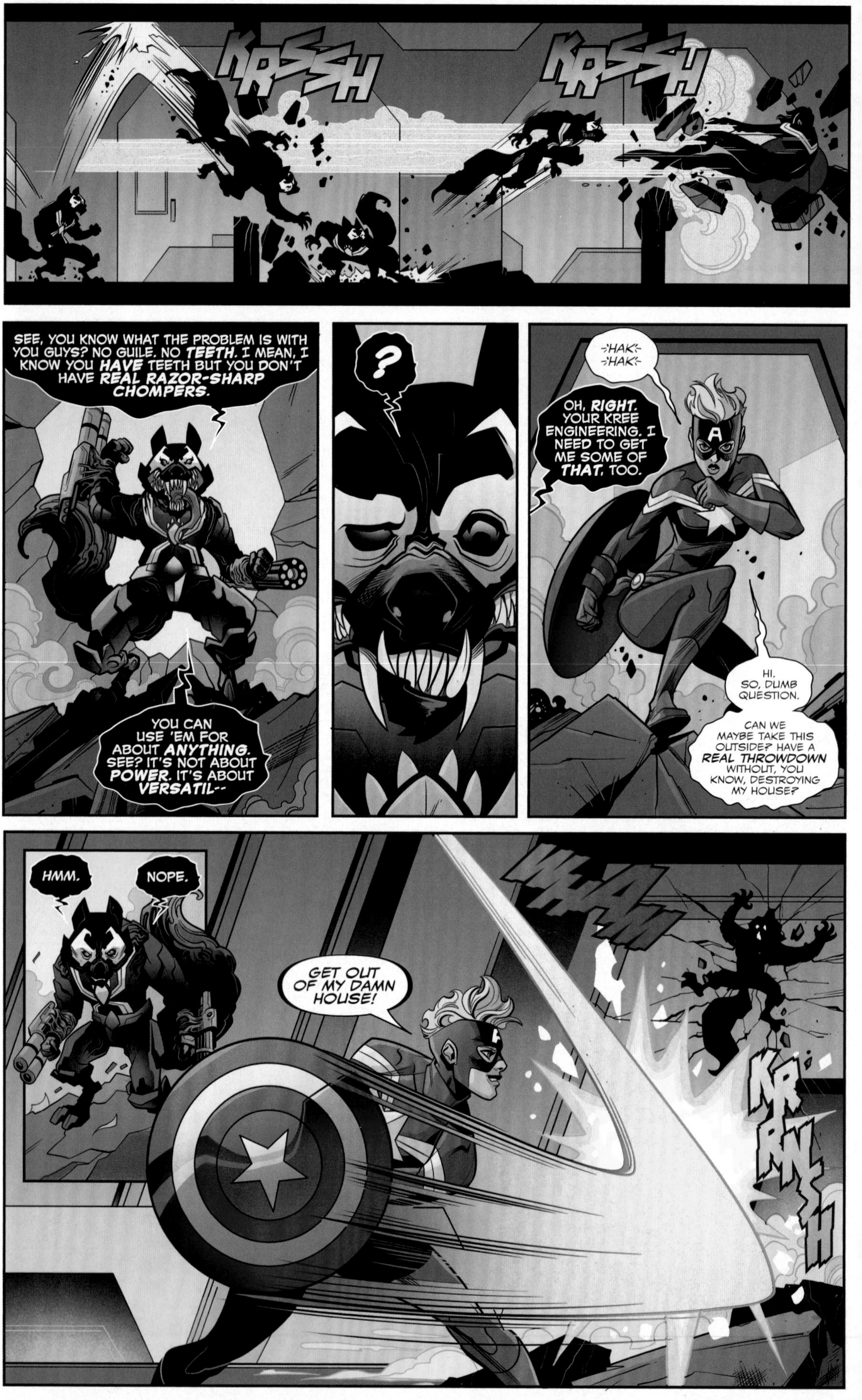
KRSSH
KRSSH
SEE, YOU KNOW WHAT THE PROBLEM IS WITH YOU GUYS? NO GUILE. NO TEETH. I MEAN, I KNOW YOU HAVE TEETH BUT YOU DON'T HAVE REAL RAZOR-SHARP CHOMPERS.
YOU CAN USE 'EM FOR ABOUT ANYTHING. SEE? IT'S NOT ABOUT POWER. IT'S ABOUT VERSATIL--
?
HAK HAK
OH, RIGHT. YOUR KREE ENGINEERING. I NEED TO GET ME SOME OF THAT, TOO.
HI. SO, DUMB QUESTION.
CAN WE MAYBE TAKE THIS OUTSIDE? HAVE A REAL THROWDOWN WITHOUT, YOU KNOW, DESTROYING MY HOUSE?
HMM.
NOPE.
GET OUT OF MY DAMN HOUSE!
KRRNSH

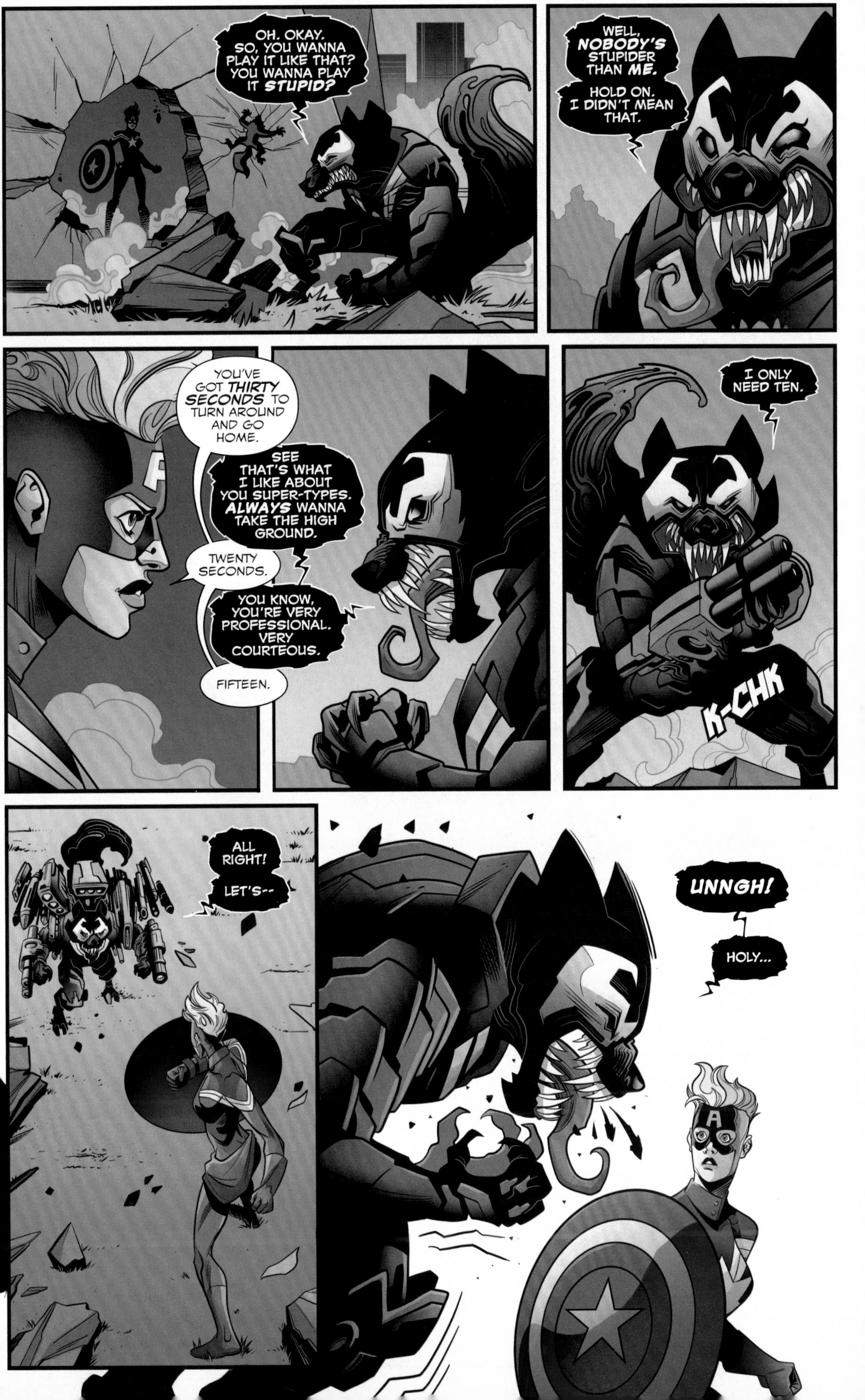
OH. OKAY. SO, YOU WANNA PLAY IT LIKE THAT? YOU WANNA PLAY IT STUPID?
WELL, NOBODY'S STUPIDER THAN ME.
HOLD ON. I DIDN'T MEAN THAT.
YOU'VE GOT THIRTY SECONDS TO TURN AROUND AND GO HOME.
SEE THAT'S WHAT I LIKE ABOUT YOU SUPER-TYPES. ALWAYS WANNA TAKE THE HIGH GROUND.
TWENTY SECONDS.
YOU KNOW, YOU'RE VERY PROFESSIONAL. VERY COURTEOUS.
FIFTEEN.
I ONLY NEED TEN.
K-CHK
ALL RIGHT!
LET'S--
UNNGH!
HOLY...

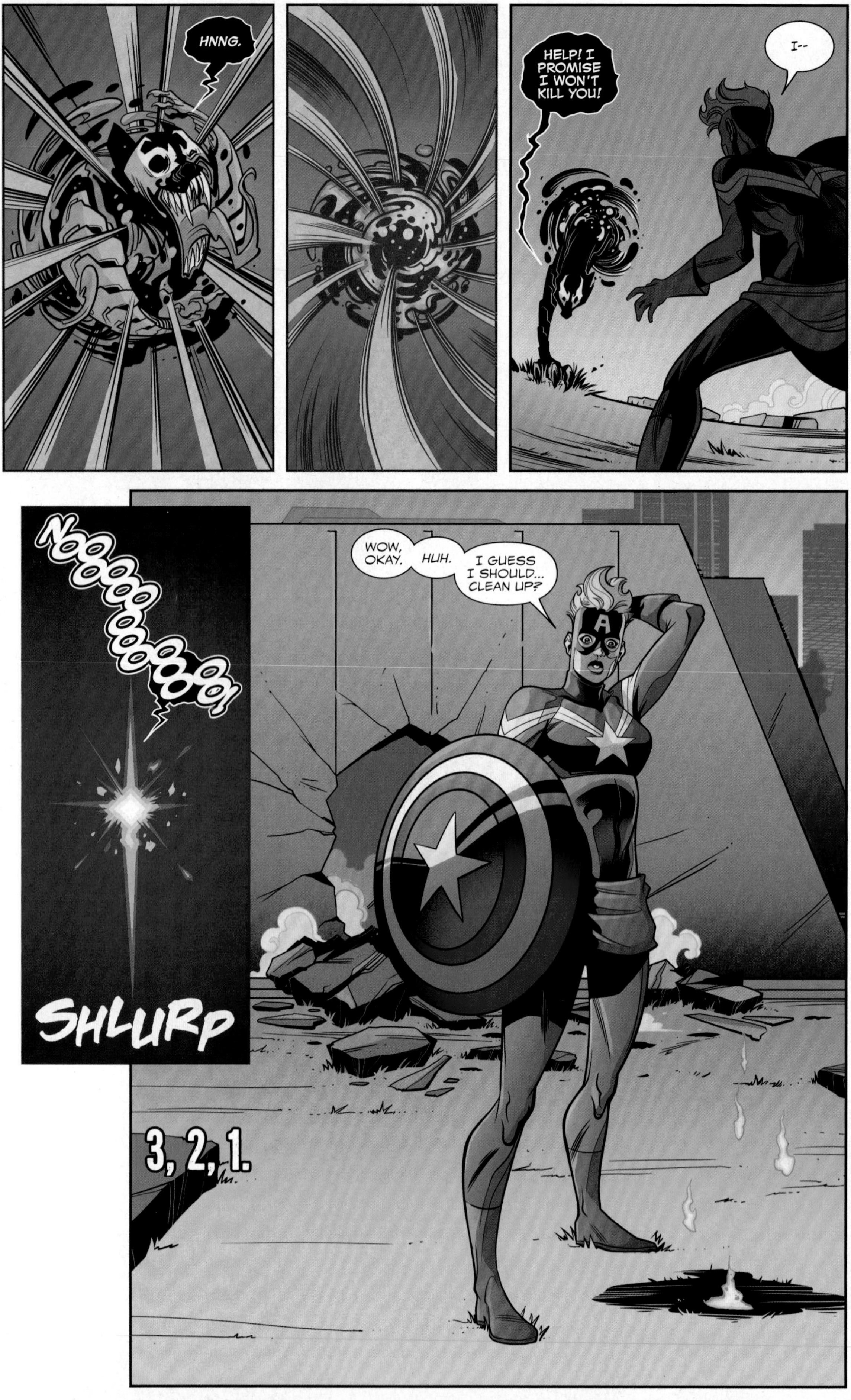
HNNG.
HELP! I PROMISE I WON'T KILL YOU!
I--
NOOOOOOOOOOOOOOO!
SHLURP
WOW, OKAY.
HUH.
I GUESS I SHOULD... CLEAN UP?
3, 2, 1.

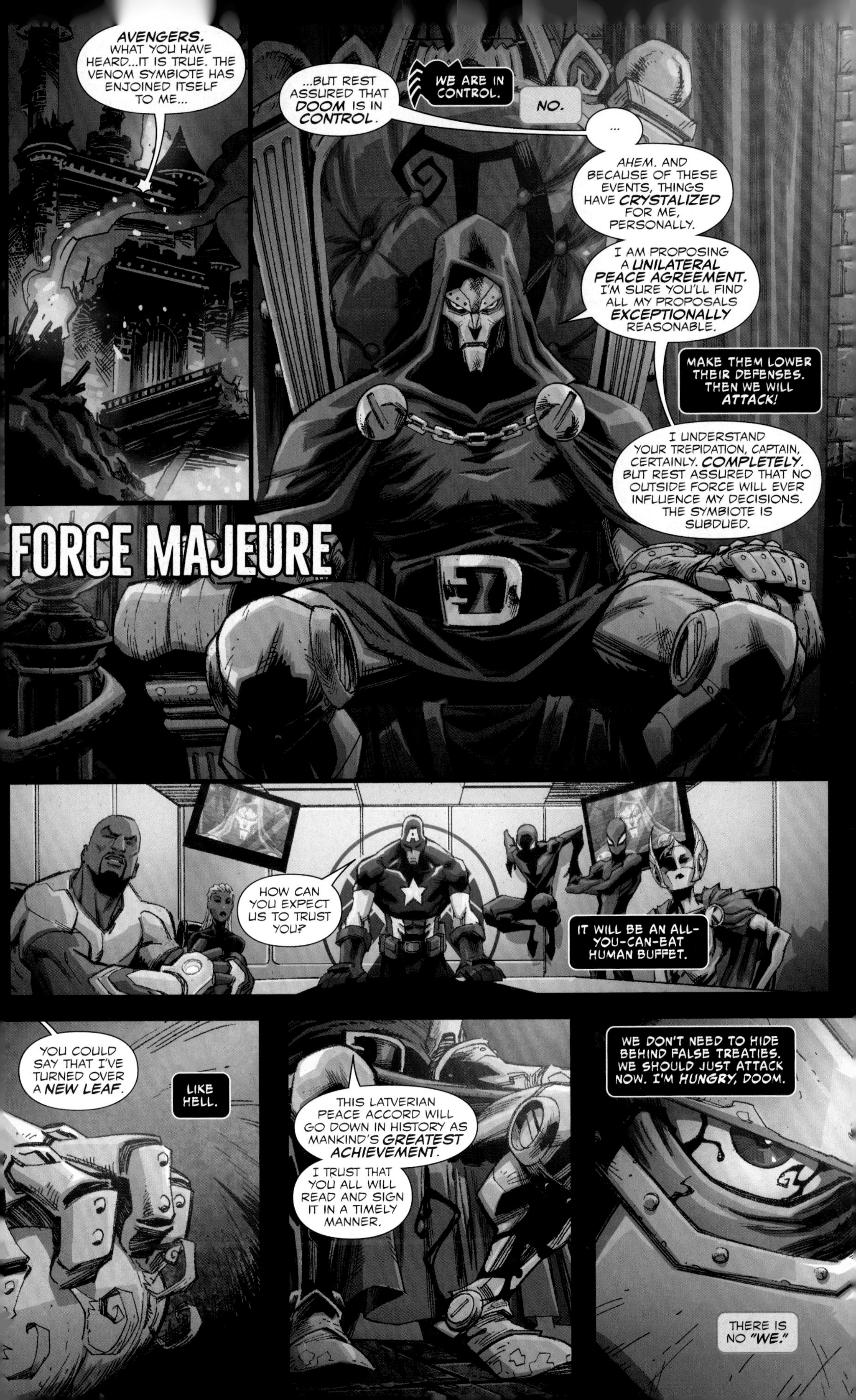
AVENGERS. WHAT YOU HAVE HEARD...IT IS TRUE. THE VENOM SYMBIOTE HAS ENJOINED ITSELF TO ME...
...BUT REST ASSURED THAT DOOM IS IN CONTROL.
WE ARE IN CONTROL.
NO.
...
AHEM. AND BECAUSE OF THESE EVENTS, THINGS HAVE CRYSTALIZED FOR ME, PERSONALLY.
I AM PROPOSING A UNILATERAL PEACE AGREEMENT. I'M SURE YOU'LL FIND ALL MY PROPOSALS EXCEPTIONALLY REASONABLE.
MAKE THEM LOWER THEIR DEFENSES. THEN WE WILL ATTACK!
I UNDERSTAND YOUR TREPIDATION, CAPTAIN, CERTAINLY. COMPLETELY. BUT REST ASSURED THAT NO OUTSIDE FORCE WILL EVER INFLUENCE MY DECISIONS. THE SYMBIOTE IS SUBDUED.
FORCE MAJEURE
HOW CAN YOU EXPECT US TO TRUST YOU?
IT WILL BE AN ALL-YOU-CAN-EAT HUMAN BUFFET.
YOU COULD SAY THAT I'VE TURNED OVER A NEW LEAF.
LIKE HELL.
THIS LATVERIAN PEACE ACCORD WILL GO DOWN IN HISTORY AS MANKIND'S GREATEST ACHIEVEMENT.
I TRUST THAT YOU ALL WILL READ AND SIGN IT IN A TIMELY MANNER.
WE DON'T NEED TO HIDE BEHIND FALSE TREATIES. WE SHOULD JUST ATTACK NOW. I'M HUNGRY, DOOM.
THERE IS NO "WE."

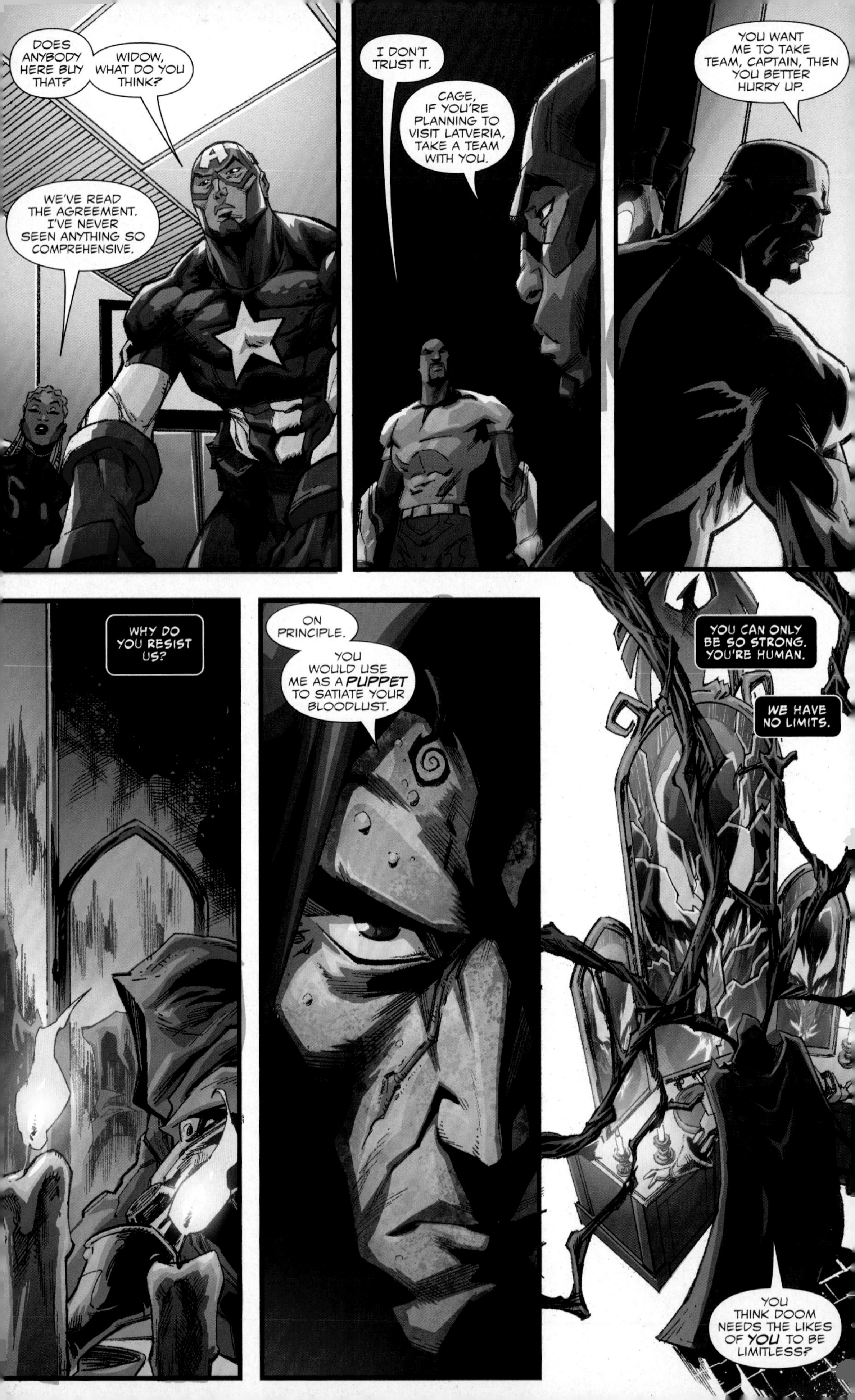
DOES ANYBODY HERE BUY THAT?
WIDOW, WHAT DO YOU THINK?
WE'VE READ THE AGREEMENT. I'VE NEVER SEEN ANYTHING SO COMPREHENSIVE.
I DON'T TRUST IT.
CAGE, IF YOU'RE PLANNING TO VISIT LATVERIA, TAKE A TEAM WITH YOU.
YOU WANT ME TO TAKE TEAM, CAPTAIN, THEN YOU BETTER HURRY UP.
WHY DO YOU RESIST US?
ON PRINCIPLE.
YOU WOULD USE ME AS A PUPPET TO SATIATE YOUR BLOODLUST.
YOU CAN ONLY BE SO STRONG. YOU'RE HUMAN.
WE HAVE NO LIMITS.
YOU THINK DOOM NEEDS THE LIKES OF YOU TO BE LIMITLESS?

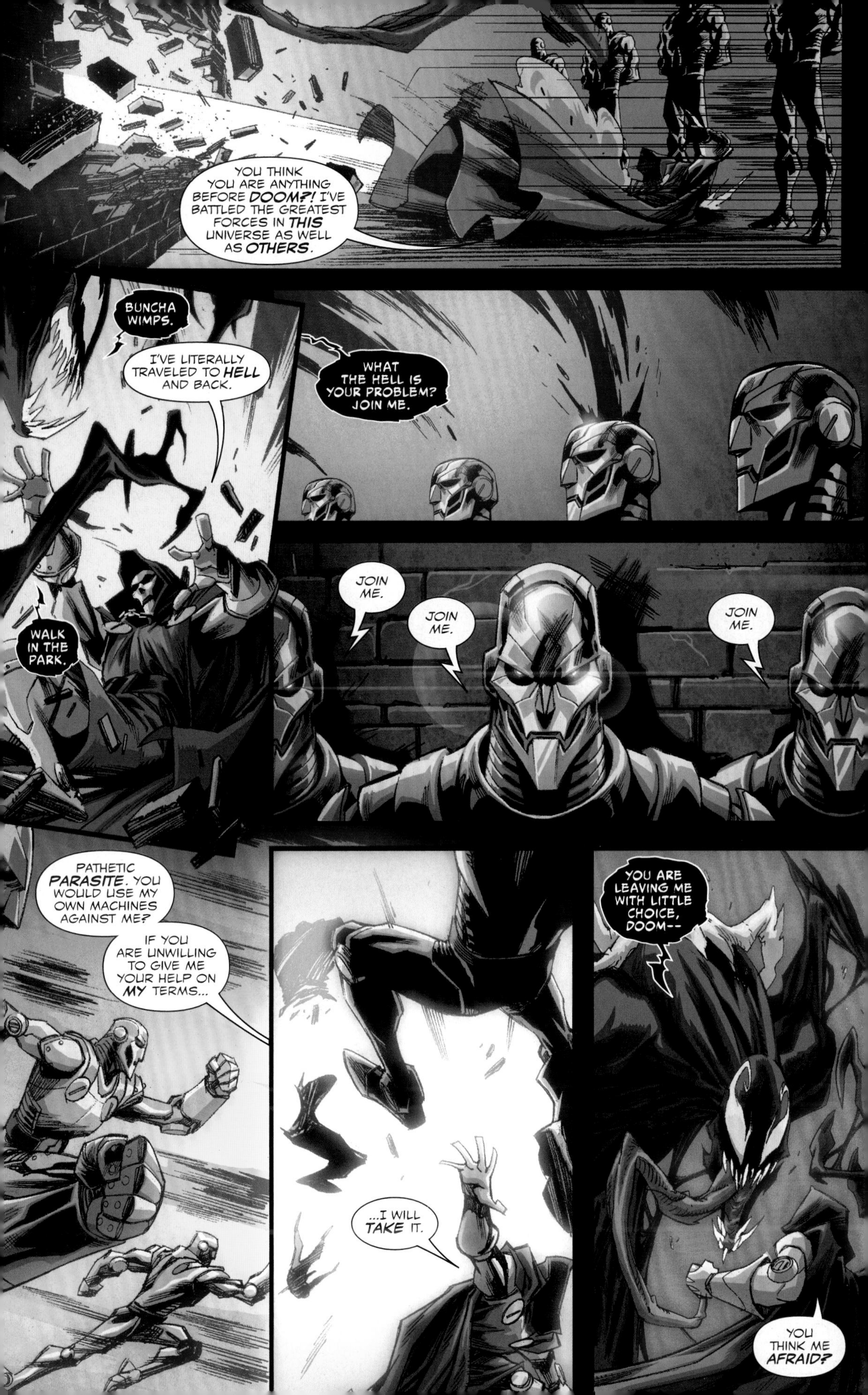
YOU THINK YOU ARE ANYTHING BEFORE DOOM?! I'VE BATTLED THE GREATEST FORCES IN THIS UNIVERSE AS WELL AS OTHERS.
BUNCHA WIMPS.
I'VE LITERALLY TRAVELED TO HELL AND BACK.
WALK IN THE PARK.
WHAT THE HELL IS YOUR PROBLEM? JOIN ME.
JOIN ME.
JOIN ME.
JOIN ME.
PATHETIC PARASITE. YOU WOULD USE MY OWN MACHINES AGAINST ME?
IF YOU ARE UNWILLING TO GIVE ME YOUR HELP ON MY TERMS...
...I WILL TAKE IT.
YOU ARE LEAVING ME WITH LITTLE CHOICE, DOOM--
YOU THINK ME AFRAID?

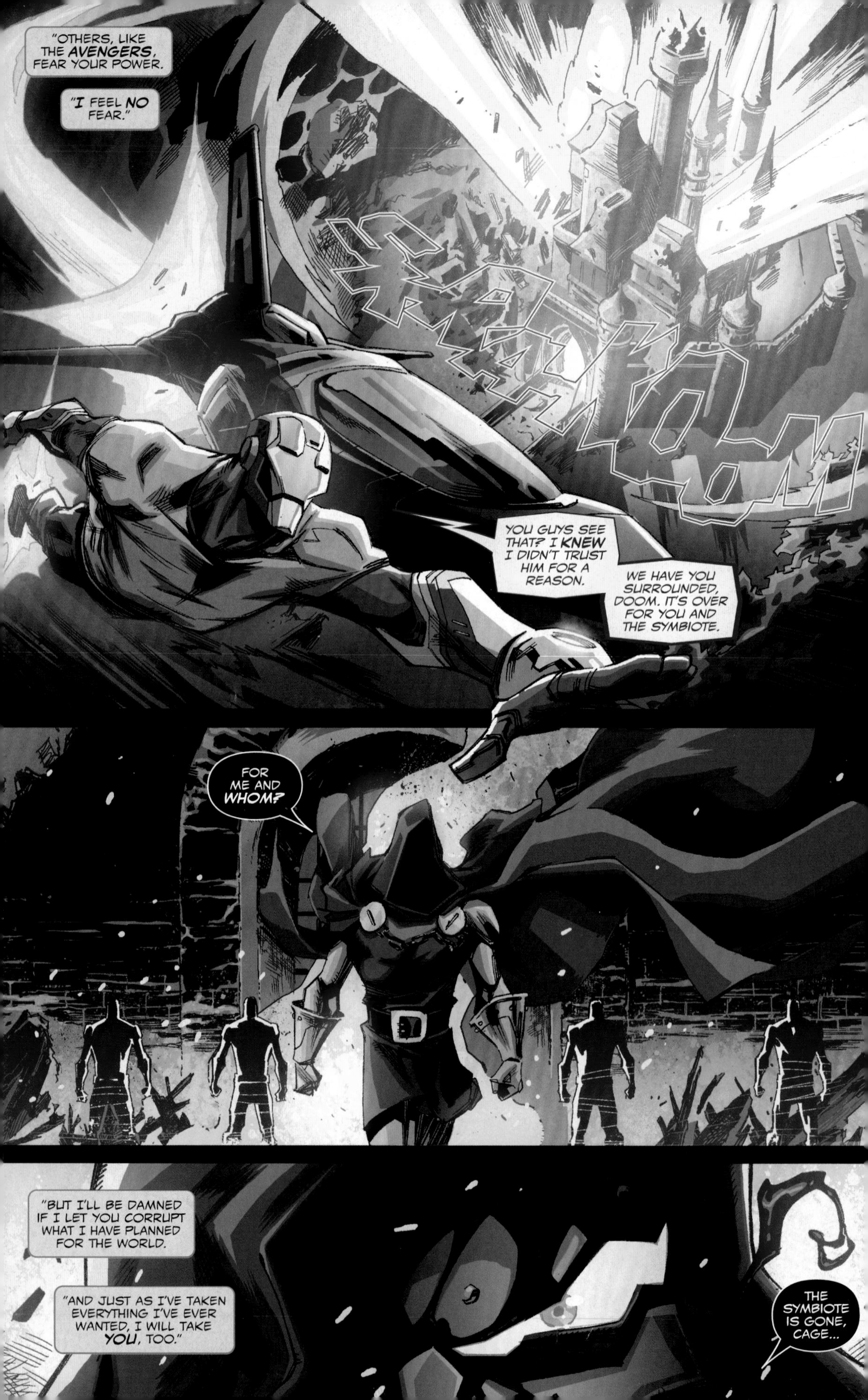
"OTHERS, LIKE THE AVENGERS, FEAR YOUR POWER.
"I FEEL NO FEAR."
YOU GUYS SEE THAT? I KNEW I DIDN'T TRUST HIM FOR A REASON.
WE HAVE YOU SURROUNDED, DOOM. IT'S OVER FOR YOU AND THE SYMBIOTE.
FOR ME AND WHOM?
"BUT I'LL BE DAMNED IF I LET YOU CORRUPT WHAT I HAVE PLANNED FOR THE WORLD.
"AND JUST AS I'VE TAKEN EVERYTHING I'VE EVER WANTED, I WILL TAKE YOU, TOO."
THE SYMBIOTE IS GONE, CAGE...

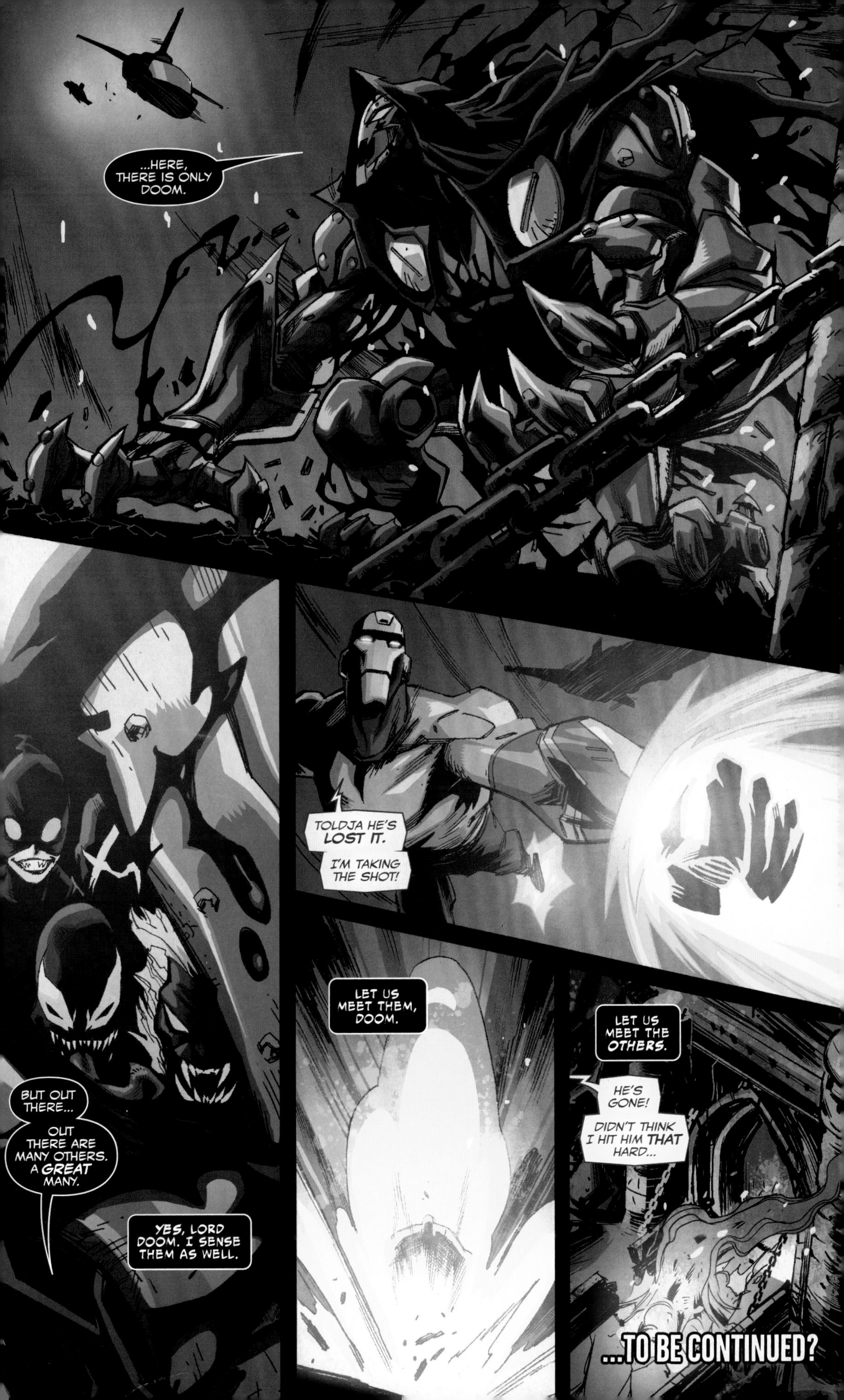
...HERE, THERE IS ONLY DOOM.
BUT OUT THERE...
OUT THERE ARE MANY OTHERS. A GREAT MANY.
YES, LORD DOOM. I SENSE THEM AS WELL.
TOLDJA HE'S LOST IT.
I'M TAKING THE SHOT!
LET US MEET THEM, DOOM.
LET US MEET THE OTHERS.
HE'S GONE!
DIDN'T THINK I HIT HIM THAT HARD...
...TO BE CONTINUED?

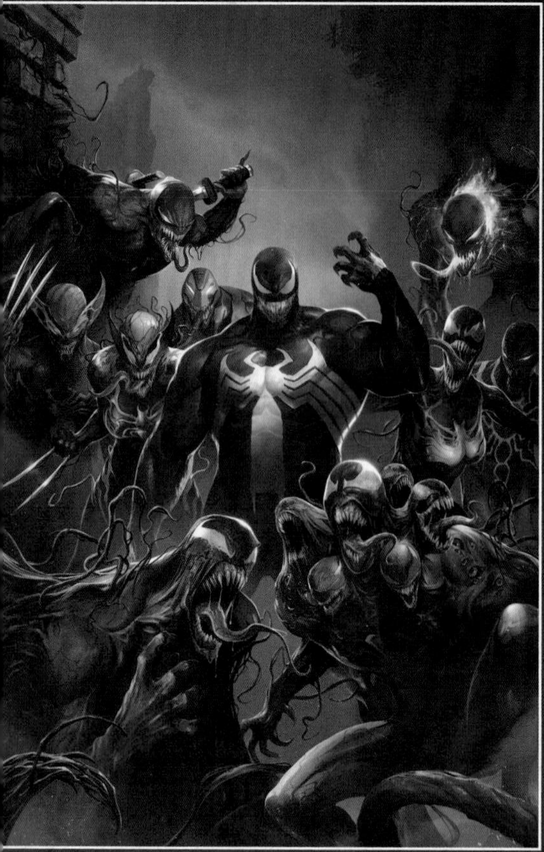

Francesco Mattina
Edge of Venomverse #1 variant

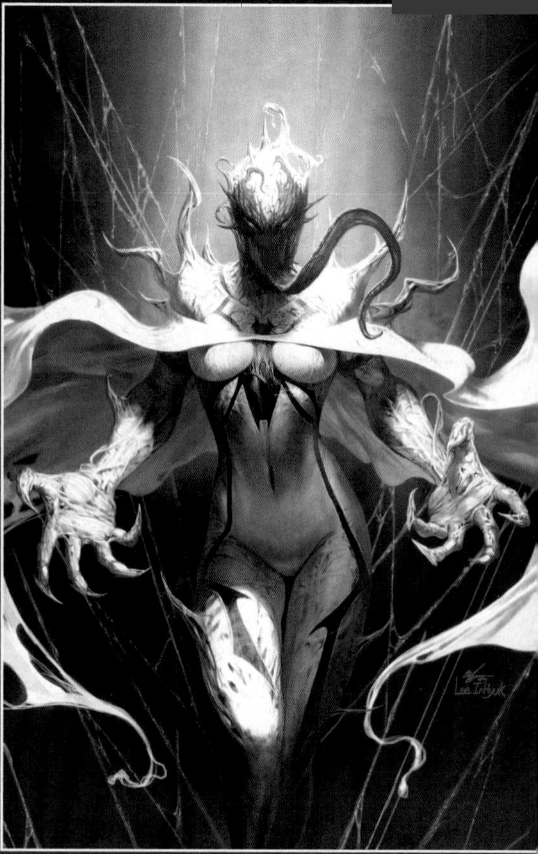

Inhyuk Lee
Edge of Venomverse #1 variant

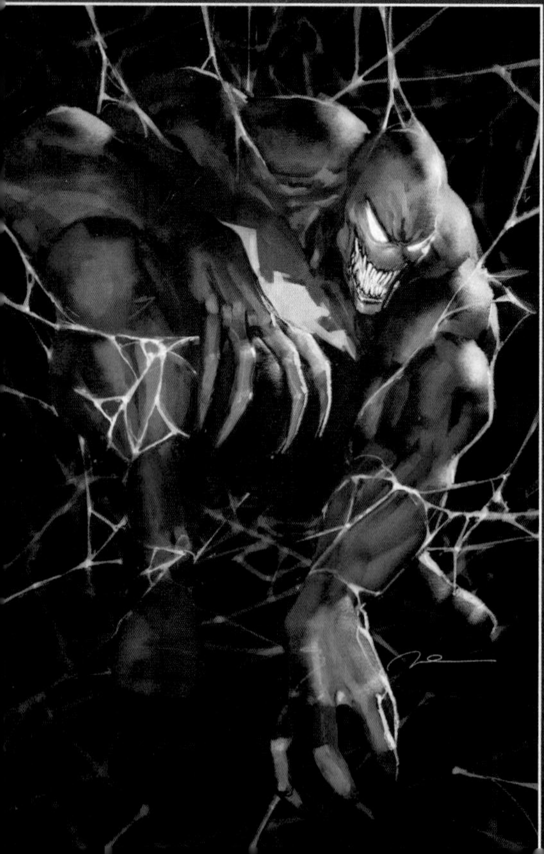

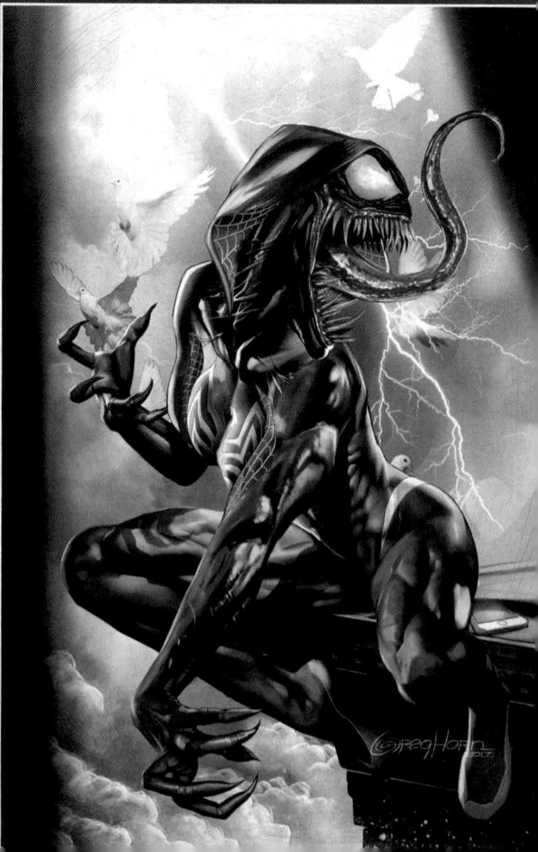

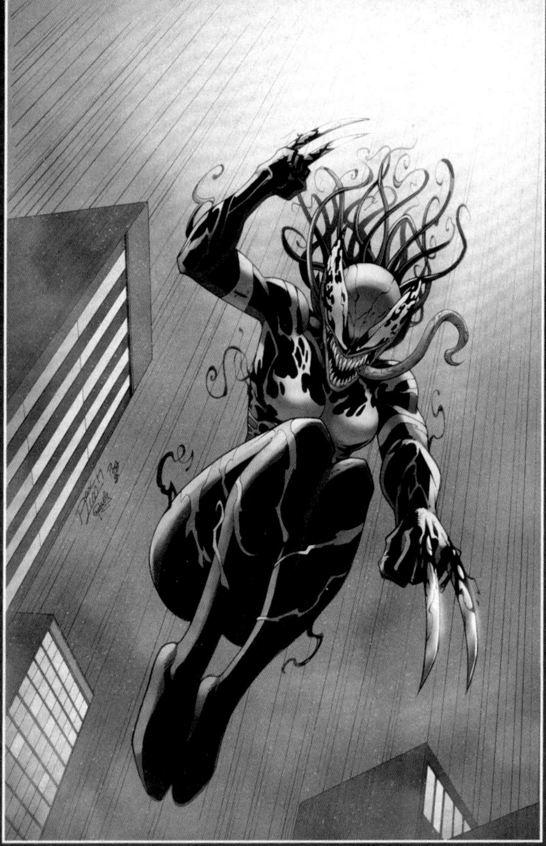

Ron Lim, Roberto Poggi & Rachelle Rosenberg
Edge of Venomverse #1 variant

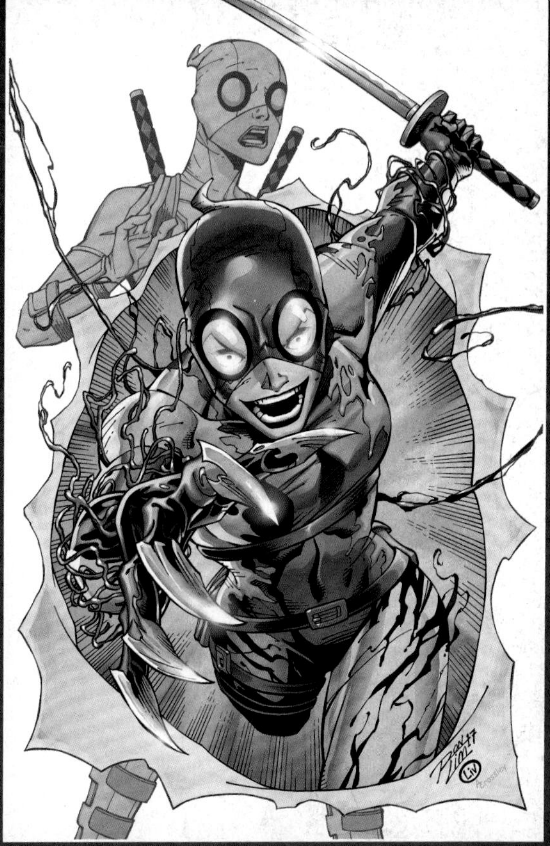

Ron Lim, John Livesay & Andrew Crossley
Edge of Venomverse #2 variant

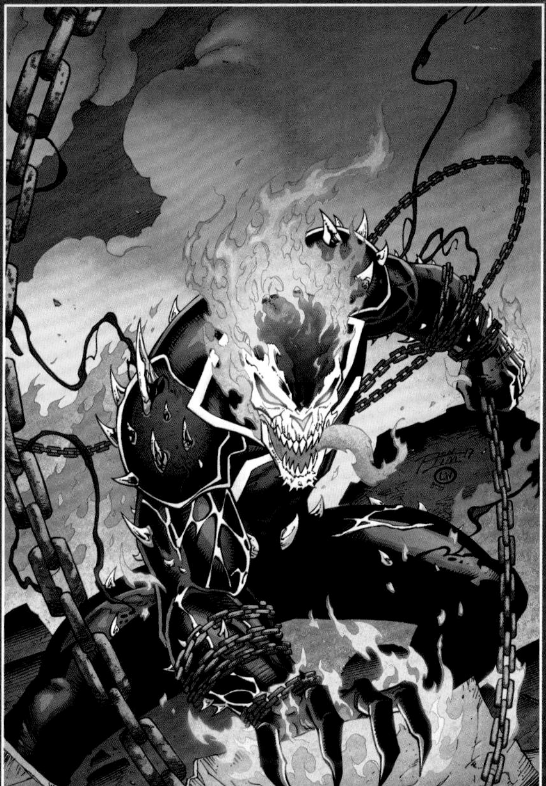

Ron Lim, John Livesay & Jordan Boyd
Edge of Venomverse #3 variant

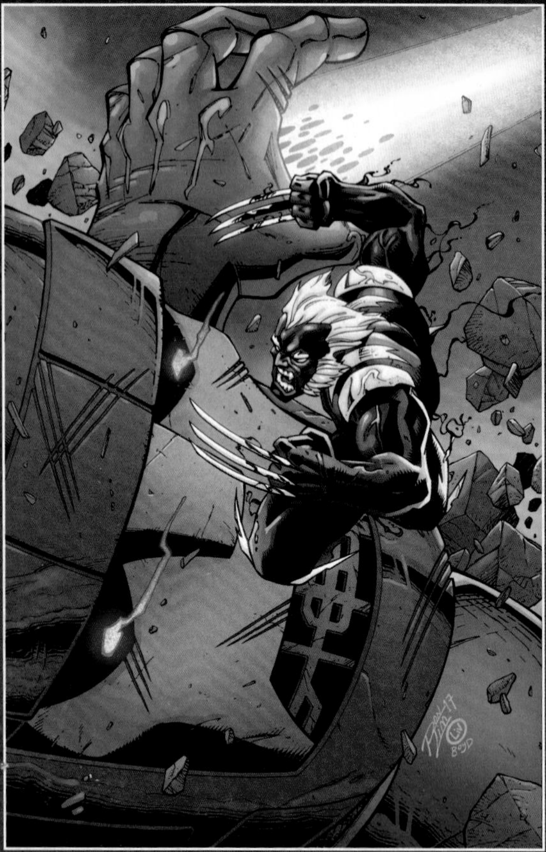

Ron Lim, Roberto Poggi & Jordan Boyd
Edge of Venomverse #4 variant

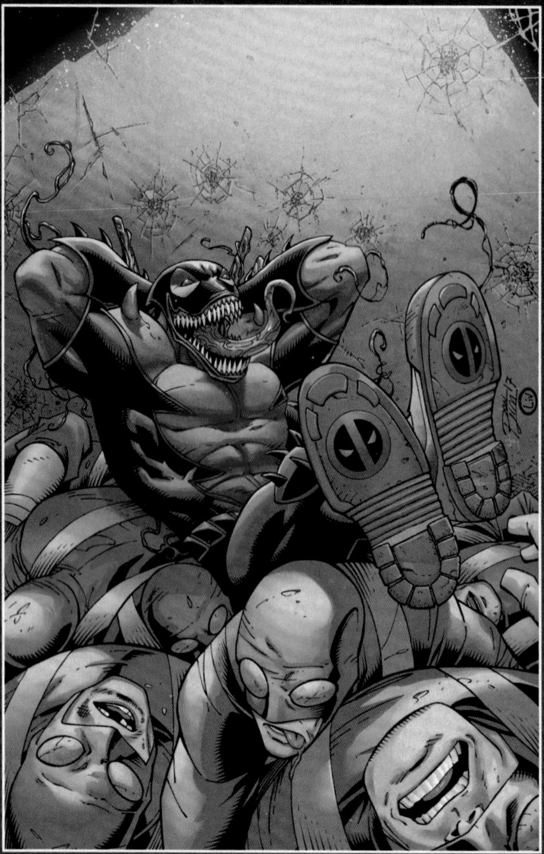

Ron Lim, John Livesay & Jay David Ramos
Edge of Venomverse #5 variant

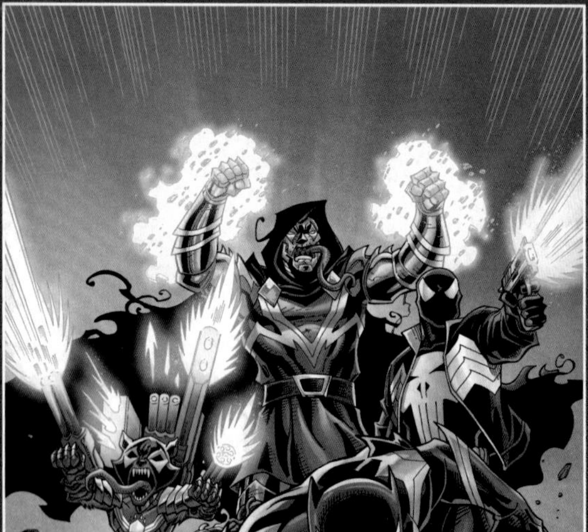

Ron Lim, John Livesay & Jay David Ramos
Venomverse: War Stories #1 variant